Me

and

Mercenaries in Medieval and Renaissance Europe

HUNT JANIN *with*
URSULA CARLSON

McFarland & Company, Inc., Publishers
Jefferson, North Carolina, and London

Hunt Janin has written or cowritten 10 other books for McFarland: *Rising Sea Levels* (and Scott A. Mandia, 2012), *Trails of Historic New Mexico* (and Ursula Carlson, 2010), *The University in Medieval Life* (2008), *Islamic Law* (and André Kahlmeyer, 2007), *Fort Bridger, Wyoming* (2006), *The Pursuit of Learning in the Islamic World, 610–2003* (2005; paperback 2006), *Medieval Justice* (2004; paperback 2009), *Four Paths to Jerusalem* (2002; paperback 2006), *Claiming the American Wilderness* (2001; paperback 2006), *The India-China Opium Trade in the Nineteenth Century* (1999)

ISBN 978-0-7864-7274-1

softcover : acid free paper ∞

LIBRARY OF CONGRESS CATALOGUING DATA ARE AVAILABLE

BRITISH LIBRARY CATALOGUING DATA ARE AVAILABLE

Cover art: *The taking of Pestien* (folio 51), Jean Cuvelier, *La Chanson de Bertrand du Guesclin,* Paris, 1380–1392 (British Library)

Manufactured in the United States of America

McFarland & Company, Inc., Publishers
Box 611, Jefferson, North Carolina 28640
www.mcfarlandpub.com

Table of Contents

Table of Contents

Now we must consider yet another category of man-at-arms who deserves much praise. That is the one who, for various compelling reasons ... leaves his locality ... before he has gained any reputation there, [even though] he would have preferred to remain in his own region if he could well do so. Nevertheless [such men] leave and go to Lombardy or Tuscany or Pulia or other lands where pay and other rewards can be earned.... Through this they can see, learn and gain knowledge of much that is good through participating in war, for they may be in such lands or territories where they can witness and themselves achieve great deeds of arms.

> — Geoffroi de Charny, a French knight and author of three
> works on chivalry, who was killed at the battle of Poitiers
> in 1356 while he was carrying the Oriflamme,
> the battle standard of the King of France,
> quoted in Caferro, *John Hawkwood*, p. 332.

Preface

Let us begin by defining a medieval or a Renaissance mercenary. These were men — some good, some bad — who came from all walks of life and who had two things in common: they were professional soldiers, and they fought not because they were members of a specific political community but because they wanted to make money or otherwise be rewarded. Since they used the same tactics, weapons, and equipment as non-mercenary troops, all our comments on these matters apply equally well to mercenaries and non-mercenaries alike.

This book is a wide-ranging survey which addresses two fundamental questions:

- Who were the medieval and Renaissance mercenaries?
- What did they do?

Neither question has an easy answer. The first question involves the complicated issue of what has been called "the mercenary identity in the Middle Ages."[1] It is very difficult for us today to say with great confidence who was a mercenary and who was not. It is not simply a question of "gain," since most mercenaries were paid in one way or another, either directly or indirectly (e.g., by capturing men who could be held for ransom, or by receiving tacit permission to rob, rape, and pillage on their own). Some more complicated cases include Merovingian antrustions, Anglo-Danish housecarls, discharged English soldiers, and Scottish soldiers in the pay of France.

Answering the second question definitively would require a more detailed knowledge of the daily life of mercenaries than is available today. What seems clear is that some adventuresome men living in troubled areas, e.g., in Flanders and northern Spain, were inclined to become

1

mercenaries because their lives were already precarious and the risks of soldiering were mitigated by hopes of gain, e.g., booty and ransom.

We know very little about the personal lives of rank-and-file mercenaries because almost all of them were illiterate and few literate people wanted to waste their time recording the experiences of mercenaries. Some of the literate mercenary commanders had a good deal to say about the conduct of battles, honor, chivalry, and other "noble" subjects. But they had almost nothing at all to say about the common soldier who was trying to endure both the boredom and hardships of military life, and the blood, sweat, and mud of the battlefield, simply in order to draw his pay.

In studying this subject one must keep in mind the habit of contemporary chroniclers of greatly exaggerating the size of battles and the number of men killed, wounded, or taken prisoner. Here is one exceptionally dramatic example: during a papal campaign in Corsica in 1445–1446, chroniclers put the papal forces at 16,000 men. However, papal financial records, which are far more accurate than the chroniclers, show that the strength of the papal army there cannot have been much above 1,000 men.[2]

This book presents a large number of vignettes focusing on mercenaries in Western Europe over a period of nearly 900 years. This approach seems to offer a couple of advantages:

- It offers some answers to the questions above; and
- It breaks up the long history of medieval and Renaissance mercenaries into manageable chunks—letting the reader focus on particularly interesting moments of mercenary history.

Most chapters begin with a short paragraph in italics highlighting the three to five vignettes to be discussed in that chapter, usually in chronological order. The chapter titles—often short extracts from the contemporary sources quoted in the text—are derived from these events or individuals.

The Introduction offers a broad overview of medieval and Renaissance warfare. Chapter I introduces some of the mercenaries and the tools of their trade. Chapters II through XI focus on a selection of the most memorable individuals and events of mercenary history—from the Merovingian mercenaries of 752, who were arguably the first medieval mercenaries known to us, to the very late Renaissance mercenaries of the Thirty Years' War, which ended in 1648 and which we shall set as the outermost limit of the Renaissance. The Conclusion offers summary remarks.

Mercenaries played violent and colorful roles in warfare but they have not received a great deal of scholarly attention compared to other aspects of medieval life. The present authors have therefore tried in a modest way to correct this situation. Toward that end, quotations from contemporary or near-contemporary observers have been used frequently. Chapter notes (at the end of the book) have been used extensively: for scholarly attribution, to explain medieval or Renaissance matters that may be unclear to the reader, and in some cases to make substantive points which are important but are too detailed to appear in the text itself. Readers who want more information on matters discussed in the text will find some excellent sources listed in the bibliography. Two appendices discuss armor and Swiss mercenaries.

The authors are grateful for the good advice we have received from Dr. William Caferro and especially from Dr. John France,who very kindly read much of the manuscript in draft and has made a number of extremely useful corrections and suggestions. We are also grateful to Dio Koolen and to Martine Kommer for their help in translating quotations from medieval Spanish and from medieval French. Alexandra Janin has earned our thanks for her indexing work. Any errors or omissions in the text are of course our own doing alone.

Introduction

An Overview of Medieval and Renaissance Warfare

During the Middle Ages and the Renaissance (i.e., from the deposition of the last Roman emperor in the West in 476 to the Italian wars of the mid–16th century) national, regional, and local leaders often found it necessary to hire highly-skilled military help, i.e., mercenaries, from outside their own organizations. They needed to be careful, however, when they decided to recruit such men: one did not always get what one expected.

In March 1095, for example, the ambassadors of the Byzantine Emperor Alexios I Komnenos appeared before Pope Urban II at the Council of Piacenza. They urgently asked the Pope for Western military help against the Seljuk Turks, who had already captured much of Asia Minor and who were invading Anatolia, i.e., what is now southern Turkey. Pope Urban responded favorably to the Byzantine request. (In practice, however, Crusader policy goals would expand to include the reconquest of Jerusalem and the Holy Land, and the freeing of Eastern Christians from Islamic rule.)

What Alexios really wanted, however, and what his envoys had asked the Pope for, was a relatively small number of experienced European mercenary troops. What he got instead was a tsunami of beginners. To the Emperor's great surprise and consternation, at the Council of Clermont in November 1095 the Pope had, quite unexpectedly, preached (that is, he had officially called for) what would become known as the First Crusade (1096–1099).[1] Most of those who initially enlisted for this campaign were not knights or men-at-arms but were, at best, simply pious peasants who wanted to gain spiritual merit by "liberating" far-flung lands from Muslim control and who were probably seeking adventure as well. The modern author J.F. Verbruggen has accurately described them as a "disorderly and reckless rabble."[2] They had few if any fighting skills.

Four main Crusader armies left Europe in 1096 and passed through Constantinople before pressing on to the Holy Land. The size of this Crusader force is difficult to estimate, but the modern military historian David Nicolle believes that it totaled some 30,000 to 35,000 men, including 5,000 cavalrymen.[3] This was of course far, far above the number of Western troops Alexios had in mind or could handle. The Byzantines were unable to provide adequate food and supplies for the vast number of Crusaders who descended on them in response to the Pope's call. Many Byzantine lands, of which Constantinople was the focal point, were therefore ransacked by the Crusaders themselves en route to the Holy Land.

In almost all other cases, however, the search for mercenaries produced excellent results. The reason was that, during the Middle Ages and the Renaissance, experienced mercenaries were willing and eager to provide military help, but usually only at a stiff price. Over the years there was a continuing demand for their services, despite the inherent risk of hiring them. As Michael Mallett, an expert on the mercenaries of this period, has explained,

> The armies of the sixteenth and seventeenth centuries differed little from those of the fifteenth century except in size and improved techniques. Men like the Constable of Bourbon, Pedro Navarro and Colonna himself [these were all famous 16th century mercenaries] were as likely to desert their employers as were Sforza and Braccio [two famous 15th century mercenaries] a century earlier. The armies they commanded were filled with Swiss and German mercenaries.[4]

Due to local shortages, mercenaries sometimes had to be recruited from far afield. Mercenaries from outside Western European Christian society, such as Saracen archers (Muslims were then known as Saracens in the West), were hired to serve in Western European armies. In fact, as early as 835, according to the contemporary cleric John the Deacon, the Neapolitans were hiring Saracens from Sicily to help defend their city-state against Prince Sicard (r. 832–839). This man was an aggressive, expansionist Lombard ruler (the Lombards were a Germanic tribe that governed a kingdom in Italy). Sicard was not a very nice man, being described by the late 11th century Monte Cassino chronicler Leo Marsicanus as "a man given to every carnal vice but, above all, consumed by greed."[5] He was eventually murdered by his own men.

European mercenaries served in Muslim armies, notably in North Africa and in the Middle East. For some years before 1147, there was a company of Christian knights in Morocco who had their own clergy and even a bishop. Christian mercenaries became one of the best fighting forces in the Turkish army. We know about them because Simon de Saint-Quentin, a Dominican priest, was sent on a diplomatic mission to the Mongols in 1246. During his journey he met Christian mercenaries in the service of Armenian princes and of the Sultan. He is thus able to tell us that a rebellion in 1240–1241 could be put down only with the help of 300 of these mercenaries. They also helped to defend Armenian borders against the Mongols. They were unimpressed by the Mongols as warriors and said that even a small Frankish garrison would have sufficed to prevent the Mongols from capturing Caesarea, a town in what is now Israel.[6]

Western European soldiers often served in armies in the fringes of or far outside Western Europe. Harald Sigurdsson (c. 1015–1066), for example, whose life story is told in six Scandinavian sagas and who later became king of Denmark is still known by his epithet, "Hardrada" (Old Norse for "hard ruler"). Before becoming king in 1046, he spent a period in exile as a mercenary commander. At one point he was chief of the Byzantine Empire's elite mercenary unit, the Varangian Guard, which is discussed later. Harald may also have commanded Norman mercenaries in Sicily. ("Norman" refers to the descendants of the Norse Vikings who raided England towards the end of the 1st millennium. They were known in medieval Latin documents as *normanni*, i.e., "northmen.")

Harald saw action against the Arab pirates of the Mediterranean and participated in the capture of 80 Arab strongholds as far east as the Euphrates. When he finally overreached himself as king by invading England with a force of about 15,000 men in 300 longships, however, he met his death at the battle of Stamford Bridge, outside York, in 1066. That battle marked the end of the Viking age, i.e., the period from the earliest recorded Viking raid on England in 789 down to the Norman conquest of England in 1066.

Mercenaries formed only a modest part — about one quarter to one third[7] — of most European armies in the later Middle Ages (1348 to 1500), but the mercenary profession was a very complicated calling which varied considerably in structure and function. Little is known about these men before about 1300 when documentary records first become clear, e.g., who they were, how they were recruited, how well they were paid in relation to other men, and whether they served as individuals before they began to be hired in groups in the 1360s.[8]

Little is known, too, about the squires and sergeants — the support troops who formed a key part of both mercenary and regular forces. They were more experienced than rank-and-file troops and, as a result, were probably more effective in combat. However, as the modern scholar Helen Nicholson has pointed out,

> the squires and sergeants remain elusive figures in the army and on the battlefield. As they lacked the [social] status of the knights, and lacked the wealth to patronize chroniclers, they were very seldom mentioned by contemporary chroniclers. Their original functions were as "support troops," either mounted or on foot. Yet epics and romances of the twelfth and thirteenth centuries indicate that squires ... could be older warriors who were given the responsibility of taking care of a young noble warrior and looking after his training. Such squires were arguably of much greater skill than their young charges.[9]

In armies today, even a very experienced sergeant is still, by definition, an enlisted man, not an officer. During the medieval and Renaissance eras, however, a sergeant filled an important "in-between role": that is, he was senior to the rank-and-file enlisted soldier but junior to the knight. Sergeants were trained to fight either as heavy or as light cavalrymen, or as professional infantrymen, e.g., spearmen or crossbowmen. They were seen as very valuable and reliable soldiers. In fact, most of the notable mercenaries, such as the Flemish spearmen or crossbowmen, were sergeants. Because crossbows were extremely expensive compared to wooden bows, they were often assigned to sergeants. These men were officially considered to be "worth half of a knight" in terms of their combat value.

An excellent example of a contemporary document extolling the value of sergeants is Jan van Heelu's chronicle of the battle of Woeringten (1288). He was a 13th century Flemish writer who was much impressed by the quality of soldiers from Brabant, a duchy covering parts of present-day Netherlands and Belgium. He wrote a poem along these lines:

> There were from Brabant
> Many courageous sergeants,
> Certainly the equals of knights,
> That seemed so in the unit
> Of the duke [i.e., John I, the Duke of Brabant], their master,
> Where they, with the most honor,
> Did the best acts of fighting
> That anyone saw in the army.
> And most of all those
> Who received from the duke
> Clothes, and were his servants,
> They showed always, without stinting,
> That they preferred to die
> Than to abandon their master.[10]

Some mercenaries were knights. Traditionally, a young man who aspired to become a knight began his training at the age of 7 as a page in a prosperous household, and then graduated into the role of a squire at the age of 14. He would become a knight at the age of 21. To prepare himself for his career as a knight, a squire had to learn the code of chivalry, the rules of heraldry, horsemanship, and the use of weapons. He also had to develop strength, speed, dexterity, and leadership skills, as well as learn how to climb (an important skill when besieging a castle), to swim, and to withstand extremes of heat and cold, tiredness, thirst, hunger.

Raymond Lulle (c. 1232–1315), a Catalan philosopher, poet, and theologian, describes the learning process of a squire in these words:

A noble man who loves the order of chivalry and will be a knight [needs] to have first a master who is a knight, for thus it is a discoverable [inappropriate] thing that a squire should learn the order and nobility from any other man than a knight. So very high and honored is the order of chivalry that a squire should suffer himself [i.e., must learn] not only to learn to keep horse and learn to serve a knight, that he will go with him to tourneys and battles; but it is necessary that he beholds the school of the order of knighthood.[11]

Not all squires made the grade and became knights. Some became too old to qualify for knighthood or were unable to afford the considerable expenses of knighthood. Nevertheless, as the earlier quote from Helen Nicholson shows, they still had an important and honored role to play on the battlefield.

The exact relationships between squires, sergeants, knights, and mercenaries will probably always remain murky to modern eyes, but today anyone who has served in the armed forces, even briefly and in peacetime, knows that all ranks must work together closely if they are to achieve the goals set out for them by their commanders. The same must have been true in the Middle Ages. It can therefore be guessed that while military discipline would have prevented officers and enlisted men from ever being on an informal first-name basis, mercenary officers probably had a more equal relationship with their regular (non-mercenary) counterparts. By the same token, mercenary troops (enlisted men) must have had close working relations with their own non-mercenary counterparts.

In the days before professional standing armies, mercenaries usually did not serve together for very long periods of time but parted company once a campaign was won or lost, or when there was no more money for their wages. However, mercenary units were composed of many different kinds of men with many different personal or feudal bonds to their leaders, so it is difficult to generalize about them.

In England, for example, "castle ward," i.e., the process of staffing a castle with the proper number of fighting men needed at any given time, involved both feudal and mercenary garrisons.[12] At the royal castles, more men probably served in them for pay, i.e., as mercenaries, rather than being obliged to do so for feudal reasons.[13] Sizeable numbers of men could be involved in this process. Hainaut is a good example. This is now one of the three regions of Belgium and derives its name from the medieval County of Hainaut, parts of which are today in France. Baldwin of Hainaut, who reigned from 1171 to 1195, is said to have hired over 3,000 mercenaries to strengthen his castles during a conflict with the Count of Flanders.[14]

Mercenaries could come from a wide variety of backgrounds. In times of warfare in Italy, for example, the lords of towns sold their military expertise to other towns; military-trained exiles could sell their own services, too. In short, the mercenary profession was inextricably linked to many other aspects of society.[15] It is also important to keep in mind that, as the modern scholar William Caferro explains,

> the most distinctive feature of warfare in Italy ... was its perpetual nature. Violence did not end with formal declarations of peace. Seeking to maintain their earnings or to make up for wages unpaid or in arrears, demobilized mercenaries coalesced into free companies [we will discuss these later] around notable commanders and corporals, who allied together by means of a formal oath. Soldiers from throughout Italy gravitated toward them.[16]

To understand the lives and times of medieval mercenaries, we first need to understand something about medieval and Renaissance warfare itself. War was a central and inescapable fact of life in a society organized chiefly for fighting and was the keystone in the arch of political power.[17] As Jean V de Bueil (1406–1477), a French warrior who will be discussed below, put it succinctly, "All empires and lordships find their origin in war."[18] He was certainly right.

During the later Middle Ages, between the years 1302 and 1495, at least 17 major battles were fought within the boundaries of the Holy Roman Empire alone as it was constituted in about 1493.[19] (The Holy Roman Empire was a German empire that existed in central Europe from 962 to 1806. The French Enlightenment writer, historian, and philosopher Voltaire famously said in 1756: "This agglomeration which was called and which still calls itself the Holy Roman Empire was neither holy, nor Roman, nor an empire.") On an earlier and lesser scale, a chronological table of warfare under the Anglo-Saxon kings lists about 30 military campaigns of varying intensity between 1066 and 1135.[20]

In addition, innumerable other acts of organized and individual violence—e.g., private wars, border conflicts, peasant revolts, battles, sieges, raids, skirmishes, vendettas, long-running feuds, murders, rapes, thefts, and arson attacks—were going on in other parts of Western

Introduction

Europe before, during, and after the Middle Ages and Renaissance. To make a very long and repetitive story very short, the times were not peaceful. Medieval men, women, and children had no choice but to accept warfare as an inevitable and unavoidable fact of their often-short lives. They were taught that warriors constituted one of the three fundamental pillars that propped up their whole world. These pillars were, in order of the contemporary importance accorded to them, (1) the clergy, (2) the knights, and (3) the commoners. Each pillar had a special and, indeed, God-ordained, role to play in life: the clergy had to pray for the people, the knight had to fight for them, and the commoner had to work tirelessly so that everyone could eat.

The authority of kings and other leaders rested chiefly on their ability to wage war successfully. Fighting was the nobleman's and, of course, the mercenary's, chief occupation. It could be highly profitable and, at the same time, it could be a gloriously exciting adventure. Bertrand de Born (1140s–c. 1215), a baron from the Limousin region of France and a renowned troubadour (a composer and performer of lyric poetry), caught this latter point very well in this famous poem, which is given here in prose:

> I love the gay season of Eastertide, which brings forth flowers and leaves, and I love to hear the brave sound of the birds, making their song ring through the thickets, and I love to see tents and pavilions set up in the meadows. And I am overjoyed when I see knights and horses, all in armour, drawn up on the field.
>
> I love it when the chargers [warhorses] throw everything and everybody into confusion, and I enjoy seeing strong castles besieged, and bastions broken down and shattered, seeing the army all surrounded by ditches, protected by palisades of stout tree-trunks jammed together.
>
> And I love just as much to see a lord when he is the first to advance on horseback, armed and fearless, thus encouraging his men to valiant service: then, when the fray has begun, each must be ready to follow him willingly, because no one is held in esteem until he has given and received blows.
>
> We shall see clubs and swords, gaily-coloured helmets and shields shattered and spoiled, at the beginning of the battle, and many vassals all together receiving great blows, by reason of which many horses will wander riderless, belonging to the killed and wounded. Once he has started fighting, no noble knight thinks of anything but breaking heads and arms—better a dead man than a live one who is useless.
>
> I tell you, neither in eating, drinking, nor sleeping, do I find what I feel

when I hear the shout "At them!" from all sides, and the neighing of the riderless horses in the confusion, or the call "Help! Help!," or when I see great and small together fall on the grass of the ditches, or when I espy dead men who still have pennoned lances [lances with long narrow banners or streamers attached to them] in their ribs.

Barons, you should forfeit castles, towns, and cities, [rather] than give up — any of you — going to war.[21]

Remarkably, warfare in the Middle Ages and Renaissance could even be seen as a route to personal salvation. As a young warrior, the famous French soldier Jean V de Bueil was nicknamed, for his prowess against the English troops, "the Flail of the English," i.e., *le Fléau des Anglais*. (In medieval warfare, a flail was a spiked iron ball attached to a wooden handle by a chain; a farmer's version of the flail was used by peasants to thresh wheat.) Jean V de Bueil served under the Armagnac mercenary captain Étienne de Vignolles, better known to history as La Hire. His unusual nickname (meaning "ire" or "anger" in medieval French) refers to his prickly disposition, which was in sharp contrast to the cool demeanor expected of an aristocrat, and may also be a play on the Latin phrase "the wrath of God" (Ira Dei). La Hire established his reputation as a mercenary leader in a daring raid during which, under cover of thick fog and thanks to an inadequate night-watch, he and his troops captured the Burgundian town of Compiègne in 1424.[22]

In about 1466 Jean V de Bueil wrote the semi-autobiographical work *Le Jouvencel*, a primer for young noblemen, in which he gives a clear picture of how as a professional soldier he thought about and conducted war at the end of the Middle Ages. He wanted to teach his readers how "always to do well and increase their honour and prowess in the marvellous adventures of war."[23] Jean V de Bueil saw military life as being potentially ennobling; indeed, as something approaching a religious experience. He wrote:

It is a joyous thing, a war.... You love your comrades so much in war. When you see your quarrel is just and your blood is fighting well, tears rise to your eyes. A great sweet feeling of loyalty and pity fills your heart on seeing your friend so valiantly exposing his body to execute and accomplish the command of our Creator. And then you prepare to go and live or die with him and for love not to abandon him. And out of that there arises such delectation, that he who has not tasted it is not fit to say what a delight it is.

Do you think that a man who does that fears death? Not at all: for he feels strengthened, he is so elated that he does not know where he is. Truly he is afraid of nothing.[24]

But, sentiments aside, Jean V de Bueil was in fact a hard-hearted realist when military operations were at stake. For example, he quotes approvingly an old captain serving the French king. The captain stressed the importance of his forces being able to live off the land and not relying on their often-inadequate supply column. The captain said:

If it please the king, our lord, to supply us with victuals and money to sustain us, we will serve him in all enterprises and obey his orders—as indeed we must do—without levying or exacting anything from the inhabitants of the countryside here. If, however, other affairs, or false counsel, prevent him from provisioning us or paying us, we ourselves must raise victuals and finance both from persons in our own obedience and from enemies, as reasonably we can. From those on our own side we will demand as modest a collection as we can, telling them that their contributions will guarantee them against everybody.[25]

Mercenaries usually did not willingly engage in siege warfare because it could take months to capture a well-defended castle or city. Instead, they were masters at hit-and-run warfare focused on relatively "soft" targets of opportunity. As Jean V de Bueil tells us,

They spy out a walled castle for a day or two beforehand; then, collecting together a group of thirty or forty brigands, they approach it from one side and then from another. At the break of day they burst in and set fire to a house, making so much noise that the inhabitants think there must be a thousand men-at-arms among them and flee in all directions. They break into the houses and loot them before departing loaded with spoil.[26]

[Men-at-arms were trained fighters who, because of the expense or the social responsibilities involved in being a knight, had never gone through the formal ceremony of investiture to become one. All knights were thus men-at-arms, but not all men-at-arms were knights.]

It is very clear that warfare in the Middle Ages and Renaissance had many attractions for ambitious men. Under "feudalism" (this term greatly oversimplifies a much more complex political and economic structure but no other "ism" has replaced it yet), military service was based on two key factors: the personal ties between lord and subject, and land-holding.[27] In practice, however, there was a great deal of variation in medieval and Renaissance warfare. Armies generally consisted of a core of highly skilled knights, together with the men of their immediate households; mounted and infantry mercenaries, usually hired for the duration of a given campaign; and locals fulfilling their feudal obligations under duress, with very few (if any) military skills.[28] During emergencies, a general mobilization could cast a wide and effective net over a local population. In 1325, for example, the Florentine state alone, with only about 400,000 inhabitants, could raise a force of 1,500 mercenary horsemen, 500 Florentine knights, and perhaps about 15,000 infantrymen.[29]

Feudalism can be defined more precisely as "an honor-based system by which the members of the aristocratic class exchanged land for military service."[30] There was plenty of room in this system for skilled mercenaries and, in fact, a real need for them. The feudal system was not all-encompassing, and mercenaries flourished in its many interstices.[31] They were often the most experienced forces military leaders could obtain.[32]

All these men, nobles and commoners alike, dealt in violence, directly or indirectly. Looking for an explanation of the endemic and, to the modern mind, often senseless violence of the early Middle Ages, the French medievalist Marc Bloch (1886–1944) concluded that violence was deeply rooted in the social structure and mentality of the times. Fundamentally, it reflected the palpable absence of any central authority able to impose peaceful solutions on situations where passions ran high. Bloch quotes a prophecy, made in the middle of the 9th century by a cleric from Ravenna, Italy, who had witnessed and deplored the collapse of the Carolingian dream of empire. This cleric predicted, "When, after the demise of the Roman Empire of the Franks, various kings shall seat themselves on the august throne, *each man will put his trust only in the sword.*"[33] Indeed, as the modern scholar Timothy Reuter has written,

> warfare was perhaps the dominant concern of the political elites of the eighth, ninth, and tenth centuries. Other medieval social orders have been described as "a society organized for war": Carolingian and Ottonian societies were largely organized *by* war.[34] [The greatest Carolingian monarch was Charlemagne, who was crowned Emperor by Pope Leo III at Rome in 800. The Ottonian dynasty (919–1024) was a dynasty of German kings, named after its first Emperor, Otto I.]

Reliance on the sword was necessary because violence played a major role on so many fronts: in the early medieval economy, in medieval law, and especially in the manners and minds of the common man. Three facts can be usefully noted here[35]:

- On the economic front, at a time when trade and travel were difficult and uncertain at best, oppression and plunder offered a well-armed, ambitious, aggressive man the quickest and surest road to prosperity. Many nobles and their warriors made their way in life by means not too far removed from those of common brigands.
- On the legal front, the principle of customary law was used to validate the usurpations—violent or peaceful, large or small—of property and land which occurred very frequently. Moreover, the right of every man and family to take the law into their own hands and to mete out justice as they saw fit led to long-running bloody feuds. When there seemed to be no other way of determining an accused person's innocence or guilt, a carefully-calibrated amount of violence was used to ferret out the truth—via the ordeals by hot water, by hot iron, or by cold water.[36]
- Finally, on the social front, violence was an accepted part of the manners and the mind-set of the age. Human life did not have a great deal of value then, since it was seen as only a brief way-station on the road to an endless hereafter, either in heaven or in hell. Writing in about 1024, Bishop Burchard of the Holy Roman Empire complained sorrowfully:

> Every day, murders in the manner of wild beasts are committed among the dependents of St. Peter [i.e., among his own parishioners]. They attack each other through drunkenness, through pride, or for no reason at all. In the course of one year thirty-five serfs of St. Peter's, completely innocent people, have been killed by other serfs of the church; and the murderers, far from repenting, glory in their crime.[37]

Medieval and Renaissance culture encouraged nobles to fight to the death about points of honor in order to win admiration for their physical prowess and to keep potential adversaries at bay. A knight's reputation preceded him and helped to protect him. Take, for example, Sir Thomas Malory's famous and moving story *Le Morte d'Arthur* (*The Death of Arthur*), which recounts the lives of the fictional King Arthur, his queen Guinevere, and his knights, especially Sir Lancelot. Malory himself appears to have been a knight in the service of the Earl of Warwick. He fought on Warwick's side at the siege of Calais in 1436; spent the last 20 years of his life in prison due to convictions for attempted murder, rape, and armed robbery; and died in about 1471.

Malory tells us that when Sir Lancelot's enemies conspired to kill him, King Arthur warned these knights that they must first have clear proof that Lancelot was in fact a traitor, i.e., that he was having an affair with Arthur's wife, Queen Guinevere. If so, this would have been a treasonable offense and would have merited the death penalty. Arthur therefore told the knights (spelling and punctuation as in the original):

> I would be loth to begin such a thing but that I might have proofs upon it; for Sir Lancelot is an hardy knight and all ye know he is the best knight among us all; and but [i.e., unless] if he be taken with the deed, he will fight with him that bringeth up the noise [i.e., whoever accuses him of adultery], and I know no knight that is able to match him.[38]

As a result of Arthur's warning, Lancelot's enemies waited until he had entered the Queen's bedroom. Then 14 of them, all heavily armed, pounded on the door and demanded that he come out and surrender. Instead, Lancelot, who had no armor in the room but did have his sword, opened the door just enough for one of the knights to blunder into the room. Malory says of this knight:

> His name was Colgrevaunce of Gore, and he with a sword struck at Sir Lancelot mightily; and he [Lancelot] put aside the stroke and gave him such a buffet upon the helmet, that he fell groveling dead within the chamber door. And then Sir Lancelot with great might drew that dead knight within the chamber door; and Sir Lancelot with the help of the queen and her ladies was lightly armed in Sir Colgrevaunce's armour....
>
> So then Sir Lancelot set all open the chamber door, and mightily and knightly he strode in among them [the remaining knights]; and anon at the first buffet he slew Sir Agravain. And twelve of his fellows after, for there was none of the twelve that might stand Sir Lancelot one buffet. Also Sir Lancelot wounded Sir Mordred, and he fled with all his might.[39]

Given the very high level of real and fictional violence in the Middle Ages and Renaissance, it is not surprising that educated men reached into the past to resurrect classical conclusions about the best military strategies and tactics. Possibly in the late 4th century, Publius Flavius Vegetius Renatus, known simply as "Vegetius," drew on Roman sources and wrote *De re militari*, a title which can best be translated as *On Roman*

Introduction

Military Matters. Although Vegetius had no military experience himself and much of what he said was simply cautious common sense (e.g., "Men must be sufficiently tried before they are led against an enemy"), *De re militari* was widely reproduced and became the bible of warfare throughout the Middle Ages and even beyond, probably because its aphorisms are so simple, so good, and so memorable.

It was also a timely warning to citizens that, in order to defend the common good, their sons had to know how to fight: relying on mercenaries to keep the peace was a short-sighted, dangerous policy. His points did strike home: Queen Eleanor of Castile commissioned a translation of Vegetius's work as a present for her husband, King Edward I of England, while they were both on crusade in the Holy Land in 1271–1272.[40] Remarkably, Vegetius is still widely quoted today. His most famous exhortation, *si vis pacem para bellum* ("if you wish peace, prepare for war"), is often evoked by military leaders and politicians. What this means is that a strong society is much less vulnerable to attack by its enemies than a weak society; for this reason, it is much to the advantage of a society to be strong. Furthermore — in a lasting tribute to Vegetius's memory — the world's most popular and widely-used military and police handgun cartridge is officially known as the 9 × 19mm Parabellum.[41]

Vegetius also addressed the Romans' use of mercenaries. By the time of the Late Roman Empire, over half of the Roman Army consisted not of Roman citizens but of contingents of auxiliaries known as federates. They were drawn from the "barbarian tribes" outside the Roman Empire who had made a treaty with it.[42] (In this context, a "barbarian" was defined as someone living outside the pale of the Roman Empire and its civilization and who probably spoke Latin badly, if at all.) The federates believed, probably quite correctly, that they were better fighters than the Romans who employed them. The late Roman aristocracy was the only one in the pre-industrial world (excluding China) that was not dominated by military prowess: its values were education and comfort, not valor and horsemanship.[43] As a result, the federates had much greater energy and aggression in battle than did their more languid Roman officers.

Vegetius says of the federates:

We shall now explain the difference between the [Roman] legions and the auxiliaries. The latter are hired corps of foreigners assembled from different parts of the Empire, made up of different numbers, without knowledge of each other or any tie or affection. Each nation has its own peculiar discipline, customs and manner of fighting.

Little can be expected from forces so dissimilar in every respect, since it is one of the most essential points in military undertakings that the whole army should be put in motion and governed by one and the same order. But it is almost impossible for men to act in concert under such varying and unsettled conditions.

They are, however, when properly trained and disciplined, of material service and are always joined as light troops with the legions of the line. And though the legions do not place their principal dependence on them, yet they look on them as a very considerable addition to their strength.[44]

In terms of military ideology, medieval and Renaissance warfare had two wellsprings. The first was Vegetius's practical advice on how to wage war in a physical sense. The second was a mixture of classical, Germanic, and Christian writings which spoke of the role of honor and of the moral foundations for legitimately waging war. These two sources mixed, mingled, and gradually (by about the 1230s) had generated among the more thoughtful members of the warrior class a composite belief which in turn had two parts.

On the one hand, fighters considered warfare to be a very positive activity because it gave men high social status; it could be very profitable; and, as Bertrand de Born so cheerfully assures us, it could also be a great adventure. On the other hand, these warriors also recognized that because of the horrendous suffering and destruction which warfare inflicted on innocent families and their property, it needed to be limited and controlled to the maximum extent feasible under the exigencies of combat. The net result of their conscious and unconscious deliberations was the body of guidelines and standards of military behavior known as chivalry.

This term first appeared in English in 1292 as a borrowing from the Old French *chevalerie* ("knighthood"). Its meaning changed over time but as the Dutch historian Johan Huizinga defined it in its purest form in his influential book *The Waning of the Middle Ages* (1919), "the source of the chivalrous idea is pride aspiring to beauty, and formalized pride gives rise to a conception of honour, which is the pole of noble life."[45]

In less poetic terms, chivalry urged warriors to practice such virtues as mercy, courage, valor, protection of the weak and poor, being faithful to God and to the church, and, last but not least, courtly love (i.e., a knight must serve a lady and show his devotion to her and, indeed, to all women, through his gentleness and graciousness). Moreover, a knight was also expected to be a *prud'homme*. There is no single English word that translates this concept adequately. In Old French, *prud'homme* connoted a man who was not merely a brave, loyal, and skilled knight but who was also a wise, experienced, and generous man of the world. As a contemporary poem says,

> Tant est prud'homme, si com semble
> Qui a deux choses ensemble:
> Valeur de corps et bonté d'âme.[46]
> ["Such is the *prud'homme* that he possesses two things at the same time: physical courage and a generosity of spirit."]

It is not amiss to conclude this chapter with a few comments on naval warfare.[47] These will necessarily be brief because very few medieval chroniclers had any experience on the sea or had much interest in it. Not many medieval naval records seem to have survived, so very little is known about the officers and the many thousands of common seamen who staffed the galleys and other ships. Probably for all these reasons, naval warfare in the Middle Ages is a subject which may not ever be fully explored.[48]

For example, although a great many soldiers of fortune and mercenary sailors and galley hands must have served in the fleets of Charles I of Anjou from about 1265 to 1285, the loss of the enormous archive of the Angevin[49] chancery (destroyed in World War II by the Germans outside of Naples in 1943) means that we can now get only faint glimpses of the nautical state of play in the days of Charles I. The maritime careers of a few notables and galley commanders can still be traced, but nothing will ever be known about the many thousands, probably the many tens of thousands, of unknown seafarers who staffed the fleets of Charles I.[50]

What maritime combat did occur was essentially land warfare played out at sea. Most ships were single-masted, slow, hard to maneuver, broad-beamed, and designed to carry cargo rather than to fight.

Indeed, the major use of ships in the Middle Ages was simply to carry warriors from one port to another on raiding expeditions. Between 1346 and 1347, for example, some 738 ships were needed to transport Edward III's forces across the English Channel to France. The French not only used their own ships for transport, but also hired galleys and galley crews from Italy.[51]

An excellent example of medieval naval warfare is the battle of Sluys, when the fleet of Edward III of England clashed with the French fleet off the Flemish coast in 1340. This fight is discussed later in the book.

I

Meeting the Warriors and the Tools of Their Trade

Changes in the supply of and the demand for medieval and Renaissance mercenaries reflected the attractiveness, or lack of it, of alternative employment.[1] Prosperity drove down the supply of mercenaries because then there were many better-paid and far less hazardous civilian jobs to be had. On the other hand, economic downturns, or even temporary and localized outbreaks of peace, increased the supply because there were fewer alternatives. That said, consistent warfare, like that of the Hundred Years' War, opened up military careers, steady employment, and the hope of ransoms.[2]

Because of the violence, importance, and duration of the Hundred Years' War, a few words on it may be useful here. This was a very bitter, protracted, and intermittent series of conflicts between England and France which extended from about 1337 to 1453 and which France eventually won. This victory was due in part to the great medieval French general Bertrand du Guesclin (ca. 1320–1380), who as commander of the mercenary companies of France used a Fabian strategy to win back most of the territory that France had lost to the English. (A Fabian strategy, named after the Roman dictator Quintus Fabius Maximus Verrucosus, avoids pitched battles and frontal assaults and concentrates instead on wearing down an opponent through a long war of attrition.)

In the broadest terms, the underlying cause of the Hundred Years' War (1337–1453) was the gradual breakdown of the feudal order in Western Europe and its replacement by a new order of nations which paid increasing attention to their own national ambitions, strengths, and weaknesses. In narrower terms and less soaring language, the Hundred

Years' War was a series of conflicts between the Kingdom of England and the Kingdom of France and their various allies for control of the French throne.

The belligerents in the Hundred Years' War included:

- For the House of Valois: France, Castile, Scotland, Genoa, Majorca, Bohemia, the Crown of Aragon, and Brittany.
- For the House of Plantagenet, also known as the House of Anjou: England, Burgundy, Aquitaine (contemporary chroniclers used the names Aquitaine and Gascony interchangeably), Brittany, Portugal, Navarre, Flanders, Hainaut, Luxembourg, and the Holy Roman Empire.

In this war, as in many other medieval and Renaissance conflicts, the differences between noble knights, on the one hand, and cutthroat highwaymen, on the other, were never very clear. The military equipment of the day could be used equally well by any man trained to handle it. The dagger of the knight, for example, was not significantly different from the dagger of the highwayman. As the modern scholar Nicholas Wright explains,

> Captains of the Free Companies, who acquired their wealth and reputation as freebooters, moved in and out of princely service with an ease which suggested no sense of impropriety: they married into the traditional aristocracy, acquired titles of nobility and offices of high command within the armies of rival kings, and they achieved immortality alongside the Black Prince and Sir John Chandos in the pages of Froissart's chronicles.[3]

Perhaps we should explain here that Jean Froissart (ca. 1337–ca. 1405) was a French historian, poet, priest, and one of the most important chroniclers of medieval France.[4] He focused very hard on his writing, describing it as being like the labor of a blacksmith. He tells us: "*je suis de nouveau entré dans ma forge pour travailler et forger en la noble matière du temps passé*" ("Once again I entered my forge [i.e., my office] to hammer out there something from the noble material of former times").

The text of Froissart's famous *Chronicles* is preserved in more than 100 illuminated manuscripts, illustrated by a variety of miniaturists. One of the most lavish of these copies was commissioned by Louis of Gruuthuse, a Flemish nobleman, in the 1470s. Its four volumes, now in

the Bibliothèque Nationale de France (BNF), contain 112 colorful miniatures by well-known Brugeois artists of the day. In the Conclusions chapter of our own book, we will specifically direct the reader's attention to
one of these volumes, namely BNF FR 2643, because it contains such
exceptionally useful pictures of medieval warfare.

Froissart's avowed purpose was to describe, for the edification of
future generations of warriors, the "great enterprises, fine feats of arms,
which took place during the wars waged by France and England."[5] To
this extent, he was not an impartial observer, being too prone to glorify
the often-sordid military events of the past as examples of true chivalry.
Nevertheless, he is such a good observer and he is still so readable that
we shall quote him frequently in this book, referring to him simply as
"Froissart."

In general, war or no war, medieval mercenaries consistently
received wages comparable to those earned by skilled civilian craftsmen.
This was not unreasonable because they were in fact skilled military
craftsmen. Unlike their civilian counterparts, however, mercenary soldiers could also profit (more or less legally, or at least with minimal fear
of any punishment) from the many opportunities to rape, loot, and pillage that came their way in the course of campaigning. This could be a
very lucrative calling. For example, an unidentified mercenary, campaigning near the prosperous towns of southwestern France in the mid–
14th century, reported that

> when we rode out seeking adventure, we captured several rich merchants
> from the towns of Toulouse, Condom, La Réole or Bergerac. Every day we
> did not fail to stuff our pockets with superfluous and pretty things.[6]

Peasants were unarmed except for their knives and were usually too
intimidated to offer any resistance to mercenaries who planned to pillage
their villages, but there are some documented exceptions. In December
1373, for example, according to the testimony of 10 "poor laborers" of
the parish of Saint-Romain-sur-Cher in the French province of Loir-et-
Cher, two strangers armed with swords and wearing heavy jackets rode
into their village with the clear intention of stealing property, demanding
ransoms, and raping women. They were known as *pillars* (i.e., pillagers)
and were part of one of the larger companies of soldiers who were then

terrorizing the district. The villagers were so terrified that all of them fled into the nearby woods and stayed there for several days. They seem to have plucked up their courage later on, however, for this account ends with the death, by drowning, of the two *pillars*.[7]

During the High Middle Ages (from about 1000 to 1300), major military operations were very complicated undertakings. Italian armies of the 13th century, for example, consisted of feudal, militia, and mercenary elements, with a gradual but steady increase of mercenary companies by the end of the century.[8] Armies could easily include a wide range of forces. The king or leader could bring his household and other close followers on campaigns with him. He might also be accompanied by the retinues of his great vassals and sometimes by allies over whom he had very limited control. Retinues were divided into horse and foot. Some men were present only because of their tenurial or other obligations to a superior, but pay was also widely used as an inducement. (Under feudal law, a tenurial obligation was one in which a person held land from a superior in exchange for providing military or other service to that superior.) By the end of the Middle Ages—and, indeed, long before then—it was not always clear which men fought because of their military obligations and which fought of their own free will. In fact, both certainly expected to be paid. As the modern scholar John France tells us,

> Perhaps the best indication that there were large numbers of knights and foot-soldiers who served for pay is the celebrated penance of Henry II for the murder of Becket [Archbishop of Canterbury], which provided that the king was to finance 200 knights to serve with the Knights Templars [one of the most famous Christian military orders].[9]

Thus while all mercenaries were paid men, not all paid men were mercenaries.[10]

The question of pay became an important one in social terms.[11] In classical Latin, the word *mercenarius* simply means "hireling" but it came to have very negative connotations in the Middle Ages because, in the Gospel of St. John, Christ describes himself as the Good Shepherd—in sharp contrast to the unreliable hired shepherd who is only a hired man (in Latin: *quia mercennarius est*), who does not own the sheep himself, and who thus feels no responsibility to take excellent care of them.

I. Meeting the Warriors and the Tools of Their Trade

In medieval times, then, to label a man as a mercenary was to imply that he was merely an unreliable paid man of lowly birth, rather than a chivalrous warrior of high social standing. Mercenaries were never to be trusted: church bells rang to alert the residents of villages and towns in southern France when they were sighted.[12] Rank-and-file mercenaries (though not their senior officers) stood only on the far fringes of society and were thought by their social superiors to lack the ethics necessary to bind them to good behavior.[13]

Perhaps for this reason, contemporary chroniclers tended to avoid applying the term *mercenarius* to real mercenaries. Geoffroy de Brueil, the abbot of Vigeois (France) from 1170 to 1184, knew many mercenaries and was horrified by the damage they caused. He was an eyewitness to their deeds and was prominent at the time of the Capuchin movement — an anti-mercenary movement by townspeople and peasants whose prosperity was threatened by mercenary depredations.[14] But when he used the term *mercenarios*, he was referring not to such soldiers but rather to clergymen who had been corrupted by rich living.[15] Indeed, many medieval chroniclers had a very low opinion of mercenaries. As the troubadour Bertrand de Born confessed in 1194,

> I have as much affection for the Basque *routiers* as for greedy prostitutes. [*Routiers* were freelance soldiers fighting on their own account; the mercenary companies to which they belonged where known as *routes*]. Sacks of sterling pennies and Capetian moutons [i.e., French gold coins] offend me when they are the product of fraud. A household knight who shows himself greedy ought to be hung, along with the magnate who sells his services. No man ought to pursue Lady Greed, who sells her favours for money.[16]

Yet, in point of fact, pay was always important. In 1261, Brother Thomas Bérard, master of the Knights Templar, complained in a letter to Brother Amadeus, the grand commander of the Order in England, that in the Holy Land the Order was having great difficulty hiring mercenaries there. These men (quite understandably, to our eyes) wanted to receive not only their daily living expenses but also danger pay as well.[17] In the late 13th and early 14th centuries many nobles hired mercenaries from the Rhineland (i.e., the lands on either side of the River Rhine in Central Europe) and from the Meuse (named after the River Meuse in northeastern France). In 1297, 1300, and 1302, hundreds of mercenaries were recruited into the army of the counts of Flanders. Although all these men fought bravely enough on the battlefield, they made a bad impression on contemporary chroniclers because they fought purely for money. The Belgian chronicler Louis of Veltham, for example, says that they loved only wine, good food, and money.[18]

The medievalist John France explains this anti-mercenary prejudice in the following terms:

> there were very strong social and cultural reasons for a framework of language which hides much reality from us. Roger of Sicily, of the Hauteville family who conquered South Italy in the eleventh century, was happy to tell his family historian that once he had lived as a brigand.[19] But in the twelfth century the European nobility [was] rather more fussy ... about how it presented itself and anxious to stand aloof from others. Hence care was taken to distance the "proper soldiers," the aristocrats and their dependents, from others who fought. Somewhere in that grey and uncertain gap a man might become a mercenary, but quite where the change took place is uncertain. In a world where a landed knight might serve both as a vassal and as a paid man, this is hardly surprising.[20]

Social niceties aside, it is clear that the combat abilities of medieval forces varied considerably. Virtually all the knights and men-at-arms were exceptionally well-trained, having begun learning their military skills as boys. At the age of seven, for example, they were sent to the castles and homes of wealthy relatives or local lords to begin the years of training needed to become a knight. From the age of seven to fourteen they served as pages in these households. From fourteen to twenty-one they were in effect apprentice knights and were known as squires. Each young man had to develop excellent equestrian skills, a very high level of physical fitness, and the ability to use a wide range of weapons effectively — beginning, perhaps, with wooden or blunt swords.[21]

It is also probable that at least some of them were taught how to swim. In 1167 King Henry II of England deployed tactical units of mercenaries at the siege of the town of Chaumont in France. In a brilliantly executed tactical operation, he secretly sent his Welsh mercenaries swimming down the River Epte towards the town, while he approached the gates of the town at the head of his army. His presence there goaded the French to sally forth to meet the English in battle. As the French troops left the gates and began to form up into their battle array, the Welsh swimmers were able to enter the town from behind and to set fire to the buildings. The French forces, trapped between Henry II's army and the burning town, rushed back into Chaumont to douse the flames. Henry II and his men followed hard on their heels, however, and victoriously took possession of the gates and thus the town.[22]

Virtually nothing is known today about how the "common mercenary," to coin a phrase, was trained. In order to be hired as a mercenary, he had to persuade his employer that he had the military skills his employer wanted. Most probably, he mastered them on his own, during earlier campaigns in the field. In this learning process, he doubtless got some friendly advice from his fellow soldiers and no end of blisteringly-harsh criticisms from his immediate superior, who was probably a corporal, i.e., the lowest-ranking non-commissioned officer.

Some knights and men-at-arms were full-time professional mercenaries. Not much is known about their tactics, but they were probably the same as those used by non-mercenary knights.[23] They could fight as well on foot as well as from the saddle. Philippe de Commines (1447-ca. 1511), a writer and diplomat in the courts of Burgundy and France and a good observer of the local scene, reported that in the late 15th century

> it was then the most honourable practice among the Burgundians [i.e., among their knights] that they should dismount with the archers, and always a great number of gentlemen did so in order that the common soldiers might be reassured and fight better. They had learned this method from the English.[24]

Most mercenaries were not knights or men-at-arms but, to use modern American or British military slang, simply G.I.s or squaddies serving temporary tours of duty. Nevertheless, when compared to the ill-armed, undisciplined, and untrained rabble that comprised the bulk of the infantry, the mercenaries—whether cavalry or infantry—were experienced, skilled soldiers. Since in medieval times there were no organized programs through which a common man could learn and develop military skills, the mercenaries' on-the-job training was such a valuable asset that a commander would pay well to have them on his side. Let us trace very briefly some of the initial stages of their rise in the medieval conflicts of Western Europe.

There are records of mercenaries in Venice as early as the 10th century.[25] In France, in 991, Count Fulk Nerra of Anjou employed mercenaries—probably experienced specialists such as engineers and crossbowmen—against Count Conan of Brittany. The Old French *chansons de geste* ("tales of heroic deeds") of the late 11th century refer to them, too.[26] Pope Leo IX (1002–1054) hired an army of mercenaries in Germany to fight against the Norman knights who had drifted into southern Italy and were working as mercenaries for the local lords. Countess Richildis of Hainault (ca. 1034–1088; Hainault is now part of modern Belgium) used mercenaries against Robert the Frisian of Flanders. William the Conqueror recruited many knights and adventurers in France when he launched his conquest of England in 1066. He hired many others there 19 years later, when Canute IV of Denmark and Robert the Frisian were planning an invasion of England in 1085.

In later chapters we will have much more to say about mercenaries in action, but it is important to note here that despite their formidable military skills, medieval mercenaries also had two important defects. The first was that they were expensive. The second was perhaps more important. While it was easy enough to hire them, it could be very dangerous to fire them. When discharged, having no other source of income, they often metamorphosed into heavily-armed bands of marauders or mercenaries who raped, looted, burned, and pillaged their way across the defenseless countryside. Especially during the Hundred Years' War (1337–1453), such men variously found employment in royal field armies, in royal and private garrisons, and in private mercenary companies—as dictated by royal policies, by local circumstances, and by their own needs. The English kings, for example, were quite happy to turn their discharged mercenaries loose on France.[27]

Henry Deifle, the great 19th century Dominican historian, wrote that his studies in the Vatican archives (regarding the destruction of churches and monasteries in France during the Hundred Years' War) revealed that this long war was "an endless and grimly monotonous succession of massacres, fires, pillaging, ransoms, destructions, losses of harvests and cattle, rapes and—to make an end of it—every sort of calamity."[28] Mercenaries must have been responsible for a good part of these losses.

Whether under contract or freelance, mercenaries used the same weapons as their non-mercenary comrades-in-arms. These can be broadly categorized as follows; a few of them will be discussed in this same order[29]:

- Bladed edged weapons (swords, daggers, and knives)
- Blunt hand weapons (various kinds of clubs and maces)
- Polearms (wooden poles with metal points or blades mounted on them, e.g., spears, lances, and pikes). In the 14th century, the development of plate armor actually encouraged the development of various pole arms: even if they could not always break through the armor, the fierce, well-focused blows they delivered often caused blunt trauma to the knights.
- Missile weapons (that is, weapons used at a distance, e.g., bows, crossbows, early firearms, stone-throwers, and cannons)
- Other medieval weapons and tools of the trade (equipment for siege warfare; chemical, biological, and psychological weapons; armor; and horses)

Because the study of medieval weapons and armor is a specialized and complex calling, in this book we will content ourselves with brief descriptions of some of the most interesting weapons and tools of the trade used by medieval and Renaissance soldiers. Our goal here will be to get a better understanding of this type of warfare.

The first and symbolically by far the most important weapon was the arming sword, also called a knight's sword or knightly sword. This was the single-handed cruciform sword (i.e., its hilt was shaped like a cross) of the High Middle Ages. A modern expert on medieval weapons writes that

> as a knight or professional soldier trained with his weapons, he developed a sense of distance and timing to set him apart from his contemporaries who were not so highly trained. Highly-trained men-at-arms, mercenaries, and the city militias of the guilds learned not merely how to cut [with a sword], or even to cut effectively, but to cut with extreme precision at full force.[30]

Not surprisingly, medieval culture attached a great deal of symbolic importance to the sword. *The Song of Roland*, a famous 11th century poem, offers proof of this point. This long poem is an important part of the "Matter of France"—a body of literature and legendary material associated with Charlemagne and the history of France. The Matter of France is one of the "Three Matters" repeatedly cited in medieval literature. As the medieval French poet Jean Bodel tells us:

> Ne sont que III matières à nul homme atandant,
> De France et de Bretaigne, et de Rome la grant.
> [There are but three literary cycles that no one should be without: the Matter of France, of Britain, and of great Rome.][31]

The Matter of France focuses on the deeds of Roland and of the paladins, sometimes known as the Twelve Peers, who were the foremost warriors of Charlemagne's court. The Matter of Britain deals with King Arthur and the legendary history of Great Britain. The Matter of Rome focuses on medieval interpretations of Greek and Roman mythology.

The Song of Roland is a *chanson de geste*, a literary form which flourished between the 11th and 15th centuries and which celebrated heroic deeds. It is based on the battle of Roncevaux Pass in the Pyrenees in 778, during the Muslim invasion of southern France. The great sword Durendal, swung by Roland, the hero of the story, was said to have contained within its golden hilt a piece of the clothing of the Virgin Mary, along with other precious holy relics. In the story, Roland heroically wields Durendal in a desperate rear-guard action against the Muslims, successfully slowing the advance of the massive Muslim army and thus giving Emperor Charlemagne and his forces the time they need to retreat safely from Spain into France.

In the interests of historical accuracy, however, we must note here that, over the years, local oral tradition seized upon this battle and began to portray it as a major conflict between Christian and Muslim armies. In point of fact, it was a large guerrilla force of local Basques, angered by Charlemagne's harsh treatment of the Basque people, who attacked Charlemagne's detachment.

When Roland feels himself near death and sees that the Muslim army cannot possibly be stopped no matter what he does, he vainly tries to break Durendal by smashing it against the mountainside — to prevent it from being captured by the Muslims. To quote *The Song of Roland*:

> Roland gazes at the twinkling sword, murmuring to himself, "Ah, Durendal, how beautiful you are, how you shine, how white you shine! How against the sun you gleam and return fire for fire! ... Together we have con-

quered Anjou and Brittany. Together we have won Poitou and Maine, and fair Normandy, Provence and Aquitaine, Lombardy and Romagna [i.e., Rumania], Bavaria and Flanders, and even Burgundy! Together we have won Constantinople and Poland, Saxony, Scotland, England.... For you, Durendal, I feel such heavy grief. May France never have to say that you are in pagan hands!" Desperately Roland strikes the brown rock with all his power and might. The sword neither splinters nor breaks, only bounces away from the rock.[32]

Since Roland cannot destroy Durendal, he hides it under his body as he sinks down into death. The place where he tried to break this famous sword — splitting the mountain in the process — is still known today as La Brèche de Roland (Roland's Breach). This is in fact a natural gap in the mountains, 131 feet wide and 328 feet deep, at an altitude of 9,199 feet, located in the Cirque de Gavarnie in the Pyrenees. Often visited by tourists, it forms part of the border between France and Spain.

The longsword (also spelled long-sword) of the late medieval period (ca. 1350 to 1550) was important in fact and fiction. Up to 4 feet long and weighing as much as 5 to 8 pounds, it had a cruciform hilt and was usually gripped tightly by both hands. Longswords — unsurpassed for hewing, slicing, and stabbing — were prized for their killing capabilities in close combat. Moreover, in hand-to-hand fighting, their long hilts could be used for tripping an opponent or knocking him off balance. A knight armed with a longsword was thus not a man to trifle with. Finally, contemporary accounts assure us that the longsword also provided the foundation for learning how to use other infantry weapons, e.g., spears, staves, and polearms.

A knight's arming sword was typically used in conjunction with a buckler (a small shield 6 to 18 inches in diameter) and was a light, well-balanced, versatile weapon which could be used both to cut and to thrust. The arming sword was worn by a knight even when he was not in armor; in fact, if he appeared in public without it he would be considered as being shamefully undressed.

Daggers were important, too. A dagger has a double-edged blade and is primarily designed for stabbing or thrusting. A knife has a single-edged blade, which is best at cutting, although some daggers and knives can be used for stabbing, thrusting, and cutting. In the Middle

Ages—and, indeed even today—daggers and knives are usually backup weapons designed for last-ditch personal survival.

With the appearance of plate armor during the Middle Ages, however, the dagger came into its own as a very useful offensive weapon. It could be used to stab through the gaps in an enemy's armor, e.g., under the arm, with the objective of piercing the heart. One type of dagger—the stiletto—was known as the "misericorde," meaning "mercy." Its pointed, strong blade was used to give a fatally-wounded opponent the *coup de grace* ("mercy strike") to end his suffering. A rondel dagger could penetrate a suit of armor either through the joints or under the visor of a helmet. This dagger had a long, slim blade tapering to a needle point. "Rondel" means round or circular; the weapon gets its name from its round hand guard and pommel. It could be used to force a wounded knight, or one who had been thrown from his horse and was stunned by the fall, to surrender and be held for ransom.

A mace is a strong shaft with a heavy head made of metal or stone. During the Middle Ages, mail and later plate armor protected the wearer from edged weapons and projectiles, e.g., arrows and crossbow bolts (crossbow bolts were also known as quarrels). Solid metal maces were able to injure or kill an armored man, bloodlessly, because the shock of a heavy blow from a mace was enough to cause a concussion (a traumatic brain injury) without actually penetrating the armor or tearing the flesh. Flanged maces, however, had protruding edges which allowed them, when swung by a strong arm, to dent badly or even penetrate the very best armor.

In the Bayeux Tapestry (an embroidered cloth, made in England in the 1070s, which depicts the events leading up to the Norman conquest of England in 1066), Bishop Odo of Bayeux is shown swinging a mace at the battle of Hastings in 1066. Clergy often used maces in warfare to avoid the religious prohibition of clerics shedding blood: maces caused wounds or death by concussion. Clergymen fought on the battlefield in person until about 1540. William the Conqueror is also depicted in the Tapestry carrying a mace. Finally, the mace was a favorite weapon of the Italian mercenaries in the 14th century.

The bayonet on a modern rifle is the descendant of ancient polearms, such as the spear. After the waning of the Roman Empire, the spear continued to be used by almost all Western European cultures. Cheap and easy to make, it remained the main weapon of the common soldier in medieval times. To withstand cavalry attacks, the butts of the shafts could be set into the ground, with the spearheads sharply angled upward toward the enemy. In the 11th century, when used on horseback with stirrups and high-canted saddles to help the rider keep his seat, the spear — now in the form of a nine-foot-long lance — became a most formidable weapon.

We must note here, in the interests of historical accuracy, that the word "lance" was also used in Italy in the mid–15th century to describe a three-man combat team. This consisted of a man-at-arms, who was the lance-bearer and sometimes — but not always — a knight; his sergeant, and his page. Outfitting a lance was always expensive: in early 15th century Poland, for example, it cost the equivalent of 30 head of cattle.[33]

In the "couched lance" technique, a mounted knight would grip his lance firmly with one hand, tucking it securely under his armpit, and would use his other hand to guide and control the horse. When mastered after long years of practice, all the momentum of horse and rider was focused on the tip of the lance. The medieval sport of jousting help knights to practice and perfect their skills with the lance.

A pike is a very long thrusting weapon used by infantrymen, both for attacks on enemy foot soldiers and to defend themselves against cavalry charges. Ranging in length from 10 feet to over 20 feet, a pike had a wooden shaft with a metal spearhead attached to its end. The great length of pikes presented an oncoming enemy with a formidable concentration of spearheads, while at the same time keeping the pikemen themselves at some distance from their targets. Pikes were too long to use in close combat, however, so a pikeman also had to be armed with a sword, mace, or dagger to defend himself if enemies broke through the wall of pikes. By 1600, musketeers had driven all but the pikemen from the battlefield because the musket was able to pierce armor at 80 meters.[34]

In the Middle Ages, urban militias such as the Flemings (natives of Flanders) and the lowland Scotts were the principal users of pikes. So long as pike formations stood their ground, mounted men-at-arms could not overrun them, but these densely-packed formations were very vulnerable to massed fire from archers and crossbowmen. If the pike formations could be weakened or broken in this manner, they could then be attacked by dismounted men-at-arms. Knights fought on foot either when the terrain was too difficult for combat on horseback or when they wanted by their example to stiffen the ranks of the foot soldiers and to encourage them. The soldiers understood very well that, when dismounted, the knights were as fully committed to the fight as they were: they had no way to escape.

The deep pike attack column was very effective in the late medieval period. The Swabian War of 1499 between the Old Swiss Confederacy and the House of Habsburg involved both Swiss and Swabian pike-armed mercenaries and in all but a few minor skirmishes the more experienced Swiss soldiers defeated the Swabian and Habsburg armies. (See Appendix 2 for more detailed information on the Swiss mercenaries.) The Swabian War was the first conflict in which both sides deployed large formations of well-trained pikemen, but the ever-improving skills of artillerymen and arquebusiers proved, later on, that the time of the pikeman was already passing.

We turn now to two of the most famous weapons of medieval warfare and thus of medieval mercenaries—the English longbow and the Italian crossbow. Both are weapons that project arrows by means of their elasticity, i.e., they are a type of spring. As the bow is drawn, energy is stored in the limbs as potential energy. Physics teaches us that potential energy is the stored energy of position possessed by an object. When the bow is not drawn, i.e., when it is in its usual equilibrium position, there is no energy stored in it. But when its position is altered from its usual equilibrium position, i.e., when an archer is ready to shoot, the bow is able to store energy by virtue of its new position. This stored energy of position is referred to as potential energy.

Draw weight is a measurement of how much effort is required to bring a bow to full draw. The most powerful English longbows had a draw weight of up to 200 pounds at 32 inches of draw. They were thus far more powerful than the average hunting bow, which traditionally had a draw weight of only about 50 pounds at 28 inches of draw. Because of their constant practice since youth, English archers could handle very heavy bows. Ninety-two fairly complete English skeletons recovered from the wreck of the warship *Mary Rose*, which sank in the Solent (a stretch of sea separating the Isle of Wight from the mainland of England) in 1545 and was raised in 1982, give proof of repetitive stress injuries of the shoulder and lower spine — almost certainly the result of constant practice with such bows.[35] English (and the Welsh) archers used their powerful longbows to great effect in the civil wars of the times and in the Hundred Years' War against the French. A skilled longbow man could release 10 to 12 arrows per minute. A modern commentator has remarked, "The longbow was the machinegun of the Middle Ages: accurate, deadly, possessed of long range and rapid rate of fire, the flight of its missiles was likened to a storm."[36]

There are many contemporary reports about the tremendous power of longbows in the hands of experts. In one such account, we are told by the archdeacon Giraldus Cambrensis that during the siege of the Welsh castle of Abergavenny in 1182, arrows pierced an oak door four inches thick. The arrows were left sticking in the door, their tips being just visible on the inner side of the door. In another account, a knight was pinned to his horse by an arrow that went through the flap of his mail shirt, pierced his mail breeches, his thigh, his wooden saddle, and came to rest in the flank of his horse.[37]

Good as the longbow was, the crossbow had its merits, too. The Saracens called the crossbow *qaws Ferengi* ("Frankish bow") because the Crusaders used it with such great success against Arab and Turkish horsemen. A crossbow had a short, very powerful bow (known as a prod), made of wood or steel and mounted on a wooden stock made of yew, ash, hazel, or elm.[38] Crossbow bolts were much shorter than arrows. Unlike a longbow, which was extremely difficult to draw and which could not be held at full draw for more than a second or two seconds, a crossbow was cocked by means of a mechanical device (a lever or a crank on a ratchet) and did not require a great deal of strength to operate.

It was thus an ideal weapon for a young soldier or even for a boy (it required much less upper body strength than a longbow) or for an exhausted adult soldier. Moreover, thanks to its trigger mechanism, it could also be kept cocked for a long period of time with no effort on the part of the crossbowman. This permitted more accurate aiming when it was finally time to shoot: there were two or three notches on the stock in which to rest the thumb, which could then be lined up with the crossbow bolt to form a rudimentary sight. Early wood crossbows in the Middle Ages had an effective range of about 350 yards; the later powerful steel crossbows were more accurate, had a flatter trajectory, and a longer maximum range (of up to 500 yards).

On the battlefield, a crossbowman was very vulnerable when reloading his weapon — a slow and complicated process. He therefore protected himself by ducking behind a broad, four-to-five-foot-high convex shield known as a pavise, which when marching he carried slung across his back. Before a battle began, he propped up the pavise in front of him so that it would stay put. A pavise could also be used as part of a defensive screen called a pavisade, which was formed by setting up a row of pavises side-by-side. In this whole process, the medieval crossbowman was often assisted by one or more helpers.

Crossbows could not be fired as rapidly as longbows (their rate of fire was only about two crossbow bolts per minute) but they released more kinetic energy. Most of these crossbow bolts could penetrate mail; sometimes, with a solid hit at close range, they could even kill a knight in full armor. Moreover, a raw recruit could be taught how to use a crossbow in only one week, whereas combat competency with a longbow required many years of constant practice. The ability to use the crossbow was widespread. For example, all Venetians learned how to fire one as part of their civic obligations, and it was the usual weapon of garrison troops and town guards.[39]

Anna Comnena (1083–1153), a remarkable Greek aristocrat who was the daughter of Emperor Alexios I Komnenos of Byzantium (and also, in her own right, a scholar, a doctor, and a hospital administrator) gives us, in her book the *Alexiad*, a description of a very powerful crossbow. It was, she says, a fearsome new weapon:

> The crossbow is a weapon of the barbarians, absolutely unknown to the Greeks. In order to stretch it one does not pull the string with the right hand while pushing the bow with the left away from the body; this instrument of war, which fires weapons an enormous distance, has to be stretched by laying almost on one's back; each foot is pressed forcibly against the half-circles of the bow and the two hands tug at the bow, pulling it back with all one's strength toward the body.... Along [a groove in the stock of the crossbow] arrows of all kinds are fired. They are very short but extremely thick with a heavy iron tip. In the firing the string exerts

tremendous violence and force, so that the missiles wherever they strike do not rebound; in fact, they transfix a shield, cut through a heavy iron breastplate and resume their flight on the far side.... Such is the crossbow, a truly diabolical machine.[40]

Although in the 12th century the crossbow almost completely replaced the longbow in most European armies, this was not the case in England. The English preferred their tried and true longbows. Under King Edward I's sponsorship, Welsh and English archers perfected, through long arduous years of frequent practice, the strength, technique and discipline required to draw the longbow to the ear and then send storms of accurately-aimed arrows into advancing cavalry and infantry formations.[41] Indeed, during the battle of Crécy in 1346, English archers may have fired as many as half a million arrows during the course of this fight.[42] Arrow wounds made horses unmanageable, thus deflecting a cavalry charge; ranks of lightly-protected foot soldiers could easily be decimated.

In the armies of Europe, mounted and unmounted crossbowmen, often supported by archers and javeliners, were assigned to a central position in battle formations. Mounted knights armed with lances were ineffective against formations of pikemen who were combined with crossbowmen, whose weapons could penetrate the armor of many knights. As better mechanisms for cocking crossbows were developed, they could also be used on horseback, leading to new cavalry tactics. Knights and mercenaries were deployed in triangular formations, with the most heavily armored knights in the forefront, some of them carrying small but very powerful all-metal crossbows.

It is interesting to note that crossbows are still said to be used today by commando forces in Serbia, Greece, Turkey, and Spain. Chinese armed forces use crossbows at all unit levels, from traffic police to the elite Snow Leopard Commandos of the Chinese army. One reason for this is the crossbow's ability to stop persons carrying explosives without the risk of causing detonation. Another is that they kill silently and at a distance — a combination which may be an asset for authorities if they are trying to break up a terrorist or criminal attack.

The rank of commanding officer of the crossbowmen was one of the highest positions in a medieval army. In most European armies, mounted and unmounted crossbowmen, together with archers and javeliners (a javelin was a light spear thrown by hand), were assigned to a central position in battle formations. The crossbowmen would open fire on enemy forces before an attack by the crossbowmen's forces of mounted knights. Crossbows were also used in counterattacks to protect one's own infantry.

The arbalest was a later and much more powerful version of the crossbow. It had a steel prod, i.e., a steel bow; was bigger and heavier than earlier crossbows; and, thanks to the greater tensile strength of steel, it delivered far greater force. A large, windlass-cocked arbalest could have up to 5,000 pounds of power and could be accurate (against a very big target, such as a fortification) at more than 900 yards. Arbalests were sometimes considered to be inhumane and unfair weapons because they allowed a lightly-trained commoner to kill, safely and at relatively long range, a noble knight who had perfected his own fighting skills over the course of a lifetime of tournaments and battles.

The same charge must have been levied against the men who learned how to use the first firearms. Soldiers using earlier weapons had needed fitness and skill to operate them effectively. When such men were killed, wounded, or simply ran away, they were very hard to replace on short notice. Gunpowder, i.e., firearms, changed all that. The earliest firearm was known as a hand cannon or as a "gonne," i.e., a gun. It was a very simple device, consisting of a barrel with some kind of handle attached. In order to fire it, the gunner held the hand cannon in both hands and pointed it in the general direction of the enemy. His assistant then ignited the charge of gunpowder in it by applying a live coal to it, a slow-burning match, or a red-hot iron rod. Alternatively, the hand cannon could be secured to a rest and the gunner could fire it by himself. Projectiles used included small rocks, shaped balls of stone or iron, or very sturdy arrows.

The earliest reliable evidence of the use of gonnes in combat in Europe comes from the 14th century, but it was not until about 1450 that technological advances made them effective on the battlefield. The value of these early firearms was four-fold:

- Unlike the longbow and the crossbow, they could be used effectively by relatively unskilled soldiers. (Flemish and German mercenaries, however, may have been the first men to master these new weapons.)

- At close range, they could pierce heavy armor plate.
- They terrified men and horses that were not used to their fiery, smoky blasts.
- They would contribute greatly to the importance of the infantry, since they spelled the beginning of the end for the armored knight astride his warhorse. In the early 1600s, the Spanish novelist, poet, and playwright Miguel de Cervantes would denounce artillery (and, by extension, firearms in general) as a "devilish invention allowing a base cowardly hand to take the life of the bravest gentleman."

In the Middle Ages, gunpowder was made from sulfur, saltpeter, and charcoal, the proportions of each varying according to different recipes. The earliest manufacturing process used lime saltpeter, which produced calcium nitrate rather than potassium nitrate. Calcium nitrate absorbs moisture very easily, so gunpowder made with it did not last very long. By the 15th century, new techniques for making potassium saltpeter were being developed and gunpowder was being "corned" into granules. This made it a much better propellant, and huge quantities were produced. In 1477, for example, the Duke of Burgundy paid for more than 14,000 pounds of gunpowder. Generous supplies of it were indeed necessary because a large bombard (discussed later) burned about 80 pounds of powder at each shot.[43]

The successor to the hand cannon was the arquebus. This muzzle-loading matchlock weapon was fired from the shoulder, rather than from the hip, which had been the practice with earlier firearms. Used from the 15th to the 17th centuries, it was the forerunner of the musket and the rifle. Good suits of armor might stop arquebus balls at long range but at close range they could penetrate even the toughest armor of knights and other heavy cavalrymen. The first European use of the arquebus in large numbers came about in Hungary under King Matthias Corvinus (r. 1458–1490): every fifth infantry soldier in the mercenary Black Army of Hungary carried an arquebus.

Medieval artillery included various kinds of stone-throwing mechanisms and, later, devices using gunpowder, e.g., petards and cannons. A traction trebuchet (a trebuchet is a type of catapult) had a range of up

41

to 1,000 yards and could hurl stones weighing up to 750 pounds. The counterweight trebuchet, developed in the 12th century, could throw 300 pound stones—or, in an early version of biological warfare, the corpses of people who had died from contagious diseases. In 1191, at the siege of Acre in what is now Israel, the English king Richard the Lion-hearted had two trebuchets built. One he named "God's Own Catapult"; the other, "Bad Neighbour."

When gunpowder weapons were first used in combat, they often had more of a psychological than a physical impact. The First Italian War (1494–1498), for example, pitted Charles VIII of France against the Holy Roman Empire, Spain, and an alliance of Italian powers under the leadership of Pope Alexander VI. Charles VIII assembled a large army of 25,000 men and invaded Italy with 8,000 Swiss mercenaries. Both sides claimed victory after a bloody fight at Fornovo, 18 miles southwest of Parma. In that battle, which was largely a stalemate, Charles VIII deployed 3,000 Swiss mercenaries and 28 pieces of artillery. The physician Alessandro Beneditti, who was an eyewitness at Fornovo, tells us in his *Diaria de Bello Carolino* (*Diary of the Caroline War*) that at the battle of Fornovo in 1495

> on every side the sky repeatedly flashed with fire and thundered with artillery and was filled with wails and cries. Iron, bronze and lead balls sped hissing aloft, and *these threw the ranks of cavalry and infantry into turmoil even without slaughter*.[44]

Designed to hurl heavy stone balls, a bombard was a large-caliber muzzle-loading cannon or mortar. (A mortar is a short range weapon with a very high-arcing ballistic trajectory.) Perhaps the best surviving example of a bombard is the huge mortar named "Mons Meg." Built around 1449 and now on public display at Edinburgh Castle in Scotland, it could fire balls weighing up to 396 pounds and was designed to bring down castle walls.

Petards, on the other hand, were small gunpowder-filled bombs which were placed against gates and walls to blow them open. In *Hamlet*, Shakespeare used a now-proverbial phrase: "hoist with his own petard." This means that if a petard exploded prematurely, the man who placed it would be "hoist," i.e., blown into the air and possibly killed, by the force of the explosion.

Armor in various shapes and forms was used extensively in medieval warfare. The most familiar (to modern viewers) style of armor is the all-encompassing plate armor associated with the knights of the Late Middle Ages. A knight thus equipped has been wonderfully described by an anonymous contemporary source as "a terrible worm in an iron cocoon." Common soldiers were not fitted out in full armor because it was much too expensive. They usually had to make do with a metal helmet — known as a "kettle hat," or *chape* (or *chapel*) *de fer*, literally an "iron hat. They also had padded clothing and, in some cases, a mail shirt.

Contrary to what we might think, a website on medieval weapons and armor assures us that

> while it looks heavy, a full plate armour set could be as light as only 20 kg (45 pounds), if well made of tempered steel. This is less than the weight of modern combat gear of an infantry soldier.... The weight was so well spread out over the body that a fit man could run, or jump into his saddle. Modern re-enactment activity has proved that it is even possible to swim in armour, though it is difficult.[45]

Armor was not light but did not slow down a very athletic man too much. A biographer of Jean le Maigre (d. 1421), marshal of France and governor of Geneva, depicts him as being able to jump onto his warhorse while fully armed, without using the stirrup, and as being able to do somersaults in full armor (except for the helmet). Wearing a mail shirt, Jean le Maigre could also climb up a tall ladder leaning against a wall without using his feet, i.e., relying only on his hands. He could then take off the mail shirt with one hand, while hanging on to the ladder with the other hand. He even is said to have worn a mail shirt when he was dancing.[46]

Armor was so critically important to medieval and Renaissance soldiers—their lives literally depended on it — that they devoted a great deal of thought and experimentation to perfecting it. One result was an extensive technical vocabulary from the early 12th to early 16th centuries. Because of the importance of armor in this era, Appendix 1 gives a partial and annotated listing of the armor used for the head, neck, torso, arms, legs, and other parts of the body. The knights and the men-at-arms of the mercenary companies would have been very familiar with all this gear.

During the Middle Ages and Renaissance, enemy forces wanting to besiege a well-situated, well-provisioned fortress or castle needed to have the right men and the right machines. Their siege devices could include scaling ladders, battering rams, and catapults. In addition, sappers (today we would call them combat engineers) were skilled at digging a tunnel under the wall of a fortress and propping up the tunnel temporarily with wooden beams. When the tunnel was judged to have reached the wall, it was packed with combustible material, the sappers withdrew, and the combustible material was set alight. In due course, the beams burned through and the tunnel collapsed, hopefully (from the attackers' point of view) bringing a big section of the wall down with it. Infantrymen and archers could then pour through the opening and capture the fortress.

Because a siege was likely to stretch out over a considerable period of time and because it required highly specialized capabilities, the attackers were happy to enlist the help of skilled mercenaries whose time and abilities were for sale. To get some idea of just what siege warfare required, let us meet a remarkable woman: Christine de Pisan, or Pizan (ca. 1365-ca. 1430). She was a poet who has been acclaimed as the first professional woman writer in Europe and even as the founder of the feminist movement.

Born in Venice, raised in Paris, married at the age of 15, and widowed 10 years later at the age of 24, Christine spent all of her adult life in France, first living in Paris and then at the Dominican abbey at Poissy, which is now a suburb of Paris. She wrote poetry because she needed to earn a living for herself and her three children. In addition to her poetry, she also wrote a treatise in Middle French on the art of war: the *Livre des faitz d'armes, ci de chevalerie* (*Book of Feats of Arms and Chivalry*). This was based on Vegetius and, we can guess, on the details of siege warfare she gleaned from the French and English officers she met in Paris.[47]

In 1408–1409, drawing from the descriptions given her by the officers who were her informants on current military practice, she compiled a list of the items she judged were necessary for a siege.[48] In her time, it was normal to give names to large artillery pieces, whether cannons or stonethrowers. Christine tells us the names of a few of these weapons and the weight of the shot that they threw: "Garite," 400–500 pounds; "Rose," 300 pounds; "Montfort," 300 pounds; and "Artique," 100 pounds.

Much like ships and bells, great cannons had their own personalities and thus, in a figurative sense, they were somehow "alive" in the minds of their users. They could bear inscriptions in verse, such as this one, translated from the French:

> I am Dragon the venomous serpent, who desires with furious blows to drive off our enemies. John the Black, master gunner, and Conrad, Coin and Cradinteur, all of them master founders, made me on schedule in 1476.[49]

All told, in her discussions of siege warfare Christine refers to some 248 cannons and 30,000 pounds of gunpowder. To move this huge mountain of gear from one place to another required a large number of men, horses, and carts. Christine also tells us that a besieging general would need 330 crossbows with 2,000 crossbow bolts, and 300 longbows with 1.2 million arrows.

Many different kinds of horses were used during the Middle Ages, e.g., chargers (war horses), palfreys (riding horses), and carthorses or pack horses. The best-known war horse of the medieval era was the destrier, a word derived from the Vulgar Latin *dextarius* ("right-sided"). This may refer to the fact that it was led by a squire at the knight's right side; that it was led with the right hand; or that, in its gait, the horse led with its right leg.

Contemporary sources describe the destrier as "tall and majestic and with great strength" and refer it as the "great horse." However, medieval horses were not huge by modern standards, so it was probably smaller than these words might suggest. What is clear is that a good destrier was very expensive. Its price varied from between 20 and 300 *livres parisis* (Paris pounds), compared to only 5 to 12 *livres parisis* for a normal courser, i.e., a light, fast, strong horse. In 1277 Florence hired a number of Provençal (French) mercenaries with clauses in their contracts that each of them must have a horse, presumably a destrier, worth at least £30, i.e., the equivalent of 133 days' wages.[50] In fact, although the destrier was highly prized by knights and men-at-arms, it was not very common and may well have been best suited to the joust.

Cavalry could be extremely important in battles and in sieges for sallies or countering them. As a website on medieval warfare explains,

> Once one side coaxed their opposing infantry into breaking formation, the cavalry would be deployed in an attempt to exploit the loss of cohesion in the opposing infantry and [would] begin slaying the infantrymen from horse-top...it is much easier to kill a man from the top of a horse than to stand on the ground and face a half-ton destrier carrying an armed knight.[51]

A cavalry charge by knights must have been (for an observer standing in a very safe position) an exhilarating spectacle. For the knights and particularly for the foot soldiers who were facing such a charge, it must have been a terrifying and sometimes fatal experience. A key element in a successful charge, and one which required great practice, disciple, and favorable terrain to pull off, was for the charging knights to ride roughly abreast of each other and gradually to accelerate to their top speed until they crashed into the enemy's battle lines. The modern scholar J.F. Verbruggen describes such a charge. He says:

> Even if some of the knights did not carry on the charge to the utmost [it was very difficult for them to force their horses to charge into formations of foot soldiers who were armed with long pikes, the butts of which rested solidly on the ground and the sharp points of which faced the horses], a terrible shock followed. This came with a hellish din when the armoured formations charged a wall of foot-soldiers, exactly as when two knightly armies met each other.
> [Verbruggen uses the following first-hand quotes from contemporary chroniclers to describe such a charge.]
> - "Four hundred carpenters would not have made so much noise."
> - "They closed in with such force that the clash of weapons and the din of blows made the air ring, just as though trees in the forest were being cut down by innumerable axes."
> - "The fighters were like woodcutters, chopping down the trees of a forest." "The din was so frightful that one could not have heard even God's thunder."
> - "It was as though all the smiths in the world in Brussels and Bruges were striking their anvils."[52]

Often the knights would charge in several successive waves, at full gallop. If the couched lance of a knight hit the shield or the armor of an enemy knight, it might easily knock him off his horse. After their initial charge, the knights would drop their heavy lances and would continue to fight on with whatever secondary weapons they had, such as swords and maces. If a foot soldier was hit by a couched lance, he would be knocked backward with such force that several of his fellow soldiers might well be killed or wounded, too.

With this brief review of the warriors and the tools of their trade behind us, let us now look at the Merovingian mercenaries and at their successors.

II

The Long-Haired kings

The first medieval mercenaries were very probably the Merovingians, in about the year 752. Later, the Duke of Naples is said to have hired Saracen (Muslim) mercenaries in southern Italy in 832. Beginning in 988, the Varangian Guard of the Byzantine Empire was one of the most famous mercenary corps of history.

The Merovingian ruling family was often referred to by contemporaries as the "long-haired kings" because their long hair set them apart from the Franks, who cut their hair short. The Merovingians were a dynasty of the Franks (a confederation of Germanic tribes) who, after the decline of the Roman Empire in the West, controlled Gaul for 300 years—until 752, when Pope Zachary deposed Childeric III, the last Merovingian ruler. Gaul included present-day France, Luxembourg, Belgium, most of Switzerland, and parts of northern Italy, the Netherlands, and Germany.

The Merovingian military structure was created in 481, when, at about the age of 16, Clovis inherited from his father, Childeric, the ruler of Tournai, a small war band of about 400 to 500 men. Clovis was then able to recruit an armed force powerful enough to take control of most of Gaul.[1] The Merovingians set up armies in Gaul, hired knights and mercenaries there, gave them lands in return for military service, and appointed counts (*comites*) to take charge of defense, administration, and legal matters. They were not men to trifle with. Sidonius Apollinari, the Bishop of Auvergne, writing in the 5th century, says of them:

> The Franks [i.e., the Merovingians] are a tall race, and clad in garments which fit them closely. A belt encircles their waist. They hurl their axes and cast their spears with great force, never missing their aim. They manage

their shields with great agility, and rush on to their enemy with such speed that they seem to fly more swiftly than their spears.[2]

The Merovingians were able to impose their rule quickly throughout Gaul for two reasons: (1) they were geographically well-placed to fill the power vacuum left by the fading Roman Empire, and (2) one of their kings (Clovis I, 466–511) was a remarkably able leader. The Merovingian dynasty was named after Merovech, the grandfather of Clovis. By the end of his life, Clovis had subjugated the different Frankish sub-groups in what is now France and he ruled between the Rhine and Loire valleys, as well as in Aquitaine. His successors conquered even more lands, e.g., in Provence, Burgundy, Rhaetia (a province of the Roman Empire approximately centered in what is now Switzerland), Alemannia (the German region of Swabia, the French Alsace, and eastern and central Switzerland), and Thuringia (southwestern Germany).[3]

The military organization of the Merovingians, including mercenaries and other paid troops, was largely based on institutions already well-established in Gaul in Roman times. Merovingian strategy involved around the taking and holding of fortified centers. These centers were staffed by garrisons of former Roman mercenaries of Germanic origin; throughout Gaul, the descendants of Roman soldiers continued to wear similar uniforms and to perform similar ceremonial duties.

One of the most effective weapons of Merovingian troops was a throwing axe known as a francisca. The Roman historian Procopius (ca. 500–565) describes the fighters and their use of throwing axes in these words:

> Each man carried a sword and shield and an axe. Now the iron head of this weapon [the axe] was thick and exceedingly sharp on both sides while the wooden handle was very short. And they are accustomed always to throw these axes at one signal in the first charge and thus shatter the shields of the enemy and kill the men.[4]

This axe was heavy enough so that, even when thrown to its maximum effective range of about 40 feet, its iron head could still cause considerable injury regardless of whether the edge of the blade itself actually struck an enemy's body. Moreover, when hurled in volleys, as they usually were, these axes would ricochet when they hit the ground and would then scythe into the shields and legs of the defenders.

Procopius also describes another formidable infantry weapon: the angon. He says:

> The angons are spears which are neither very short nor very long; they can be used, if necessary, for throwing like a javelin, and also, in hand to hand combat. The greater part of the angon is covered with iron and very little wood is exposed. Above, at the top of the spear, on each side of the socket itself where the staff is fixed, some points are turned back, bent like hooks, and turned toward the handle.
>
> In battle, the Frank throws the angon, and if it hits the enemy the spear is caught in the man and neither the wounded man nor anyone else can draw it out. The barbs hold inside the flesh causing great pain and in this way a man whose wound may not be in a vital spot still dies. If the angon strikes a shield, it is fixed there, hanging down with the butt on the ground. The angon cannot be pulled out because the barbs have penetrated the shield, nor can it be cut off with a sword because the wood of the shaft is covered with iron.
>
> When the Frank sees [this] situation, he quickly puts his foot on the butt of the spear, pulling it down and [as] the man holding it falls, [his] head and chest are left unprotected. The unprotected warrior is then killed either by a stroke of the axe or a thrust with another spear. Such is the equipment of the Frankish warriors....[5]

Regrettably, it is not possible for modern scholars to distinguish between the Merovingian fighting men who clearly were mercenaries and those who clearly were not. It is clear that the chief lords of the Merovingians had their own personal retinues of professional soldiers[6], who were selected with care and were probably well-rewarded for their ability and loyalty. A fundamental problem here, however, is that there was no widely-used, unambiguous technical vocabulary in Latin to denote mercenaries during the later Roman Empire and in Merovingian Gaul.

The Romans used two terms, *conducticius* and *miles mercenarius*. Both terms mean "payment for hire" but their more detailed meanings depended on the context in which they were used. Neither term was used very often. Given a lack of documentary evidence, it seems impossible now for scholars to give any precise dates for mercenary involvement in this part of the world. Only educated guesses can be made.

The best summary (shortened, edited, and annotated here) of this complicated issue makes the following points:

There was no unambiguous vocabulary used to define mercenaries during the Merovingian *Francia*, i.e., during the Frankish kingdom. This fact indicates a continuity of Roman thought patterns and, probably, of Roman institutional structures as well. It is clear that during the later Roman Empire and the Merovingian dynasty there were groups of fighting men, as well as individual fighting men, who could offer their services for hire and who were recruited to perform military duties for pay. Some of the *foederati* ("federates," i.e., Germanic soldiers in the service of the Roman Empire) can be considered to have been mercenaries, as well as some of the household forces employed by both lay and ecclesiastical magnates. Militia troops and expeditionary levies, on the other hand, cannot be considered as mercenaries because they did not have a choice whether to engage or not engage in military service.[7]

Merovingian mercenaries may, or may not, have included the fighters known as antrustions: modern scholars seem to be unsure on this point. What is clear is that antrustions were carefully-selected members of the bodyguard or military households of the Merovingian kings; fittingly, their name comes from the Old High German *trost*, meaning fidelity or trust.[8] Any man who aspired to enter this elite band of fighters had to present himself, fully armed, at the royal palace; to place his hands between those of the king; and to take a special oath (*trustis*), as well as the usual oath of fidelity to the king. In return, as a member of the royal retinue he was a person of considerable importance, was fed and clothed by the king, and was entitled to royal assistance and protection.

The modern scholar J.F. Verbruggen describes the antrustions in these words:

> Among the Franks private retinues ... existed up to the sixth and seventh centuries. The royal *trustis* corresponds to the *comitatus* [the bond existing between a Germanic warrior and his lord, which stipulated that neither could leave the field of battle before the other] described by Tacitus. The bodyguard was a sort of permanent little army which had to protect the king, but which could also be set to other tasks.[9]

Antrustions were held in great respect. If one was killed by another Frank, his *wergeld* (literally "man-fee"), i.e., the price that was set on his life and that had to be paid as compensation by the family of the slayer to free the culprit from further punishment and to prevent a blood feud, was three times that of an ordinary citizen. Thus a man who killed an ordinary Frank had to pay 200 gold *solidi*, but a man who killed an antrustion had to pay 600 *solidi*. (This was a very large sum of money: the pay of a Roman cavalryman was only about 1½ *solidi* per month.)

Antrustions played a key role in Merovingian life at the time of Clovis and initially made up much of his army. They became less important, however, as later rulers formed armies in which the Gallo-Romans mingled more and more with the Franks. Antrustions gradually became a small bodyguard and were also used to staff garrisons in the frontier towns. They seem to have disappeared around the beginning of the 8th century.

The recruitment of men who were clearly mercenaries begins to come into sharper focus around the year 832, when the Duke of Naples is said to have hired Saracen (Muslim) mercenaries in southern Italy.

A bit of background may be needed here. "Saracen" is a loosely-defined historical term for a group of Arab Muslims, and its meaning has shifted over time. Initially, in early Greek and Latin, it referred, apparently non-pejoratively, to the peoples living in the desert areas in or near what the Romans called "Arabia." By the Early Middle Ages, however, this term was being used in a more negative sense to describe all the Arab tribes.

In 827, the Arabs began their conquest of Sicily; a local revolt against the Byzantine authorities gave them the opportunity to land there. By 877, all the major cities of the island were in their hands. The Arab conquest of Sicily would not be completed until the last Byzantine fortresses there finally fell in 902, but as early as 832 some Muslims had already been hired as mercenaries by the Duke of Naples.[10]

Details on them are few but when civil war broke out in Sicily in 839, the two princely rivals for power (Prince Radelchis in Benevento, and his brother Prince Siconulf, or Sikenolf, in Salerno) both hired Saracen mercenaries in about 842 to fight for them in Campagnia (southern Italy). Benevento was the first one to hire mercenaries, apparently engaging some North African Berbers who had been raiding around Bari. Salerno promptly responded by hiring some Spanish Muslims who had been pillaging the Taranto region.[11] Writing 20 years after the fact, a chronicler recounted their princely succession dispute and how one of Radelchis's officials had invited the Saracens into the port city of Bari. The Saracens promptly took the town for themselves and, as the chronicler dryly and laconically noted, "from then onwards everything rapidly got worse."[12]

In 842–843, Prince Siconulf seized from a local monastery large quantities of gold and silver, thousands of gold coins, and many valuable objects made of gold or silver. He needed this loot both to pay his Saracen mercenaries and to try to buy the friendship of the Duke of Spoleto and of Carolingian King Louis II in his struggles with Radelchis.[13] A colorful story is told about Prince Siconulf in a contemporary work known as the *Chronicon Salernitanum*. The modern scholar Barbara Kreutz recounts the tale as follows:

> Apolaffar [an Arab mercenary leader] had begun his mercenary career not with Radelchis but with Sikenolf, but had stormed off from Salerno in a rage one day because Sikenolf insulted him when they were returning together from a military foray. As the *Chronicon* describes it, the two were clambering up the outer stairs of the palace when Sikenolf, exuberant over their success, impulsively grabbed Apolaffar, a small man, and hoisted him up to the next step. Apolaffar, very sensitive about his size, found this an unpardonable humiliation.[14]

Much later, the Saracens came into the limelight again as a result of a Saracen settlement in the southern Italian mainland city of Lucera. This settlement was the result of Holy Roman Emperor Frederick II's decision to move 20,000 unruly Sicilian Saracens there in hopes that their expulsion would bring social and religious peace to Sicily itself. Although most of the affluent and powerful Muslims had already returned to North Africa by then, in 1220 Frederick II resolved to ship the remaining Muslims from Sicily to the southern Italian mainland. In 1224, Lucera was one of the seven resettlement sites chosen.[15]

The total Saracen population of Lucera (which alone had 20,000 Muslims) and the other resettlement areas are thought to have been some 60,000 people, which was enough to generate a theoretical maximum of about 14,000–15,000 men fit for military service. Contemporary sources report that 7,000 to 10,000 of them did indeed fight at the battle of Cortenuova in 1237, where Frederick II defeated the Second Lombard League. Saracens also fought at the battle of Benevento in 1266. This was a clash between two factions: the Guelfs, who were Angevin French troops (some of them mercenaries) supported by Italian mercenaries, and the Ghibellines, who were Kingdom of Sicily troops supported by German and Italian mercenaries.

One can pause here to remark that the bloody and essentially meaningless feud between the Guelfs and the Ghibellines is a good example of the gratuitous violence that characterized so much of the Middle Ages and provided so many excellent employment opportunities for mercenaries. A later French Governor of Genoa described the feud in these words:

> For with no other quarrel of land or seigneury, they have only to say, "You are Guelf and I am Ghibelline; we must hate each other," and for this reason only and knowing no other, they kill and wound each other every day like dogs, the sons like the fathers, and so year by year the malice continues and there is no justice to remedy it....
> And from this come the despots of this country, elected by the voice of the people, without reason or right of law. For as soon as one party prevails over the other and is the stronger, then those who see themselves at top cry "Long live so-and-so!" and "Death to so-and-so" and they elect one of their number and kill their adversary if he does not flee. And when the other party regains the advantage, they do the same and in the fury of the people, from which God protect us, all is torn to pieces.[16]

To return now to the Saracens: most of the Saracen mercenary troops were lightly armed archers but they were also trained in the use of the sling. They formed a skilled personal bodyguard of 5,000 to 6,000 bowmen, mostly on foot but some mounted, for Frederick II and his successors.[17] The Saracens were politically reliable because they had no ties to any of the rival Italian claimants for power and, in the relatively controlled environments of the resettlement areas, they had no way to challenge royal authority. They were highly valued as mercenaries. If they fought well, they were rewarded: in fact, by demonstrating unusual bravery in battle, Saracens could earn individual or family exemptions from taxes.

This favorable situation later changed for the worse, however. When Charles II of Naples came to power in 1289, he had already planned to expel the Jews from his lands in Anjou and Maine in France. In 1300 he decided to do the same thing to the Saracens in Lucera. His reasons are a bit opaque but it seems likely he hoped that by seizing and selling the Saracen holdings in Lucera he would be able to settle some of his debts with Florentine bankers. His attack on Lucera, aided by treachery inside the city itself, was a decisive victory.

II. *The Long-Haired Kings*

The majority of the city's Saracens were slaughtered or sold into slavery, though some found asylum across the Adriatic Sea in Albania. The political and social leaders of the Saracen community were imprisoned in Naples. Charles II replaced Lucera's Saracens with Christians, chiefly Burgundian and Provençal soldiers and farmers. The cathedral of Lucera was built on the ruins of a destroyed mosque. The Civic Museum in modern Lucera still displays shards of evidence, such as pottery with Arabic inscriptions, recalling the Saracen presence there.[18]

Turning now to the Varangian Guard of the Byzantine Empire, in order to see it in its proper context, beginning in 988, a few words about the Byzantine Empire itself are needed first.[19]

The Byzantine Empire (also known as Byzantium, as the Eastern Roman Empire, and as the medieval Roman Empire) was the Roman Empire during Late Antiquity and the Middle Ages. It was centered on the capital of Constantinople but scholars cannot say precisely when the Roman Empire ended and when the Byzantine Empire began. If a date is needed, however, the year 395 can conveniently be used. It was then, after the death of Emperor Theodosius I, that the Roman Empire was divided for the last time and its western and eastern halves were permanently separated.

The western half came to an end in 476, when the Germanic Roman general Odocar deposed the titular Western Emperor Romulus Augustulus. The eastern half, however, would go on to become the most powerful economic, cultural, and military force in Europe. Indeed, it would endure until the Ottoman Turks captured Constantinople in 1453.

The Byzantine Army was the direct descendant of the Roman army and was among the most effective military forces in western Eurasia for much of the Middle Ages. One of the reasons for its great success is that every time it came up against a strong enemy, it welcomed that enemy as a potential new source of mercenary recruits. Its opponents included Goths; Huns; Vandals; Ostrogoths; Avars; Slavs; Rus, i.e., Vikings from what is now Sweden; Normans; Seljeks; Anatolian beyliks, i.e., the inhabitants of a small Turkish principality; Ottomans; and warriors from Sassanid Persia, the Muslim Caliphate, Bulgaria, and the Crusader states. The Byzantine Empire recruited mercenaries from among its own allies, too. These soldiers included Bulgars, men from the Crusader states, Anatolian beyliks, Khazars, Avars, Rus, and Magyars [Hungarians]. It will be noted that some of the above were both the Byzantine Army's opponents and its allies, though at different times.

The mercenaries hired by the Byzantines were first known as the *foederati* ("allies" in Latin — by the 6th century this term came to mean units of non–Roman, as well as Roman, mercenaries brigaded together) and then as the Hetairoi ("Companionships" in Greek). They were mainly assigned to the Imperial Guard. This formidable force was structured into "Great Companionships," "Middle Companionships," and "Minor Companionships," each commanded by their respective "Companionship lords." Mercenaries may also have been recruited along religious lines, e.g., from the Christian subjects of the Byzantine Empire, from Christian foreigners, and from non–Christians. Mercenary units were organized by their place of origin: Inglinoi (Englishmen), Phragkoi (Franks), Skythikoi (Scythians), and Latinikoi ("Latins," referring here to Germans and Normans), and Ethiopians. The Skythikoi were often used as a police force in Constantinople.

The Varangian Guard, an elite unit of the Byzantine Army in the 10th to the 14th centuries, was one of the most famous mercenary corps of history and was certainly the most famous of all the Byzantine regiments. It is thought that the term "Varangian" comes from an archaic Norse word variously translated as "confidence," "vow of fidelity," or "ally," and refers to a group of warriors and traders who had sworn allegiance to their leader and fellowship to each other. Interestingly, what is now the Baltic Sea was in earlier times known as the Varangian Sea.

The first clear glimpse of them comes in 988, when the Emperor Basil II (978–1025) asked Vladimir I of Kiev for military assistance to help defend his throne. Vladimir sent 6,000 warriors, known as "Rus," to the Emperor. The word "Rus" may have come from an Old Norse term meaning "the men who row." They were such excellent fighters that they soon became the Emperor's personal bodyguard.

Under Basil II, the Byzantine Empire built up a largely mercenary army, generally abandoning the earlier system under which territorial forces defended the provinces and regulars from Constantinople reinforced them when needed. Because Basil II regarded mercenaries as politically more dependable than regular troops, his reliance on them would persist for a long time. The Varangian Guard greatly profited from his support and was paid very well indeed. The Icelandic Laxdale Saga, for example, gives this report on the homecoming in 1030 of the folkloric hero Bolli Bollason, who went to Byzantium as a mercenary recruit and eventually rose to become a senior officer of the Varangian Guard.

The saga says:

> Bolli brought back with him much wealth and many precious things that lords abroad had given him. Bolli was so great a man for show when he came back from this journey that he would wear no clothes but those made of scarlet and fur, and all his weapons were adorned with gold: he was called Bolli the Great....
>
> Bolli rode from the ship with twelve men, and all his followers were dressed in scarlet, and rode on guilt saddles, and were a trusty band, though Bolli was peerless among them. He had on the clothes of fur which the Garth-king [i.e., the Emperor] had given him, he had over all a scarlet cape; and he had Footbiter [the name of his sword] girt on him, the hilt of which was adorned with gold, and the grip woven with gold; he had a gilded helmet on his head, and a red shield on his flank, with a knight painted on it in gold. He had a dagger in his hand, as is the custom in foreign lands; and whenever they took quarters the women paid heed to nothing but gazing at Bolli and his grandeur, and that of his followers.[20]

Anna Comnena wrote of the 11th century Varangian Guardsmen:

> They regarded loyalty to the Emperors and the protection of their persons as a family tradition, a kind of sacred trust and inheritance handed down from generation to generation; this allegiance they preserve inviolate and will never brook the slightest hint of betrayal.[21]

The commander of the Varangian Guard was awarded the title of *Akolouthos*. Literally, this meant the "Follower" of the Emperor, but in practice it meant the man who stood closest to the Emperor on formal occasions and who served as his most important bodyguard. The tall, fierce men of the Varangian Guard were initially of Scandinavian origin but after the Norman Conquest of 1066, many displaced Anglo-Saxons joined the Varangian Guard, too.

The Varangian Guard demonstrated its worth in the battle of Beroia in 1122 in what is now Bulgaria. Led by Emperor John II Komnenos of the Byzantine Empire, the Varangian Guard won that fight against the Pechenegs. These were men from the Russian steppes who had invaded the

Byzantine Empire by crossing the Danube frontier and entering Byzantine territory. The Pechenegs fought as waves of horse archers, shooting arrows continuously and using their laager [wagon fort] as an arrow-depot; as a rallying-point; and, if necessary, as a holdout for a last stand.

After a very hard fight, the Byzantines forced the Pechenegs to take refuge in their laager, but there they put up such a stiff resistance that the Byzantines could not overrun them until the Varangian Guard arrived and used their broad-axes (also known as Danish axes) with shafts up to 6 feet long to hack their way through the circle of wagons, forcing the Pechenegs to flee for their lives. Rather than massacring the surviving Pechenegs, however, the Varangian Guard simply took them prisoner and enrolled them in the Byzantine army.

In 1167 in what is now Serbia, the Byzantine Empire decisively defeated the Kingdom of Hungary at the battle of Sirmium. According to the contemporary Byzantine historian John Kinnamos, the Byzantine army then consisted of one-third foreign and two-thirds native units. This battle involved regular Byzantine troops, Turks, Cumans, Imperial guard units (including the Varangian Guard), Italian mercenary lancers from Lombardy, Serbian infantry and cavalry, German mercenaries, and even some Western mercenary knights. The net result was that the Hungarians were forced to sue for peace on Byzantine terms; to recognize Byzantine control over Bosnia, Croatia, and related areas; and to pay tribute to Byzantium and to provide troops for it whenever so requested.

The Varangian Guard was also instrumental in repelling the Crusader assaults of the First Crusade (1096–1099). In 1204, however, combined Crusader armies of Franks and Venetians besieged and captured Constantinople during the Fourth Crusade (1202–1204). Bad weather had delayed the initial Crusader attack on the city but later a strong north wind and good seamanship allowed Venetian ships to moor right alongside the city's wall. This feat enabled the attackers to seize some of the towers along the wall. After short but sharp battle, about 70 Crusaders managed to fight their way into Constantinople itself. At the same time, other Crusaders were busy knocking holes through the wall — just big enough for a few knights at a time to scramble through them. The Venetians also managed to scale the wall from the sea, in the face of extremely bloody fighting with the Varangians.

The victorious Crusaders burned, looted, and vandalized Constantinople. Under the terms of a prearranged treaty, the Byzantine Empire was then divided between Venice and the Crusader leaders, and what was called the Latin Empire of Constantine was thus established. Much of the Byzantine aristocracy, which was exceedingly unpopular with the common people of the city, fled from the city. The contemporary Byzantine historian and eye-witness Nicetas Choniates (himself an aristocrat) says:

> The peasants and common riff-raff jeered at those of us from Byzantium and were thick-headed enough to call our miserable poverty and nakedness equality.... Many were only too happy to accept this outrage, saying "Blessed be the Lord that we have grown rich," and buying up for next to nothing the property their fellow-countrymen were forced to offer for sale....[22]

After the loss of Constantinople, the Varangian Guard was disbanded as a permanent major fighting force and subsequently performed only secondary or ceremonial duties.[23] Some of its men served the Nicean Empire and the Despotate of Epirus in 1205–1261. Others defended Ainos against the Bulgarians in 1265 and were bodyguards for Emperor John V in 1351. The Varangian Guard was mentioned as participating in imperial ceremonies in Byzantium in 1351. Finally, there is some evidence that English mercenaries and mixed-blood descendants of Varangians served together. For example, "axe-bearing soldiers of British race" are mentioned by Byzantine envoys in Rome in 1404.

III

"Human thoughts are inclined to greed"

Norman pilgrims in Salerno helped defend it against a Muslim attack in about 999. The Norman mercenary Rainulf Drengot began as a bandit but ended up as ruler of most of southern Italy. Mercenaries played important roles in Anglo-Norman warfare, e.g., in William the Conqueror's invasion of England in 1066 and in keeping him in power thereafter. The Norman adventurer Roussel de Bailleul refused to send his own mercenaries into the battle of Manzikert in 1071 because he foresaw (correctly) that this was going to be a major disaster for his employers, the Byzantines. The Spanish hero El Cid, who served as a mercenary captain for both Christian and Muslim leaders, carved out his own fiefdom in Valencia in 1094.

The Norman conquest of southern Italy took place in bits and pieces from the arrival of Norman mercenaries there in about 999 until the conquest of Naples in 1139. This was not a simple process. Unplanned and unorganized, it involved confusing arrays of battles, few of them decisive, and glimpses of many independent warriors risking their lives to carve out lucrative territories for themselves and their descendants. Here little else can be done than touch on some of the highlights of such a long and complicated process.[1]

It is not known precisely how and when the Normans first came to southern Italy. The problem here is not a shortage of early historical sources but rather too many of them — and a significant lack of agreement among them. Nevertheless, as the modern scholar G.A Loud says of the Normans in Italy, "it is possible to reconcile the various traditions and to suggest a plausible (if ultimately unprovable) explanation for their arrival."[2]

The first and most dramatic account comes from the chronicler-monk Amatus of Montecassino, a Benedictine monk at the abbey of Montecassino, who was writing more than 80 years after the fact. In his *L'Ystoire de li Normant* (*History of the Normans*), he says that a small group of Norman pilgrims returning from the Holy Sepulcher in Jerusalem arrived in Salerno (southern Italy) "before the year 1000." At about that time, e.g., in 999, Salerno was under fierce attack by Muslims, who were reacting to the fact that tribute was no longer being paid to them. The city was at the point of surrender. The Normans allegedly intervened, killed many of the Muslims, and drove off the rest. The prince of Salerno and his subjects were said to be so impressed by the Normans' fighting skills that they asked them to remain permanently in Salerno as their protectors. When the Normans declined to do so, the prince reportedly sent them home to Normandy, laden with presents and begged them to encourage their colleagues there to come to southern Italy, which he said was "the land flowing with milk and honey and so many good things."

There are a number of problems with this and with other near-contemporary accounts of the coming of the Normans to southern Italy but these scholarly issues need not be detailed here. The Muslim attack on Salerno in about 999 appears to be confirmed and it is not unlikely that Norman pilgrims were in fact present and did indeed help to defend the city, though probably in a more modest way than Amatus of Montecassino would have people believe. In any case, Norman mercenaries were apparently being employed in southern Italy by the early years of the 11th century. The excellent job prospects for mercenaries there, coupled with the good climate, food, and drink, encouraged many other Normans to follow them later on.

For example, the Norman adventurer Rainulf Drengot (his first name can be spelled in other ways) led a band of warriors and other adventurers into the Mezzogiorno (southern Italy) in 1017. He and his motley crew supported themselves by protecting, for a price, the bands of pilgrims heading for the shrine of the soldier-archangel Michel at Monte Sant'Angelo sul Gargano. Later, Rainulf and his men supported the local prince, Pandulf IV of Capua, but they were a mixed blessing for him. As Amatus of Montecassino writes,

Under his [Pandulf's] protection, they hastened to plunder the neighboring places and to harass his enemies. But since human thoughts are inclined to greed and money always triumphs in the end, from time to time they abandoned him.... They sold their services as they could, .according to circumstances, offering most to him who gave most.[3]

Rainulf did so well that in 1030 the duke of Naples, Sergius IV, felt obliged to pay for his aid by presenting him with the county of Aversa, slightly north of Naples. This was the first "official" Norman possession in Italy. Soon, however, Robert Guiscard (ca. 1015–1085), a Norman adventurer of the Hauteville family, would become even more successful than Rainulf and more famous. His family would play a major role in the Norman conquest of southern Italy. In 1046 or 1047 Robert led a small band of mercenary knights there; his older brothers had already preceded him in the mid–1030s. This Norman migration seems to have been due both to the hope of booty and to population pressures at home. As a monk writing in Sicily in about 1100 said of these Norman adventurers,

They saw that their own neighbourhood would not be big enough for them, and that when their patrimony was divided not only would their heirs argue among themselves about the share-out, but the individual shares would not be big enough.... They decided that since the elders [i.e., the elder members of Robert's clan] were at that time stronger than those younger to them, they should be the first to leave their homeland and to go to other places seeking their fortune through arms.[4]

When Robert arrived in southern Italy, however, his brothers could do little to help him, so he had to make his own way in the world. He began as a mere bandit, albeit a very intelligent one (his nickname, "Guiscard," means "the cunning one" or "the weasel"). When Anna Comnena wrote the *Alexiad*, a historical account of her father's reign, she described Robert as follows:

This Robert was Norman by descent, of insignificant origin, in temper tyrannical, in mind most cunning, brave in action, very clever in attacking the wealth and substance of magnates, most obstinate in achievement, for he did not allow any obstacle to prevent his executing his desire. His stature was so lofty that he surpassed even the tallest, his complexion was ruddy, his hair flaxen, his shoulders were broad, his eyes all but emitted sparks of fire, and in frame he was well-built where nature required breadth, and was neatly and gracefully formed where less width was necessary. So from tip to toe this man was well-proportioned, as I have repeatedly heard many say.

Now, Homer says of Achilles that when he shouted, his voice gave his hearers the impression of a multitude in an uproar, but this man's cry is said to have put thousands to flight. Thus equipped by fortune, physique and character, he was naturally indomitable, and subordinate to no one in the world. Powerful natures are ever like this, people say, even though they be of somewhat obscure descent.

Such then was the man, and as he would not endure any control, he departed from Normandy with only five followers on horseback, and thirty on foot all told. After leaving his native land, he roamed amid the mountain-ridges, caves, and hills of Lombardy, as the chief of a robber-band, and by attacks on travellers acquired horses, and also other possessions and weapons. Thus the prelude of this man's life was marked by much bloodshed and many murders.[5]

Despite these modest beginnings, by the time of his death in 1085, Robert would be a great warlord and would be courted by popes and emperors. One reason for his meteoric rise was that he learned early on how to capitalize on and, indeed, how to deliberately prolong the endless mini-wars of the region. William of Apulia, a chronicler of the Normans (only his name is known, not who he was or what he did), said of these mercenaries:

> The Normans never desired any of the Lombards [the local inhabitants] to win a decisive victory, in case it should be to their [own] disadvantage. But [by] now supporting the one, and then aiding the other, they prevented anyone being completely ruined. Gallic cunning [i.e., French cunning] deceived the Italians, for they [the Normans] allowed no one to be at the mercy of a triumphant enemy.[6]

Desiderius, the famous abbot of Montecassino from 1058 to 1087, held a similar opinion about Norman mercenaries. "For the Normans are avid for rapine and possess an insatiable enthusiasm for seizing what belongs to others."[7]

Before long, Robert was well-established as the *de facto* ruler of most of mainland southern Italy, but he also wanted the papacy to recognize formally the ducal status he had earned by force of arms. This he achieved in 1059, when he swore fealty to Pope Nicholas II and was invested by the Pope as "by the grace of God and St. Peter, Duke of Apulia and Calabria, and in the future, with the help of both, of Sicily."[8]

When Robert died in 1085, he was duke of Apulia and Calabria, prince of Salerno, and suzerain of Sicily. He used his ducal power to put down many baronial revolts but did not have time to organize carefully the broad territories he had conquered. Nevertheless, he is still remembered in history as the hero and founder of the Norman kingdom of Italy. This was a remarkable achievement for a man who had begun as a mere bandit with only a handful of followers.

Mercenaries were very active, too, in most of the episodes of Anglo-Norman warfare, e.g., under the leadership of three Anglo-Norman kings. These kings were: (1) William I, who was at first simply Duke William of Normandy but is now better known as William the Conqueror, 1066–1087; (2) William II Rufus, 1087–1100; and (3) Henry I, 1100–1135. As the modern scholar Stephen Morillo explains,

> The institutional strength of the government was in large part responsible for its wealth, and the influence of money on the military system is clear. Mercenaries appear in most episodes of Anglo-Norman warfare.... Money was, in fact, the fuel that made the military machine run.... And the money was available. England was a rich country with a strong, developed, specialized economy.... The Anglo-Norman military system, then, was built on a large supply of money put to use by an efficient, powerful government.[9]

A defining moment in medieval history came in 1066, when Duke William invaded England and conquered it. As he planned his attack, his supporters in Normandy were very worried about manpower: England had a much greater supply of soldiers than Normandy did. To deal with this shortfall, Duke William called on his own feudal tenants to form the nucleus of his force and also actively recruited mercenaries from many regions far beyond Normandy itself—for example, from Flanders, Aquitaine, Maine, Brittany, Picardy, Poitou, and probably from Burgundy, Anjou, and even from the Norman colonies in southern Italy.

Some of these men were prosperous and of established social position, but many of them were landless knights, e.g., the younger sons of nobles who had been disinherited by their fathers and who were unwilling or unable to enter the Church as a way to get a first step up the social ladder.[10] Instead, they enlisted with William for pay because they had heard of his generosity.[11] A few of these volunteers may also have been motivated to join Duke William because the Pope supported his planned invasion and because the propaganda surrounding this exercise struck a crusading and semi-religious note. By far the greatest number of them, however, must have joined him simply in hope of plunder.[12]

One of the most pressing problems both Duke William and his English opponent, Harold Godwinson, the reigning king of Anglo-Saxon England, faced was how to keep their large military forces well-fed and in a high state of readiness without devastating the lands on which these forces were based and thereby permanently alienating the population. Harold was quite unable to solve this problem: he could not provision the force he had drawn up to oppose the invasion and had to disband it. Duke William, however, was much more successful. William of Poitiers, a Norman chronicler known for his hero-worshiping accounts of Duke William, claims that for a whole month the Duke "utterly forbade pillage" and that

> he made generous provision both for his own knights and for those from other parts, but he did not allow any of them to take their sustenance by force. The flocks and herds of the peasantry pastured unharmed throughout the province. The crops waited undisturbed for the sickle without either being trampled by the knights in their pride, or ravaged out of greed by plunderers. A weak and unarmed man might watch the swarms of soldiers without fear, and following his horse singing where he would. [13]

Duke William promised his troops that, once he was victorious, he would give land to those who followed him into England, and he offered immediate cash payments to those who needed them at once and who could not afford to wait for this windfall later on.[14] A large part of his invading force (estimated at 7,000 men, 2,000 to 3,000 of whom were mounted warriors[15]) consisted of mercenaries, e.g., knights, foot soldiers, archers, and crossbowmen. Although these mercenaries were an important element in the Duke's successful invasion, it was basically his own Norman knights who, together with his archers, were chiefly responsible for the victory.[16]

In any case, William of Poitiers claimed, with no little pride and with a good deal of overstatement, "With his Norman troops and not much foreign help Duke William overthrew all the cities of England in one day between nine o'clock and sunset."[17] In point of fact, it actually took Duke William (now, of course, King William I) much longer — from 1067 to 1072 — to conquer England completely.

Once he was firmly established in power in England, an impressive array of potential fighters was available to him. In 1068 he had disbanded many of the mercenaries hired for the expedition of 1066, but he hired more mercenaries in 1069–1070.[18] In 1078 William used the profits of estates confiscated from his continental enemies to increase the numbers of his mercenaries even further; later, he would be forced to resort to a terribly heavy taxation of England in order to pay for them.[19]

On a more positive note, as King of England he could now draw at will upon three different pools of manpower:

- The first pool was the fyrd — a militia called up from districts threatened with attack. Service in the fyrd was generally of short duration; participants were expected to arm and feed themselves. By Henry I's reign, some of these men were mercenaries, though probably not of very high caliber.

- The second pool consisted of soldiers enfeoffed in England and Normandy. (Under the feudal system, enfeoffment was the deed by which a person was given land in return for a pledge of military service.) An enfeoffed soldier could be hired for military service in place of, or in addition to, being required to discharge his own feudal duties. In this case, he may be considered, at that time, a mercenary. Anglo-Norman kings liked to hire enfeoffed men because they knew these men would remain in military service as long as they were paid, and not only as long as feudal custom dictated. Enfeoffed men, for their part, might volunteer for the king's service because it gave them an extra source of income. They frequently needed more money to support themselves in style as knights — a very expensive way of life because of the high costs of armor, weapons, attendants, and horses.

- The third and perhaps the biggest and deepest manpower pool was the stock of potential mercenaries ready and eager to be hired. The best of these were what might be called in modern terminology "officer-candidates," e.g., second sons of well-established families, who had to make their own way in the world; ambitious adventurers; and able, upwardly-mobile members of the king's mounted household troops (the *familia regis*).[20] There was a considerable overlap between this mercenary pool and the enfeoffed pool: some of the potential mercenaries were Normans who had settled in England after the conquest and who now lived on English land for which they owed military service. What is clear is that William continuously maintained a large body of mercenary troops and that he financed them by imposing heavy taxes on his English subjects.[21]

In addition, a wide range of other mercenaries was available: Breton and Flemish troops, as well as men from Wales and from the whole of France. Taken collectively, these mercenaries were valuable assets to medieval leaders because they had experience and impressive combat skills. The Anglo-Norman kings, for example, could hire, as they liked, heavily-armed infantrymen; archers; crossbowmen; mounted troops, artillerymen; combat engineers; and miners, i.e., men who could bring down a wall of a besieged castle by digging a tunnel under it and then later, by burning the wooden pit-props they had used to keep the walls and roof intact, force the tunnel to collapse.

In the autumn of 1085, William faced the threat of an invasion from Denmark, led by King Cnut and possibly supported by Count Robert of Flanders. At a meeting convened in England about 1085, he decided to split up a large mercenary army which he had brought with him to England and to quarter its members in the households of the magnates— a move which the magnates had to accept.[22]

More fundamentally, he also had to find a way to pay this mercenary army, which he needed to keep himself and his supporters in power. The only feasible way to pay it was to tax the English people. To do this, however, it was first necessary to find out who owned what, how much it was worth, and how much of this worth was owed to him in his capacity as king of England. At Christmas 1085, William I therefore commissioned a great survey to ferret out the resources and taxable values of all the boroughs and manors in England. The record of this historic survey, completed in 1086, is now held at the National Archives in Kew in southwest London. It has long been known as the Domesday Book, a reference to the

Biblical Day of Judgment ("doomsday") from which there can be no appeal.

The *Anglo-Saxon Chronicle* (a collection of annals, i.e., yearly summaries of important events, which were distributed to monasteries across England and which record the history of the Anglo-Saxons since the 9th century) describes the taxation process in these famous words:

> [The king] sent his men all over England into every shire and had them find out how many hundred hides [a hide was a unit used to calculate how much tax was owed] there were in the shire, or what land and cattle the king himself had in the country, or what dues he ought to have annually from the shire. Also, he had a record made of how much land his archbishops had, and his bishops and abbots and his earls—and though I relate it at too great length—what or how much everybody had who was occupying land in England, in land and cattle, and how much money it was worth. So very narrowly did he have it investigated that there was no single hide nor yard of land nor indeed (shame to relate it but it seemed no shame to him to do) was one ox or one cow or one pig left out, that was not put down in his record. And all these writings were brought to him afterwards.[23]

In the end, it was the mercenaries, and not the soldiers generated by the fyrd and the system of feudal obligations, who ultimately formed the strongest backbone of the military forces of the Anglo-Norman kings. Mercenaries could be used year-round and could be discharged when their services were no longer needed. They were well-trained, reliable, and could exhibit a high degree of professional pride. A good example of this pride can be seen in the account by Orderic Vitalis of Henry I's successful siege of a castle at Bridgnorth, a town in Shropshire, England, in 1102. Orderic Vitalis (1075-ca. 1142) was an English chronicler-monk who wrote one of the great contemporary histories of 11th and 12th century Normandy and Anglo-Norman England.

The garrison of this castle, according to Orderic, consisted of two different groups: a feudal contingent, led by three captains and some burgesses; and 80 mercenary knights. The feudal contingent, without revealing to the mercenaries what they were doing, made a secret deal with Henry I to surrender the castle and town to his besieging forces. Upon learning of this plan and enraged by what they considered a betrayal, the mercenaries immediately tried, by force, to prevent the surrender, but the feudal contingent shut them up them in a remote part of the castle and then admitted the king's forces.

This is what Orderic says happened next:

> The king allowed the mercenary troops to leave freely with their horses and arms, because they had served their master as was right. As they rode out through the besieging forces they bewailed their fate, loudly complaining that they had been unfairly let down by the deceit of the garrison and their masters, and called on the whole army to witness the tricks of these plotters, so that their [own] downfall might not bring contempt on other mercenaries.[24]

Mercenaries were also present on both sides at the battle of Manzikert, which took place on the borders of Armenia in 1071, between the Byzantine forces led by Emperor Romanus IV Diogenes and the forces of the Seljuk Turks, led by Sultan Alp Arslan.[25] In this clash, the Byzantines were decisively defeated and their Emperor was captured. This defeat did not bring the Byzantine Empire to its knees but it did undermine Byzantine authority in the region and thus encouraged the growth of Turkish influence in Anatolia.

Byzantine forces are thought to have numbered about 40,000 men. This may have been the biggest army ever fielded by the late Roman Empire. These forces included about 5,000 Byzantine troops from the eastern provinces; some Turkish, Bulgarian, and Pecheneg mercenaries; infantrymen under the duke of Antoich; a contingent of Armenian troops; some, but not all, of the Varangian Guard; and, finally, 500 Frankish and Norman mercenaries under Roussel de Bailleul, a remarkable Norman soldier-of-fortune.

Anna Comnena writes of this man:

> Now this man was a Frank by birth who had been enrolled in the Roman army, reached a high degree of prosperity, and after gathering a band, or rather quite a considerable army, of men from his own country, and also of other races, he immediately became a formidable tyrant. For when the hegemony of the Romans had received several checks, and the luck of the Turks was in the ascendancy, and the Romans had been driven back like dust shaken from their feet, at this moment this man attacked the [Roman] Empire. Apart from his tyrannical nature, what more especially incited him to openly establish his tyranny just then was the depressed state of the imperial affairs, and he laid waste nearly all the Eastern provinces. Although many were entrusted with the war against him, men of high rep-

utation for bravery, and of very great knowledge of war and fighting, yet he openly baffled even their long experience. For sometimes he would take the offensive himself and rout his opponents by his meteor-like attacks, and at others he obtained help from the Turks, and was quite irresistible in his onrushes, so that he actually overpowered some of the most powerful chieftains, and utterly confounded their phalanxes.[26]

Bailleul was present at the battle of Manzikert but refused to commit himself or his mercenaries to the fight, probably because he foresaw, correctly, that it was going to be a disastrous defeat for the Byzantines. He had previously been a mercenary leader in Italy; later, he would try to carve out an independent kingdom in central Anatolia for himself and his men; and eventually (in 1077) he would be executed by the Byzantines as a traitor.

Returning now to the Battle of Manzikert, a contingent of 2,000 to 3,000 Turkish mercenaries fought for the Emperor to the bitter end and was virtually annihilated as a result. On the Sultan's side there were Pecheneg and Cuman mercenaries but their losses are not known. In the end, the Byzantine mercenaries turned out to be a mixed blessing for their employers. Large numbers of them fled before the battle began and thus survived unbloodied but unutilized.

A long-running problem here was that, over the years, the quality of the Emperor's troops had declined greatly. Rather than strengthening its own army, however, the Byzantine government had hired mercenaries instead. Since they were outsiders, mercenaries were thought to be less likely to stage coups or to become involved in factional fighting. A further difficulty was that the government usually disbanded its mercenaries whenever an immediate danger had passed. Even when still employed, however, the mercenaries were never an easy bunch to handle. Indeed, the Emperor had to fire his Frankish mercenaries because they were plundering the local people.

When the Emperor Romanus was captured at the battle of Manzikert and was brought before Sultan Alp Arslan, the Sultan put his boot on the Emperor's neck and forced him to kiss the ground. Remarkably, despite this inauspicious beginning of their relationship, the Sultan in fact treated the Emperor extremely well. This famous conversation is recorded to have taken place between them:

ALP ARSLAN: "What would you do if I were brought before you as a prisoner?"
ROMANUS: "Perhaps I'd kill you, or exhibit you in the streets of Constantinople."
ALP ARSLAN: "My punishment is far heavier. I forgive you, and set you
free."[27]

In retrospect, it is clear that Romanus should have remained indefinitely as the guest of the kindly Sultan. Soon after Romanus returned to his own subjects, he was deposed, blinded, and exiled to an island, where he died as a result of an infection caused by an injury during his blind-ing. After the deposition of Romanus, the empire dissolved into civil war, in which both sides bought Turkish support by handing over land and cities. This is how the Turkish "conquest" of Anatolia came about.[28]

On balance, while the battle of Manzikert was a serious blow to Byzantine prestige, it did not then endanger the Empire as a whole. The Byzantines probably suffered no more than about 8,000 casualties. This was only 20 percent of their military strength and could easily be reme-died by recruiting native soldiers from the Empire's military estates. Service with the Byzantine army would continue to attract mercenaries from all around the medieval world.

Nevertheless, in retrospect the long, slow decline of Byzantium seems to have begun with the battle of Manzikert. This fight is also held to be one of the causes of the later Crusades, since the West saw the Byzantine defeat there as a clear sign that Byzantium would no longer be able to protect either Eastern Christianity or the travels of the many Christian pilgrims making their way from Europe to Jerusalem to visit the Holy Sepulcher.[29]

Turning now to Spain, Rodrigo Diaz de Vivar (1043–1099) is known in Spanish history as El Cid Campeador, a compound of two separate sobriquets, one meaning "Sir" or "Lord," and the other meaning roughly "the champion of single combat on the battlefield."[30] Tradition-ally referred to simply as El Cid, he was a Castilian nobleman, military officer, mercenary leader, diplomat and in later life a ruler in his own right. He is also remembered as the clever folk hero celebrated in *El Cantar de Mio Cid* (*The Poem of My Cid*, ca. 1207), which is the oldest preserved Castilian poem and is based on folkloric tales about

El Cid during the Reconquista, i.e., the reconquest of Spain from the Moors.

One of these tales recounts how, after he was exiled from the court of the Spanish Emperor Alfonso VI of Léon and Castile in 1080, El Cid had virtually nothing of value left in his castle and therefore could not pay his soldiers. The above poem says,

> Tears stood in the eyes of the Cid as he looked at his pillaged castle. The coffers were empty, even the falcons were gone from their perches.... Little hope then had the Cid of mercy from King Alfonso; and sooner than bring suffering to his beloved people of Burgos he betook himself without the city and sat him down to think of what to do. [He therefore said to his friend Martin Antolinez] "I have no money with which to pay my troops. Thou must help me to get it, and if I live I will repay thee double."
> Then the two together fashioned two stout chests covered with red leather and studded with guilt nails, and these they filled with sand. Then Martin Antolinez without delay sought out the money lenders, Rachel and Vidas, and bargained with them to lend the Cid six hundred marks, and to take in pawn for them the two chests filled with treasure that he dared not at that time take away with him. For a year they were to keep the chests and pledge themselves not to look in them. Glad were the hearts of the money lenders as they lifted the heavy chests, and happy was the Cid when he saw the six hundred marks counted out before him.[31]

To return to a more factual account: after being exiled, El Cid went to Barcelona looking for a job as a mercenary captain, but the local leaders refused to hire him. He then, in 1081, offered his services, this time successfully, to the Moorish king Yusuf al-Mu'taman ibn Hud and served both him and his successor, Al-Mustain II. But later, after a crushing Christian defeat at the battle of Sagrajas in 1086, Alfonso VI found that he urgently needed a very competent general to prevent further defeats, so he recalled El Cid to his service. Yet El Cid was exiled anew in 1089. He then decided to go it alone and commanded a combined Christian and Moorish army, using it to carve out his own fiefdom in the rich, Moorish-controlled, Mediterranean coastal city of Valencia in 1094.

An anonymous Latin work, written at some point between 1102 and 1238 and known to historians of Spain as the *Historia Roderici* (i.e., the *History of Rodrigo*, but a better translation would be *The Deeds of Rodrigo*), is the primary source for El Cid's historical — as opposed to his legendary — exploits.[32] According to the *Historia Roderici*:

III. "Human thoughts are inclined to greed"

Rodrigo continued to press the siege of Valencia ever more closely for no little time. At long last he took possession of it by assault. At once he subjected it to sack. He found and took possession of vast and innumerable riches; immense, uncounted quantities of gold and silver, precious jewellery, gems set in fine gold, treasures of various sorts, silken textiles decorated with precious gold. So vast were the hoards of riches which he seized in the city that he and his followers were rendered wealthier than it is possible to say.[33]

El Cid lived in Valencia after his capture of the city until his death in 1099. The *Historia Roderici* sums up his eventful life:

It would take too long — and perhaps would tax the patience of readers — to narrate in order all the battles which Rodrigo and his companions fought and won, or to list all the lands and settlements which his strong right arm wasted and destroyed with the sword and other weapons. What our limited skill can do we have done: written of his deeds briefly and in a poor style, but always with the strictest regard for truth. While he lived in this world he always won a noble triumph over the enemies who fought him in battle. Never was he defeated by any man.[34]

IV

"They went about in bands of thousands"

In the 11th century, Scandinavian armies were drawn from the "ship's levy" and from a body of men known as the hird. *The father of modern Sweden, Gustav Vasa, would seize power by hiring mercenaries. In England, William of Ypres commanded a contingent of Flemish mercenaries; the high point of his career probably was the Rout of Winchester in 1141. When the Second Crusade ended in failure, unemployed mercenaries and common criminals jeopardized law and order in France itself after 1149. Across the Channel, Henry II had to rely on mercenaries known as Brabanters to bring his own family into line when they rebelled in 1173.*

There is not much literature in English about medieval mercenaries in Scandinavia but the following points can confidently be made here in a brief overview.[1]

The most widely-studied period of the military history of medieval Scandinavia is known as the Viking Age, which ended in the late 11th century when Christianity had spread to much of but not to the entire Scandinavian world. Initially, most Scandinavian armies were based on the traditional concept of the "ship's levy" (*ledung*), which was a form of conscription used to organize coastal fleets for seasonal excursions and armies for the defense of the realm. These armies were rather small compared to those of continental Europe, usually averaging about 500 men but sometimes reaching a high of perhaps 4,000 men. Military equipment did not change a great deal from the mid–11th to the late 13th centuries, probably due to the relative poverty of the region, but a powerful weapon new to this region — the crossbow — was very well-received.

Indeed, by the end of the medieval period every free man of the peasant militias would own a crossbow.

Military forces were also drawn from another important institution of the Viking age — the *hird*, a term which meant "a body of men." Originally, in Norwegian history the *hird* was only an informal retinue of the king's personal armed companions, e.g., known as hirdsmen or housecarls, who were free men (essentially mercenaries) hired and paid for by him, but it gradually grew into both the nucleus ("Guards") of the royal army itself and into a formal royal court household based on the knightly ideal of a community of warrior-equals, with the king as the first among these equals.

It should be noted here that after Anglo-Saxon England was conquered by Denmark in the 11th century, housecarls appeared in England, too, probably in about 1016–1018. They were brought or recruited there as a royal bodyguard, either by Sweyn (or Swein) Forkbeard or by his son Cnut.[2] Frank Stenton (1880–1967), perhaps the best-known historian of Anglo-Saxon England, explained their importance as follows:

> Cnut was surrounded by a large company of specialized fighting-men, which formed the nucleus of his armies, and from which individuals could be dispatched on unpopular or dangerous business. From later Danish evidence it is clear that the members of this body formed a highly organized military guild, united, not only by loyalty to the king, but by a code of behaviour intended to secure that each man respected the interests and, above all, the honour of his fellows.... This force as a whole was set apart from other men by the severity of its discipline, its elaborate constitution, and its intimacy with the king.[3]

There seem to have been between 3,000 and 6,000 of these men. Many were constantly in attendance on the king. Others were deployed as garrison troops in places of strategic importance or were granted gifts of land on which to settle. The Bayeux Tapestry depicts at least three of them in action — one is wielding a long-hafted axe; another is simultaneously (sic) using a bow and arrow and is slashing downward with a long-bladed sword (this feat would require three hands, but allowances must be made here for artistic freedom); and the third, shown upside-down and turning in mid-air, is obviously a casualty.[4]

In England, the royal housecarls played both military and administrative roles, being governed both by Norse traditions and by canon (church) law. They were in effect a mercenary force: contemporary sources refer to them as "men receiving wages," as "salarymen," and as "paid men." A special tax was levied to provide pay in coin for the royal housecarls, who were paid each month. They were not bound to indefinite service to the king but were free to leave his employment once a year — on New Year's Eve, the day on which it was customary for Scandinavian kings to reward their retainers with gifts.

In contrast to Norway, the *hird* system in Denmark and Sweden was replaced in the mid–14th century by professional mercenaries paid in cash. Such men were considered by the court to be more reliable than soldiers drawn from the nobility, whose primary allegiance was to their own families rather than to the king himself.[5]

Sweden did not have any domestic mercenary companies of its own. Instead, it hired many mercenaries from other countries during the 15th through 17th centuries. In fact, the father of modern Sweden, Gustav Vasa, seized power in the 1520s by taking large loans from the Hanseatic League (a commercial and defensive confederation of merchant guilds and market towns); hiring mercenaries with that money; and then, during the Swedish War of Liberation (1521–1523), successfully deposing the Danish king Christian II as regent of the Kalmar Union in Sweden.

More and more mercenaries were used in Scandinavia during the 15th century conflicts that raged in Sweden, the Baltic, and the southern reaches of Denmark. For example, the Danish monarchy relied heavily on professional German mercenaries — a trend that had begun in the 14th century due to the close proximity of what has been called the "mercenary markets" of northern Germany. Danish nobles were not required to take to the battlefield themselves: they could support the war effort simply by contributing money to it. As a result, the commanders of Danish units were often not Danes but minor German princes or counts hired for the tasks at hand.

The downside of this policy for the Danish crown was the high cost of paying these mercenary troops. If there was no money to pay them, the mercenaries either had to make their way back to their own homes, if any, and face a very uncertain future there, or take matters into their own hands by raiding the crown's holdings.

The situation in Sweden was different, largely because it was a poorer country than Denmark. The large scale use of mercenaries did not begin there until the early years of the reign of Gustav Vasa (r. 1523–1560). An internal uprising of peasants in south Sweden in 1542–1543, however, led Gustav Vasa to conclude that foreign mercenaries were too costly to hire and, moreover, were very poorly-suited to warfare in the freezing, heavily-wooded countryside. As a result, he eventually decided to discharge the mercenaries and to rely instead on a newly-formed national army.

Mercenaries were of much greater importance to William of Ypres (ca. 1090–1164) at the Rout of Winchester in 1141. William was a very successful Flemish mercenary who was King Stephen of England's chief lieutenant and who commanded a contingent of Flemish mercenaries during the English civil wars of 1139–1154. Taken collectively, these wars are traditionally known both as the "Nineteen-Year Winter" and as the "Anarchy." Political, economic, and social conditions were so horrific then that the *Anglo-Saxon Chronicle* reports, probably with some over-statement, that during Stephen's reign,

> all was warfare, wickedness, and robbery, for right away all the powerful men who were traitors rose up against him.... They oppressed the wretched people greatly on castle works [i.e., they forced the common people to build castles for them]. When the castles were built, they filled them with devils and evil men. Night and day they seized anyone who they thought possessed any wealth (both men and women), and put them in prison, and tortured them with unspeakable tortures to get their gold and silver.... Wherever the ground was tilled, the earth bore no grain, for the land was ruined by such acts. It was openly said that Christ and his saints were asleep. Such things—and more than we can tell—we suffered nineteen winters for our sins.[6]

In England, mercenaries played key roles in Stephen's struggles against Empress Matilda (also known as Matilda of England, she was the daughter and heir of King Henry I of England). William had recruited Flemish mercenaries to support him in his struggle for the comital throne, i.e., the count's throne. He failed in this bid but when Stephen became king in 1135, Stephen hired William and his men to fight for him in the English civil wars. William rose to become Stephen's chief confidant, much to the opposition of Stephen's barons, who must have seen him as a potential threat. This would not be surprising, because

William's mercenaries were described by William of Malmesbury, the foremost historian of the 12th century, as "looters and wild ruffians who did not hesitate to desecrate cemeteries, rob churches, and carry off priests as prisoners. They lived on their pay and their plunder."[7]

William fought on Stephen's side in Normandy in 1137 and later, in 1141, he and the Count of Aumêle jointly commanded part of Stephen's royal army in the battle of Lincoln. The royal army was defeated there, however, and as soon as Stephen saw how the tide was turning, he fled from the battlefield. With a sardonic turn of phrase, the 12th century English historian Henry of Huntingdon says of William's performance: "He was a very able commander, but when he saw that he could no longer help the king, he postponed his help until a more propitious moment."[8]

Stephen was taken prisoner in this battle. William went to Kent, where he joined Stephen's queen, Matilda of Boulogne and raised new troops. The high point of his mercenary career probably came in 1141 during a fight known as the Rout of Winchester, where he commanded a contingent of Flemish mercenary cavalry.

In this affray, Stephen's army, led by William and Stephen's queen, defeated the army of a rival faction (the Angevin faction of Empress Matilda, who is not to be confused with the Queen Matilda, mentioned above) commanded by Earl Robert of Gloucester. At the climax of the battle, Earl Robert — who was at that point surrounded by William's mercenaries and was facing a bridge over the River Test at Stockbridge which was impassable because the bridge was so crowded by refugees — was forced to surrender and was taken prisoner. Stephen was exchanged for Earl Robert in 1141. Stephen considered himself indebted to William for his liberation; once free and back on his throne again, Stephen rewarded William with an annual income of £450 from the royal lands in Kent, a very sizeable sum in those days. This was money well-spent because William's mercenaries were always Stephen's strongest prop during the civil wars.

The *Dictionary of National Biography* says that for a few years after Stephen's restoration, William became "a fear and terror to all England."[9] In about 1143, William and three high-ranking fellow bandits even threatened to burn St. Albans Abbey and had to be bought off by a valuable gift from its treasury. At some later point, when Stephen sent a treasure chest to William, apparently for safe-keeping, William broke the chest open with a hatchet and helped himself to whatever he wanted. When Henry II ascended the throne in 1154, he banished William's mercenaries but allowed William himself, who had become blind, to remain in England and continue to draw his income from Kent until 1157.[10] William's last years were spent in the monastery of St. Peter in Loo in what is now the Netherlands. He died in 1165.

In 1146, the French king, Louis VII, and his wife, Queen Eleanor, "took the cross"[11] (i.e., they formally volunteered for the Second Crusade) and the next year they left France for the Holy Land. The Second Crusade (1145 to 1149) was a great humiliation for the Crusaders and a great victory for their Muslim opponents.[12] This crusade had significant impacts in France itself in terms of social unrest and by providing new opportunities for mercenaries and brigands. It had been launched in 1145 by Pope Eugene III in his bull (a papal document) *Quantum praedecessores*[13] in response to the loss of the County of Edessa the year before. (Edessa was the first of the three Crusader states to be established. The other two were the Kingdom of Jerusalem and the Principality of Antioch. Edessa was the first one to be captured by the Muslims.)

The Second Crusade was the first crusade to be led by European kings in person, namely, Louis VII of France and Conrad III of Germany, with help from other European kingdoms. In 1148, the senior officers of the crusade would meet at Acre in what is now Israel and would decide to attack Damascus instead of Edessa. Their siege of Damascus would fail utterly, however, and they would be forced, ignominiously, to retreat to Jerusalem under the constant fire of Turkish archers. German monk-historians were so impressed by the failure of the Second Crusade that they decided it could only have been the work of the Devil himself. An anonymous chronicler-monk in Würzburg also added that, for decades after this battle, noble families were still ransoming back the European knights who had been taken prisoner in it.[14]

As soon as the king and queen and their entourage left for the Holy Land in 1147, conditions in France itself began to slip downhill. The 19th century French scholar Hercule Géraud (1812–1844) was only 32 years old when he died and did not have time to write enough to place himself in the very front ranks of medievalists, but he has left such an excellent description of what happened in France as a result of the Second Crusade that it deserves to be quoted here at some length.

We are calling what follows a "free translation," i.e., an informal translation, because liberties have been taken in editing and annotating Géraud's prose to make it more readable in English.

> Until the end of the 12th century, and even later, lords who had a good deal of independence used military campaigns as an escape from the boredom of daily life in their castles. Relieving travelers of their valuables, pillaging churches, ravaging the lands of neighbors too weak to defend themselves— these were the normal pastimes of the most powerful barons....
>
> In 1146, in an assembly of senior clergymen and lords, Louis VII and his queen Eleanor took the cross from the hands of St. Bernard. They left in 1147, trailing behind them the elite of the clergy and nobility. They would be gone for two years....
>
> No sooner had the King and his entourage left France, however, than many men who were eager to pillage the country found, during his absence, the chance to practice with impunity the brigandage they had long planned. Some openly seized goods from churches and poor people; others plundered more secretly. The lands of all the lords who followed Louis VII on this crusade were subjected to the same disorders....
>
> Those men who were eager to plunder — or who were perhaps pushed into disorder by their blind desire to take revenge, in the absence of the great barons, for the injustices and violence that had been inflicted on them — were the first kernel of the terrible bands which, later on, ravaged certain French provinces. Their ranks were swollen, in 1150, by a crowd of miserable people — the sorry residue of the Second Crusade, whom the disasters of the Crusade left no alternatives other than begging or brigandage.
>
> Events outside France continued to give birth, in the heart of France itself, to terrible problems of order and of peace [here Géraud cites numerous examples of gratuitous violence, e.g., "the war ignited between Duke Godfrey the Courageous and two rebellious vassals— a war which lasted for nearly 20 years and which covered the region with ashes, blood, and ruins."]
>
> Thus from about 1147 to 1160 there spread throughout the whole of France, like a bloody network, an army of partisans [Géraud lists them as "Aragonais, Basques, Navarrais, Mainades, Triaverdins, Bracançons, Cotereaux or Routiers"]. These men were armed and consisted of diverse factions, but they were united in their pursuit of disorder and pillage. From that point on, they began a war of extermination against all kinds of property: the Catholic Church above all, which in this era was rich but was too weak to protect its treasures, was exposed to the full fury of those eager to pillage.[15]

Géraud's "army of partisans" included many mercenaries as well as many desperate men and common criminals. The threats they posed to civic law and order were very great and could not be suppressed very easily, if at all: local governments were simply too weak and had no armed forces at their disposal. As an example of the resulting anarchy, Géraud mentions that in about 1162 a certain Count "H" (only his initial is given)

> ravaged the city of Reims with an army of mercenaries. According to Henri of France, the archbishop of Reims, these brigands completely ruined the area, massacring the inhabitants or taking them prisoner. At one point they confined 36 people to a church, set the church on fire, and burned the people and the church.[16]

Mercenaries caused so much havoc in southern France in the 12th century that the Third Lateran Council (i.e., the third ecumenical council of the Church) denounced in 1179 the mercenaries who were preying on churches, the countryside, and on the poor and the innocent without any distinction of sex or social status. Canon 27 of the Council stated firmly that anyone who hired these mercenary bands or was otherwise associated with them would be subject to excommunication. On the positive side, however, it added that

> whoever, following the council of holy bishops and priests, takes up arms against them, will enjoy a remission of two years penance and will be placed under the protection of the Church just like those who undertake the journey to Jerusalem.[17]

King Henry II of England has been cited in modern scholarly studies as the medieval leader who was most dependent on mercenaries.[18] He used them when, for varying reasons, three of his four legitimate sons; his wife, Queen Eleanor of Aquitaine; and their noble supporters all rose in rebellion against him in 1173. This revolt failed after 18 months; the rebellious family members and their allies then had no choice but to resign themselves to Henry II's continuing rule.

Before looking at this rebellion, consider what Roger of Hoveden, a royal clerk who began in about 1192 to compile his *Chronica*, a general history of England from 732 to his own time, has to say about Henry's sons. This excerpt from his work paints a very clear picture of the intense training that all young men had to undergo in order to become men-at-arms or knights. Roger says of Henry II's sons:

They strove to outdo the others in handling weapons. They realized that without practice the art of war did not come naturally when it was needed. No athlete can fight tenaciously who has never received any blows: he must see his blood flow and hear his teeth crack under the fist of his adversary, and when he is thrown to the ground he must fight on with all his might and not lose courage. The oftener he falls, the more determinedly he must spring to his feet again. Anyone who can do that can engage in battle confidently. Strength gained by practice is invaluable: a soul subject to terror has fleeting glory. He who is too weak to bear this burden, through no fault of his own, will be overcome by its weight, no matter how eagerly he may rush to the task. The price of sweat is well paid where the Temples of Victory stand.[19]

To bring his family into line, Henry II relied very heavily on his Brabanters (*Brabançons*). These were mercenaries nominally recruited from Brabant (as noted earlier, Brabant was a duchy of the Holy Roman Empire covering parts of present-day Netherlands and Belgium) but they actually came from all across northern Europe.[20] They cost more than feudal forces but they had much greater military abilities and, unlike feudal forces whose utility was limited by custom (feudal forces had to serve in the ranks for only a short period of time each year), they were prepared to maneuver and to fight all year long — provided that they were paid. Roger of Hoveden says:

Immediately after Easter, in this year [1173], the whole of the kingdom of France, and the king, the son of the king of England, Richard his brother, earl of Poitou, and Geoffrey, earl of Bretagne, and nearly all the earls and barons of England, Normandy, Aquitaine, Anjou, and Brittany, arose against the king of England the father, and laid waste his lands on every side with fire, sword, and rapine; they also laid siege to his castles, and took them by storm, and there was no one to relieve them. Still, he [Henry II] made all the resistance against them that he possibly could: for he had with him twenty thousand Brabanters [estimates of their strength vary greatly but reasonable guesses range from 500 to 1,500 men] who served him faithfully, but not without large pay which he gave them.[21]

Yet not all the Brabanters were on the king's side. Writing in about 1180, this is what Walter Map (1140-ca. 1208–1210), a Welsh author who wrote in Latin, comments:

A new and particularly noxious sect of heretics arose. The fighters of these *rotten* [i.e., wandering detachments of armed men] were protected from head to foot by a leather jerkin [a close-fitting jacket], and were armed with steel, staves and iron. They went about in bands of thousands and reduced monasteries, villages and cities to ashes. With violence, yet thinking it was no sin, they committed adultery, saying "There is no God." This movement arose in Brabant, hence the name Brabançons.

From the start these marauders drew up for themselves a curious law, which properly speaking was based on no concept of right. Fugitive rebels, false clerks, renegade monks and all who had forsaken God for any reason, joined them. Their number has already risen so sharply ... that they can with impunity stay where they are or wander about all over the land, greatly hated by God and man.[22]

The Pipe Rolls (English financial records dating from the 12th century) show that Henry II employed more than 6,000 mercenaries. Ironically, one of his sons, known as Henry the Young King (who predeceased him), met his death — if only indirectly — as a result of these mercenaries. During the course of a campaign in the Limousin region, Henry the Young King pillaged the local monasteries because he desperately needed to raise money to pay his mercenaries. In the process, however, he contracted dysentery, weakened fast, and died in 1183 at the age of only 28.

V

"All the foreign knights, bowmen, their attendants and the mercenaries"

In 1199, Mercadier — a bloodthirsty French mercenary captain — avenged King Richard of England's death by flaying alive the young cross-bowman who had shot the king. Another mercenary commander, a Provençal soldier named Lupescar, was blamed for England's loss of Normandy to France in 1204. A clause in Magna Carta, the great charter of English liberties, called in 1215 for the expulsion of all foreign mercenaries from England. Two years later, the good luck of the mercenary-sailor Eustache the Monk finally ran out when English sailors captured him and gave him the choice of which side of his own ship he preferred for his beheading.

Mercadier was a ferocious French Provençal mercenary commander who first surfaces in medieval history in 1183 as chief of the Brabant mercenaries in southern France.[1] In October of that year he besieged Pompadour (now a commune in the Corrèze *département* of France) and ravaged the surrounding countryside. He retreated, however, as soon as he learned that other mercenaries from the Auvergne planned to attack him.

In 1184 he entered the service of Richard, who was then Duke of Aquitaine and later became king of England as Richard I. Under Richard's protection, Mercadier laid waste to the lands of Count Adhémar of Limoges. Four years later, Richard joined forces with Brabançon mercenaries against the Count of Toulouse; in that clash, Richard captured 17 castles near Toulouse, which he entrusted to Mercadier, who faithfully defended them and was put in command of Richard's army.

Mercadier left with Richard on the Third Crusade but Richard sent him back when Philip II Augustus, the French king, left Acre to return to France. (The Third Crusade, conducted from 1189 to 1192, was an effort by European leaders to regain the Holy Land from the Muslims. It was generally successful but failed to achieve its ultimate objective — the reconquest of Jerusalem.) Mercadier's assignment upon his return from the Holy Land was to deploy his mercenaries wherever necessary to defend Richard's lands.[2] From 1194 to Richard's death nearly five years later, Mercadier served as his right-hand man and did a brilliant job.

The modern historian J.F. Verbruggen summarizes Mercadier's subsequent achievements in these words:

> Together they [Mercadier and Richard] gained a great victory at Fréteval in 1194 [at that battle, Richard reconquered his French fiefdoms from Philip Augustus], and early in the following year Mercadier took Issoudun and placed a garrison in the fortress. [Mercadier] also fought in Brittany, and carried out a raid on Abbeville, where he robbed the French merchants and took much booty. In 1197 he ambushed the martial bishop of Beauvais and took him prisoner. [In another source, Mercadier is described as a *felon veisin* — "cruel neighbor" — to the city of Beauvais.]
> The following year Richard and Mercadier cut off the retreat of the French at Vernon, and drove the defeated troops into the [River] Epte. After that they took the castle at Courcelles, and intercepted the army of Philip Augustus, who had hastened to help. They won another victory and chased the fleeing troops to the castle of Gisors. There was so great a crush before the castle gate that Philip Augustus fell into the moat when the bridge collapsed under his knights.[3]

It is evident that Mercadier and Richard valued each other highly. Mercadier described himself as Richard's *famulus* (a close attendant) and added that

> I fought for him with loyalty and strenuously, never opposed to his will, prompt in obedience to his commands; and in consequence of this service I gained his esteem and was placed in command of his army.[4]

Richard generously rewarded Mercadier's loyalty. He ordered that his bailiffs in Normandy must guard carefully all the booty that Mercadier had collected. In the castle of Château-Gaillard, which was designed by Richard himself, he even named one of its bridges after Mercadier.[5]

In 1199, Richard was severely wounded in the shoulder by a crossbow bolt fired during the siege of Château de Châlus-Chambrol in Limousin. Before he died of an infection a few days later, it was Mercadier's doctor who cared for him. Mercadier then savagely avenged Richard's death by storming the castle, hanging the defenders, and flaying alive the young crossbowman (a boy named Pierre Basile) who had shot the king. He did this despite the fact that, as his last act, Richard had pardoned the lad, who claimed that he had fired at Richard only because both his father and his two brothers had been killed earlier in the battle.

After Richard's death, Mercadier became a mercenary leader for King John, ravaging Gascony (southwestern France) and punishing the renegade city of Angers. On Easter Monday in 1200, however, while on a visit to Bordeaux to pay his respects to Eleanor of Aquitaine he was assassinated by a mercenary who worked for a man-at-arms named Brandin, a rival mercenary captain in John's service.

Being a mercenary could be a very hazardous calling, not only in military but also in political terms. In 1204, during the reign of England's King John, mainland Normandy was captured from England by Philip II of France. The captain of the great band of mercenaries hired by King John in his vain effort to retain mainland Normandy was a Provençal leader known as Lupescar (or Lupescair).

This nickname ultimately comes from *Lupus*, the Latin word for "wolf." The 19th century French scholar Hercule Géraud has already been mentioned. He fittingly translated this brigand's name as *louvart* — a French hunting term meaning "young wolf." The king was obviously very impressed by the lupine qualities of this mercenary. King John commanded his bailiffs in Normandy to guard carefully all the booty collected by Lupescar; moreover, he later ordered that the Seneschal of Gascony should assist "our beloved and faithful Lupescar" in all possible ways.[6] (A seneschal was an official having full charge of domestic arrangements and the administration of justice in the household of a medieval dignitary.)

In the Normandy campaigns of 1200–1204, the Kingdom of England fought the Kingdom of France and, at the same time, had to beat down rebellions from its own nobles. These campaigns ultimately ended in victory for France. Lupescar himself played a leading role in John's final and failed efforts to retain control of the Duchy of Normandy but in the process he also became a convenient scapegoat for this debacle.

More is learned about Lupescar from "John the Troubadour." Writing in late 1226, this author produced a long poem glorifying William the Marshal (1147–1219), an Anglo-Norman soldier and statesman who was one of the most powerful men in Europe. The poem explains John's loss of Normandy in these damning words:

> But you should know first of all why it was that the king could not win the hearts of his men and draw them to him. Why? By my faith, he allowed Lupescar to treat them so harshly that he seized whatever he came across in the land, as if the land were at war. But that was nothing; for if he dishonourned the men's wives and daughters, not twopennyworth was paid in compensation.[7]

As if this were not enough to shift all the blame to Lupescar's shoulders, a petition drawn up by the Norman barons and sent to John shortly after this defeat also strongly condemned Lupescar's behavior in Normandy.[8]

Mercenaries may have been popular with medieval leaders but much of the rest of the population held them in fear and distrust. King John had been forced to resort to very high levels of taxation of his English subjects to pay for his mercenaries, described as "robbers, plunderers and fire-raisers," whom he had hired from the regions of Louvain, Brabant, and Flanders.[9] Moreover, these warriors were foreigners who knew nothing about English customs, who had no desire to learn anything about them, and who exploited the local people or at best treated them with disdain. There was therefore a great deal of hostility towards the mercenaries which King John brought to England when he left Normandy after his unsuccessful campaigns to regain the lands he claimed there.

A clear sign of this underlying hostility was Magna Carta (1215) or, more formally, Magna Carta Liberatatum ("The Great Charter of the Liberties of England"). This was the first document ever forced upon an English king (King John, in this case) by his own subjects, i.e., the rebellious barons. Magna Carta has long been considered as the great charter of English liberties and has had an enormous impact on constitutional law, including the United States' Bill of Rights. It is important to recognize, however, that it was not written as a stirring defense of individual freedom but chiefly because lay and religious magnates wanted to make sure that their own customary rights were officially acknowledged by the king. They also wanted to make sure that the collapse of central government and the rise of lawlessness which had prevailed in the past under King Stephen did not resurface.

Fundamentally, then, the magnates wanted to limit, by law, the king's power and thus protect their own privileges. Although mercenaries were only a minor issue in this historic document, Magna Carta did promise, in what is now known as clause 51, that

> as soon as peace is restored, we will remove from the kingdom all the foreign knights, bowmen, their attendants, and the mercenaries that have come to it, to its harm, with horses and arms.[10]

Since there was an enormous and well-founded amount of distrust between the barons and King John, it is not surprising that Magna Carta was legally valid for no more than three months. This document also provided, in what is now known as clause 61, that a committee of 25 barons could meet at any time and could overrule the will of the king if he defied Magna Carta's provisions. This was a very serious challenge to John's authority as the ruling monarch, so he quickly denounced it. Pope Innocent III objected to this clause, too.

The barons eventually decided that since King John would never agree to Magna Carta voluntarily, they would have to overthrow him. The result was the First Barons' War (1215–1217)—a civil war in England between pro–Angevin forces, on the one hand, and, on the other, the rebellious barons, supported by a French army under Prince Louis and by the Kingdom of Scotland under Robert Fitzwalter.

In preparation for this war, John went to southeast England to recruit more mercenaries, but these do not appear to have played a significant role in the conflict. His own strategy seems to have been many-sided: to try to isolate the rebellious barons by bottling them up in London; to protect his own supply lines to Flanders, which was the main source of his mercenaries; to prevent the French from landing troops in southeastern England; and, slowly but surely, try to wear down the barons through a war of attrition.

What in fact happened was that John died in 1216 and was succeeded by his young son, Henry. Louis, for his part, suffered several defeats, including the loss of a reinforcement convoy captained by a mercenary, Eustace the Monk (see the next section for more on this interesting character). This loss made it nearly impossible for Louis to continue fighting.[11] The war, however, would drag on until 1217, when Louis signed the Treaty of Lambeth, accepted a symbolic sum to relinquish his English dominions, and returned home to France.

One of the most colorful mercenaries was Eustache Busquet (ca. 1170–1217), known to history as Eustache the Monk, who was variously known as a French knight, monk, sorcerer, outlaw, sailor, and mercenary.[12] A manuscript blending fact and fiction, written in Old French between the years 1223 and 1284, recounts his many adventures in France, Spain, England, and the Channel Islands after being unjustly outlawed by Renaud de Dammartin, the Count of Boulogne.

Eustache was trained as a knight in Boulogne in northern France and probably acquired his impressive nautical skills in Italy. After traveling in Spain, where he is said to have studied black magic in Toledo, he became a monk at the Benedictine Abbey of St. Samer near Boulogne. However, when his father was murdered by a nobleman named Hainfrois de Heresinghen, Eustache abandoned his religious vocation and demanded justice from the Count of Boulogne. He tried to avenge his father by hiring a champion to fight a judicial duel on his own behalf, but his champion was defeated.[13]

Despite this setback, in 1203 Eustache was appointed seneschal by the Count of Boulogne during the latter's expedition with King Philip Augustus to win back lands in Normandy held by King John of England. When the count returned in 1204, however, Eustache was accused of financial mismanagement by his enemy Hainfrois. Eustache was summoned by the Count of Boulogne to give a full account of himself but, fearing treachery, he refused to appear before the Count and instead fled into the forests of the Boulonnais, where he became an outlaw. The Count retaliated by seizing his properties.

Because he was so outnumbered by the Count's knights and men-at-arms, Eustache had to rely on his own intelligence, stealth, deception, and clever trickery to avoid capture and to get his revenge. By donning 17 different disguises, he terrorized the Count by burning his mills, stealing his horses, and mutilating or killing his men. Several of these exploits closely resemble episodes told later in other outlaw tales—in, for example, the stories of Robin Hood.

Eustache was an outlaw only for a short time—from early 1204 to early 1205. He left France for the English Channel later in 1205 and became a pirate there and preyed upon English shipping. By November of that year he was in England, where he offered his services to King John as a naval commander. When his services were accepted, he patrolled the English Channel, looking for prey on behalf of the English—and, of course, for himself as well. The fact-and-fiction manuscript mentioned earlier describes his adventures and tells how he conquered the Channel Islands. Despite its exaggerations, it is worth quoting because it gives such a good feel for hands-on medieval combat. The manuscript states:

> So Eustache became one of King John's retainers and was given command of a fleet of ships. With some thirty galleys given to him by the king, Eustache then set sail. His first destination was the islands of Jersey and Guernsey. But as he approached one of these Channel Islands he found the islanders waiting for him and assembled with their leader Romerel, the lord of one of the island manors. When he saw Eustache's fleet approaching, the leader said to his men, "Now wait until they've landed. The moment we see them coming ashore, we'll attack and destroy them at once" ...
> Heavy fighting broke out and many men were knocked off their horses. One side attacked fiercely and the other side defended itself very well. After the mêlée, began, it soon became savage, violent and arduous. On the battlefield Eustache held a huge axe in his hands and with it he struck countless heavy blows. He smashed and split many a helmet, and more than one warhorse lost its shoulder. First to his right and then to the left he struck blow after blow, making himself lord and master of the battle. Eustache shouted out [to his own forces], "Don't stop striking your blows! They'll all take flight, as you'll soon see."
> So the great battle raged on ever more fiercely. That day many coffins were to be made. In the end, Eustache expelled everyone he found there. All the inhabitants of the Channel Islands were sent into exile. In fact, so complete was the destruction he wrought that there was nothing left to burn in any of the castles or manors.[14]

Eustache captured the island of Sark and set up his base there. During this period, he received two safe-conduct passes from King John, which allowed him to return to England when he wished. Eustache was highly valued by the English. In fact, he was given lands in Norfolk and in 1209 he was still in King John's service and had become an English ambassador to the Count of Boulogne. When King Philip learned of his presence in France, however, he outlawed him.

In 1212 Eustache was in London when the Count negotiated there a charter of allegiance with King John. Again fearing treachery, however, Eustache left England for France, changed sides, and joined forces with King Philip. He reportedly led a fleet of ships across the English Channel and may have been involved in a naval disaster at Damme in 1213. If so, there he may have lost the *Nef de Boulogne*, a huge ship built in the shape of a castle, when the English attacked and destroyed King Philip's fleet. Eustache was accused of betraying the fleet but the charges against him were dropped for lack of proof. The next year, when the English barons began their rebellion against King John, Eustache supplied them with arms. As a result, his holdings in Norfolk were confiscated.

In 1215 Eustache continued to control the English Channel. The next year a French fleet of 800 ships set sail for England to support the Barons' War and Eustache transported King Louis from France to the Isle of Thanet, the most easterly point of Kent, England. In 1217, however, Eustache's good luck finally ran out. He sailed to England to support King Louis but at the battle of Sandwich his ship was attacked and was captured by English ships. The English sailors hurled big pots of finely-ground lime onto the French ships. When these smashed against their railings, they generated such great clouds of dust that the French crews were blinded and were forced to surrender.

It was said that after this attack Eustache was found hiding in his ship's bilges and that he offered his English captors huge sums of money if they would spare his life. Probably because of his history as a turn-coat mercenary, however, they refused to do so. The best they would do for him was to offer him — as his place of execution — a choice between the ship's rail on one side of the boat, or the edge of a trebuchet (a catapult that was being carried to England as deck cargo), on the other side. History does not record which side Eustache chose, but he was beheaded there and then.[15]

VI

"An escort of galloglas armed with battle-axes"

Irish mercenaries consisted of three groups — the galloglas, the kerns, and the redshanks — who were sequentially active from 1290 until the late 1500s. The Catalan Company (the first "free company") was set up by the mercenary Roger de Flor in 1303. Genoese mercenary crossbowmen and galleys could not prevent France from losing most of its fleet at the battle of Sluys (1340). Two years later, a German captain would found the first Great Company of mercenaries.

Ireland has had a long and very turbulent history. By the 12th century, it was already a land of divided kingdoms. Power lay in the hands of a few regional dynasties, which fought each other for control of the island. In 1169, a huge force of Normans, backed by Welsh and Flemish mercenaries, came ashore in southeastern Ireland at Wexford. King Henry II of England, worried about the establishment of a hostile Norman state so close to England, landed at Waterford in southeastern Ireland in 1171. The English would eventually conquer Ireland. After a Gaelic resurgence in the 12th century, more than 60 years of intermittent warfare in the 1500s would finally lead to English dominance after 1603.

Ireland was always considered a difficult area in which to fight wars. Listen to what Froissart has to say:

> I must tell you that Ireland is one of the worst and most unfavourable countries in which to carry on warfare; it abounds in deep forests and in lakes and bogs, and much of it is uninhabitable. It is often impossible to come to grips with the people, for they are quite ready to desert their towns and take refuge in the woods, and live in huts made of branches, or even among the bushes and hedges, like wild beasts.... They have pointed, two-edged knives, with broad blades, and they never regard an enemy as dead

until they have cut his throat, like a sheep.... They never allow prisoners to be ransomed, and when they have the worst of any skirmish, they scatter and hide in hedges or bushes, or underground, and seem to disappear without trace.[1]

"Galloglas" (this word is variously spelled as "galloglas," "gallowglas" or with one "s" or with two of them) is a term derived from the Anglicized form of an Irish word meaning "young warrior."[2] In modern colloquial British English, the galloglas might accurately be called "Viking lads," a reference to their historical Norse origin. Drawing on the 19th century cowboy-history of the American West, they could be thought of as "young guns." In any case, these hardy fighters drifted into Ireland after the Wars of Scottish Independence, a series of military campaigns fought between the Kingdom of Scotland and the Kingdom of England in the late 13th and early 14th centuries.

The galloglas are first mentioned in the *Annals of Connacht* and in the *Annals of Loch Cé* in 1290. Much later, Shakespeare refers to them, although anachronistically, and to their mercenary colleagues, the kerns (see below), in *Macbeth* (Act 1 and Act 5):

...the merciless MacDonald–
Worthy to be a rebel, for to that
The multiplying villainies of nature
Do swarm upon him —from the Western Isles [i.e., the Hebrides and the West
    Highland coastland]
Of kerns [lightly-armed Irish infantrymen] and galloglasses is supplied....
Mark, king of Scotland, mark:
No sooner justice had with valour arm'd
Compell'd these skipping kerns to trust their heels,
But the Norwegian lord surveying vantage,
With furbish'd arms and new supplies of men
Began a fresh assault....
I cannot strike at wretched kerns, whose arms
Are hired to bear their staves; either thou, Macbeth,
Or else my sword with an unbattr'd edge
I sheathe again undeeded.

The galloglas were a heavily-armored, well-trained aristocratic infantry that could be relied on to hold their positions tenaciously in the heat of battle. The importation of galloglas into Ireland was a key factor in slowing the Anglo-Norman invasion during the 12th century because

93

they strengthened the hands of the local Irish lords. Galloglas were hired by Irish chieftains not only because of their military skills but also because, as outsiders, they were less likely to get caught up in local feuds. Over time, however, many Irishmen joined their ranks, so "galloglas" eventually came to mean a type of warrior, rather than having any specific ethnic connotation.

The most detailed information about the galloglas comes from contemporary English observers. William Camden (1551–1623) was an English antiquarian, historian, and topographer. His *Annales* contains this description of the retinue of Shane O'Oneill, the rebel lord of Tyrone who came to London to negotiate with Queen Elizabeth in 1562:

> And now Shane O'Oneill came from Ireland, to keep the promise he had made a year before, with an escort of galloglas armed with battle-axes, bare-headed, with flowing curls, yellow shirts dyed with saffron, large sleeves, short tunics, and rough cloaks, whom the English followed with as much wonderment as if they came from China or America.[3]

Writing in the last years of the sixteenth century, John Dymmok, who was in the service of the Earl of Essex, depicted them as follows (spelling and phrasing as in the original):

> The Galloglass ar pycked and scelected men of great and mightie bodies, crewell [cruel] without compassion. The greatest force of the battell consisteth in them, chosinge rather to dye then to yeelde, so that when yt cometh to handy blowes they are quickly slayne or win the feilde. They are armed with a shert of maile [mail], a skull [helmet], and a skeine [a linen shirt, often saffron-dyed]: the weapon they most vse [use] is a batle axe, or halberd, six foote longe, the blade whereof is somewhat like a shoemakers knyfe, and without pyke [this means that a halberd is an axe blade topped with a spike and mounted on a long shaft], the stroake whereof is deadly where yt lighteth. And beinge thus armed, reckoninge to him a man for his harnesse bearer, and a boye to carry his provision, he is named [known as] a spare, of his weapon so called [i.e., a battle axe, which was also known as a spare], 80 of which sparres make a battell [fighting formation] of Galloglass.[4]

Writing in 1584, Richard Stanyhurst, the Oxford-educated son of a prominent Dublin family, offered these observations:

> Their weapons [i.e., the blades of their weapons] are one foot in length, resembling double-bladed hatchets, almost sharper than razors, fixed on shafts of more than ordinary length, with which when they strike they

inflict a dreadful wound.... They are men of great stature, of more than ordinary strength of limb, powerful swordsmen, but, at the same time, altogether sanguinary and by no means inclined to give quarter...In every sharp and severe engagement, should they come close to fighting, they either soon kill, or are killed.[5]

The high point of the galloglas way of life arguably came in 1504, when these rough, heavily-armed men played important roles on both the Hiberno-Norman and the Anglo-Norman sides during the battle of Knock-doe (its name translates as "Hill of the Axes") in Galway, Ireland. A modern scholar has labeled this clash as "the greatest battle fought by these professional axemen."[6] A contemporary chronicle, the *Book of Howth*, gives this account of what has gone down in history as the battle of Axe Hill:

> And at morrow they prepared to battle in such order as their custom was; they set forward their galloglas and footmen in one main battle, and all their horsemen on their left side.... With that the Irish galloglas came on, to whom the English archers sent such a shower of arrows that their weapons and their hands were put fast together [i.e., they grasped their weapons very firmly and got ready to fight].
> MacSweeney [also spelled as MackSwine], Captain of the Irish galloglas, came foremost and asked where was Great Darcy [a famously big and powerful champion on the English side]. Darcy answered that he was at hand which he should well understand. With that MacSweeney struck Darcy such a blow upon the helmet that he put Darcy upon his knees. With that Nangell [a baron on the English side], being a lusty gentleman that day, gave Mac-Sweeney such payment that he was satisfied ever after [i.e., Nangell killed MacSweeney]. They fought terrible and bold a while. The Irish fled....[7]

Much of what is known about the galloglas as fighters comes from English observers who knew Ireland in the 16h century. For example, Sir Anthony Sentleger, Lord Deputy of Ireland, reported to Henry VIII in 1543 on the favored weapon and the warrior ethos of the galloglas. He told the King:

> As to their footmen [i.e., their rank-and-file soldiers], which be harnessed in mayle [mail] and bassinettes [helmets], having every one of them his weapon, called a sparre, much like the axe of the Tower [the Tower of London], and they be named galloglasse...these sort of men be those that do not lightly abandon the field, but byde the brunt to the death.[8]

Contemporary Irish sources agree that the kern (this term — an Anglicization of a Middle Irish word meaning a collection of fighting men—can be used either in the singular or in the plural) was a light infantryman. Kern formed the largest component of medieval Irish armies. They did not wear armor but variously carried javelins, axes, slings, and bows. Their Anglo-Irish overlords found it next to impossible to defeat them militarily.

By the end of the 16th century, the galloglas had virtually disappeared: they were simply too vulnerable to pikes and arquebuses. Writing in 1618, Thomas Gainsford, an English writer who had served as a soldier in Ireland, reports that at the time of the battle of Kinsale in 1601 "The name of galloglass is in a manner extinct."[9]

On the other hand, their military descendants, as it were, would thrive. By the 16th century, the first influx of Scottish mercenaries had settled down into rural life in Ireland. The political situation there was still in considerable flux, however, and mercenaries were still needed. As the modern scholar Muríosa Prendergast states,

> The sixteenth century was the era of the "redshank"—a mercenary distinctly different from his predecessors. [The nickname "redshank" refers to the fact that these men wore kilts and during their campaigns unflinchingly waded into the coldest streams.] The redshank was a mercenary in the truest sense of the word—they offered their services to those who would pay the most, providing loyalty of sorts for a required period of time, leaving as soon as their period of service had ended. Settlement was not an immediate priority.... The evolution of the role of the Scots mercenary force in the sixteenth century caused the development of a semi-politicised mercenary ideal that ultimately aided the destabilisation of the north of Ireland.[10]

The eventual outcome of this destabilization process was, as noted earlier, that 60 years of intermittent warfare in the 1500s led to English domination of Ireland after 1603.

Now for the Catalan Company and the mercenary leader Roger de Flor.

A "free company" (known in Italy as *compagnie di ventura* and sometimes, in English, as a "free lance" company) was a small army of medieval mercenaries acting independently of any government control, often led by a captain from the lower nobility or by a bastard son of the higher nobility, though commoners could lead a free company, too. It was called "free" not because it worked for nothing but because it was free to serve any leader or faction it liked and could charge for its services whatever the traffic would bear.

Free companies were highly professional units when compared to the average mercenary bands of the age. In the first place, they were much bigger. For example, the mercenary captain Piero Gianpaolo Orsini, in papal service in 1437, had 800 cavalrymen and 200 infantrymen. Micheletto Attendolo's company in 1441 numbered 561 lances, i.e., 1,683 men, since lance was a three-man combat team. Tiberto Brandolini had 400 lances and 300 infantrymen in 1460.[11]

In the second place, they had an established command structure; financial officers known as "butiniers" to make sure that the booty was divided fairly; secretaries to record the booty and to write out the captain's demands; and, in some cases, such as the company of the Archpriest Arnaud de Cervole (covered later), even to provide uniforms.[12]

When not employed, i.e., when peace had broken out, at least temporarily, the men of such companies had no choice but to live by plunder, since they had absolutely no other means of support. In France they were known and feared as *routiers* (bands of mercenaries) and as *écorcheurs* (literally this means "flayers of dead bodies" but in this context it refers to the destruction visited by mercenaries on villages and crops in France and in the western parts of Germany). The term "free company" is now generally used to describe the suddenly-reemployed mercenary groups which came together after the Peace of Brétigny (1360) during the Hundred Years' War, but it can be applied equally well to earlier mercenary organizations, such as the Catalan Company.[13]

Known in Catalan as the *Companyia Catalana d'Orient* and in English as the Catalan Company or as the Catalan Grand Company, this was the first free company. Made up of Aragonese and Catalan mercenaries known as "Almogavars,"[14] it was a light infantry unit organized by Roger de Flor (1267–1305), an Italian military adventurer who began his military career at the tender age of eight, when he was sent off to sea in a galley belonging to the Knights Templar.

A contemporary chronicler (Ramon Mutaner, see below) says that Roger quickly distinguished himself, first by his ability to make his way up the rigging of a ship "as lightly as if he were a monkey," and then as "one of the best mariners in the world" by running missions to the Holy

Land and thereby earning a sizeable fortune.[15] He was eventually fired by the Templars for malfeasance and then sought more promising work as a mercenary captain in Sicily and in the Byzantine Empire in the early 14th century. Roger formed a new mercenary brigade, which he termed the Great Company, by recruiting soldiers who found themselves out of work after the Peace of Catabellotta in 1302 (the last in a series of treaties designed to end conflicts in the Mediterranean between the Houses of Anjou and Barcelona).

The next year he offered his services and those of his men to the Byzantine Emperor Andronicus II, whose lands were being threatened by the Ottoman Turks then invading Anatolia.[16] His offer was accepted and he signed an elaborate *condotta*. This is the Italian word for "contract."[17] A *condotta* spelled out in precise legal terms the relationship between a mercenary and his employer, with detailed sub-clauses covering compensation for injury or loss of limbs in battle. Roger thus agreed to work for the Emperor in a specific military capacity and, indeed, some scholars consider him to have been the first *condottiere*, i.e., "mercenary captain."

A literal translation of the Italian term *condottiere* is "contractor." It comes from the *condotta* or contract signed between mercenaries and their employer. These Italian mercenary companies were at the same time both semi-feudal ventures and purely commercial undertakings. Many of the followers of a *condottiere* were linked to him by family ties and by personal loyalty; many others were tied to him by contract and by hopes of profiting from what was essentially a commercial venture.[18]

Roger organized an armada of 39 galleys and transports to carry some 1,500 knights and 4,000 foot soldiers to Constantinople. He defeated the Turks but in the process his forces engaged in such widespread violence and looting that the Byzantines began to consider them as mere brigands and freebooters, not as reliable allies. Their indiscipline, coupled with Flor's own soaring ambitions (he wanted to carve out a domain for himself in Anatolia), soon led to his death. In 1305 he was ambushed and killed by the Alans, another group of mercenaries in the Emperor's service, reportedly along with 300 of his cavalrymen and 1,000 infantrymen while he was attending a banquet given by Emperor Michael.

The Catalan Company itself survived the loss of its founder and continued to function as a military force in Greece until 1390, when it was finally defeated by the rival Navarrese Company. Ramon Mutaner (1270–1336), a Catalan soldier and writer, has left, in his *Crònica* (*Chronicle*), a 614-page-long (in printed form), very detailed first-hand account of his own adventures, including his experiences as a senior officer of the Catalan Company. Ramon served as the Company's "master rationer" (that is, as the officer in charge of administration and accounting) and distinguished himself in battle during the defense of the city of Gallipoli. The enduring value of his *Crònica* is that, in the words of the modern historian Philippe Contamine, it is

> one of the rare medieval texts which shows life from the inside of a military company with its human and economic problems, the relationship of men to their leaders, the pressing search for supplies, the thirst for power and riches, tensions with the civilian population, the many faces of war, its risks, profits and fatigues and, finally, the complexity of political problems.[19]

Contamine also gives the Catalan Company very high marks for surviving for so long. He says:

> Under its successive leaders, the Catalan Company, thanks to conspicuous Byzantine weakness, was able to conserve its cohesion and compensate for the inevitable erosion of its numbers by the addition of new elements. But above all..., relying on distant Aragonese patronage, [it] was able to found for its own profit a principality [namely, the Catalan Duchy of Athens] which was to survive until 1388. This was indeed an exceptional success of which no equivalent can be found either in the time of the Brabançons and Cotereaux [these were other medieval mercenary bands] or in that of the Companies during the Hundred Years War.[20]

It is worthwhile here to add a brief word about the rise and decline of the Duchy of Athens.[21] In 1311, the battle of Cephissus (also known as the battle or Hambros or of Orchomenos) was fought between the Frankish Greek forces of Walter V of Brienne and the mercenaries of the Catalan Company.[22] Walter had hired the Catalan Company to defend his Duchy of Athens from hostile neighbors, including the Byzantine Empire. However, when he fired most of the Company — keeping only 200 of the best horsemen and 300 of the best infantrymen, whom he paid very well but expelling the rest without any pay — the rest of the Company rebelled.

In retaliation, Walter assembled a huge force — said to have included 700 Frankish knights, thousands of Greek horsemen, 24,000 Greek infantrymen, and the 500 mercenaries he had hand-selected from the Catalan Company. His opponents could muster only some 2,000 cavalrymen and 4,000 infantrymen. To make a long story short, the Catalans won this battle decisively. They then proceeded to occupy the Duchy of Athens, which they placed under the protection of a prince of the House of Aragon and ruled it until 1379. The Duchy subsequently passed through other hands until the Ottoman conquest of 1458.

Most of the mercenary personalities and events discussed in this book are land-based, but since Flor began his own career at sea, it is not amiss here to look briefly at mercenaries on the sea, namely the battle of Sluys in 1340.

This took place on the coast of what is now the Netherlands—in front of the town of Sluys on the inlet (or, accurately, in the open roadstead) between West Flanders and Zealand. It was one of the opening salvos of the Hundred Years' War. The decisive English victory there was important because it resulted in the destruction, at least temporarily, of most of France's fleet. It was then impossible for France to invade England; as a result, the rest of the war was fought chiefly on French soil.

To summarize this battle: some 200–250 English ships attacked some 190 to 213 French vessels in the open roadstead in front of the town of Sluys (or Sluis). Part of the French fleet consisted of Genoese mercenary galleys and Genoese mercenary crossbowmen serving under Egidio Bocanegra (also known as Barbavera). The French chained most of their ships together — a very ill-considered move because it immobilized the ships and thus allowed the English to attack them at will.

The battle itself centered on bloody hand-to-hand combat, the desperate boarding of ships, and the equally desperate repelling of borderers. This is what Froissart says about the fight:

> The battle then began very fiercely; archers and crossbowmen shot with all their might at each other, and the men at arms engaged hand to hand ... in order to be more successful, they [the French] had large grapnels, and iron hooks with chains, which they flung from ship to ship to moor them to each other. There were many valiant deeds performed, many prisoners made, and many rescues.... This battle was very murderous and horrible. Combats at sea are more destructive and obstinate than upon land, for it is

not possible to retreat or flee — every one must abide his fortune and exert his prowess and valour.[23]

In medieval shipbuilding, a ship of war was usually equipped, in the bow, with a high multi-deck structure known as a "castle." This provided an excellent platform for archers, who could stand on it and shoot down onto the decks of enemy ships below them. During the battle of Sluys, English longbows rained storms of arrows from the castles of their ships down upon the decks of the French ships. The English archers, who could fire five times as fast as Genoese crossbowmen, quite overwhelmed the French with their firepower. By the end of the battle, most of the French fleet had been destroyed and the English had lost only two ships, both of them boarded and captured by the hardy Genoese crossbowmen. King Edward himself was wounded by a crossbow bolt. A vast number of men on both sides were killed: estimates range from 16,000 to 18,000.[24] Indeed, the water of the Sluys roadstead was dark with blood and was bobbing with floating corpses.

Over the years, and especially after the Treaty of Brétigny in 1360, several different bands would call themselves and would be known to friend and foe alike as "the Great Company."[25] The first of these mercenary organizations was chiefly composed of the Germans who were readily available for hire in the troubled Italian peninsula. Such mercenary companies responded to no authorities other than their own commanders. The only way for local governments to get rid of them was either to destroy them militarily, which was usually impossible because they were too strong, or to pay them off and encourage them to go elsewhere.

Froissart sets the stage in these words:

Although the truces [in the wake of the Treaty of Brétigny] which had been arranged [between] the kings of France and England were properly observed between the persons of the kings themselves, and between people, too, where their power and authority were recognized, none the less many adventurers, who were really brigands and thieves, became active, especially in the far corners of France, where the local knights were not up to fighting [them], or were not ready to take up arms against them.
There they captured [the knights'] towns and castles, and gathered around them a considerable number of similar sorts of people, bearing arms, men of the German nation and others who, under the guise of war, perpetuated their wicked deeds and enterprises; none opposed them and it was said by

some that they were openly tolerated and endured by the royal officers, knights, and esquires in the areas in which they were active, and that those shared the loot and the booty with them.[26]

During the Renaissance, much of Italy was often at war. The five major Italian city-states, i.e., the Republic of Venice, the Republic of Milan, the Republic of Florence, the Papal States (located in central Italy), and the Kingdom of Naples (located in southern Italy), could rarely settle their differences peaceably and were eager to hire mercenaries to do their fighting for them. There were also many lesser Italian political entities, e.g., the republics of Siena, Luca, and Genoa, plus lordships ranging in size and importance from the large holdings of the Duke of Ferrara to tiny fiefs of only a few square miles in area.[27] These lesser entities wanted to hire mercenaries, too. Fortunately for all these consumers, there were many mercenaries right at hand: indeed, to mention only the most visible "nationality," during the years between 1320 and 1360, over 700 German cavalry officers were active in Italy, as well as about 10,000 German men-at-arms.[28]

The first Great Company was founded in 1342 by Werner von Urslingen (ca. 1308–1354), a highly successful German mercenary captain who reportedly wore a breastplate engraved with a remarkable motto: it proclaimed that he was the "Enemy of God, Enemy of Piety, Enemy of Pity." In 1339, contemporaries denounced Werner and his band as a "plague of societies."[29] At its high point, his Great Company numbered about 6,000 men, mainly armored cavalry. It was so powerful that it would become the role-model for the *condottieri* who would later dominate Italian warfare during the Renaissance years.

After Werner died in 1354, a Provençal knight known as Fra' Moriale took his place. ("Fra" is a form of the monastic title "Frère," i.e., "Brother.") More Italians, Provençals, and other nationalities joined the Company, so it and other mercenary groups were rarely homogeneous. When Fra Moriale was executed in Rome in 1354, Konrad von Landau became the new commander-in-chief. Under his leadership, the Company raided Lombardy and Romagna frequently and successfully, holding whole cities to ransom and raking in a good deal of money in the process. As Konrad explained patiently to the papal legate Albornoz just before invading church lands,

VI. "An escort of galloglas armed with battle-axes"

It is our custom to rob, sack, and pillage whoever resists. Our income is derived from the funds of the provinces we invade; he who values his life pays for peace and quiet from us at a steep price.[30]

In 1363, however, while hired by the Visconti family which ruled Milan from 1277 to 1447, this Great Company was defeated by the White Company (la Compagna Bianca) led by Albert Sterz. The name of "Great Company" would live on. Four years later, in 1367, as part of his campaign to rid France of the pillaging free companies, the great French mercenary commander Bertrand du Guesclin — who began his career by organizing a guerrilla campaign against the English army besieging the city of Rennes and who would later rise to the high post of Constable of France[31] — led a reconstituted Great Company into Spain to support Henry of Trastámara in his war against Pedro the Cruel. This Spanish adventure would be the last Great Company's final act: it would be decimated during the Trastámara campaign.

VII

"Drink thy blood, Beaumanoir"

Neither the mercenary Genoese crossbowmen nor the French knights fought very well at Crécy (1346), one of the major battles of the Hundred Years' War. The Combat of the Thirty (1351), however, which involved both mercenaries and knights was long hailed as an example of the finest chivalry. The career of a French mercenary known as the "Archpriest" began in the early 1350s and ended when his own men murdered him. German mercenary pikemen and Scottish mercenaries saw action at the battle of Poitiers (1356), the second of the three great English victories of the Hundred Years' War. The Jacquerie (1358) was a violent but short-lived peasant revolt in northern France, stimulated in part by the inability of the French government to suppress the depredations by unemployed mercenaries and by outlaws.

The battle of Crécy in 1346 was one of the most important battles of the Hundred Years' War. It took place in northern France and pitted the Kingdom of England and its allied knights from the Holy Roman Empire, on the one hand, against the Kingdom of France, its Genoese mercenaries, and the Kingdoms of Navarre, Bohemia, and Majorca, on the other. Froissart gives a good picture of the wide range of geographical and social origins of the French forces:

> Orders were issued [by the king of France] to the duke of Lorraine, the count of Sarrebuck, the count of Namur, the count of Savoy and Sir Louis de Savoy, his brother, the count of Geneva and all the great barons the king thought owed him service or would do it, as well as to the men of the cities and *bonnes villes* [literally "good towns," but in fact these were towns that enjoyed a privileged legal status from the king which gave them more independence than other towns], the provostships, bailiwicks, castellanies and municipalities of the kingdom of France so they might make ready. Then a day was appointed on which each one should appear to be mustered, for he

wished to fight the English.... Then there came, indeed poured in, soldiers from every region to serve the king of France and the kingdom, some who were obliged by homage to do so, others in order to earn their wages and money.[1]

Thanks to the effectiveness of the lethal, sky-darkening volleys of arrows fired from English longbows, however, the smaller English army of 10,000 to 15,000 men was able to defeat decisively the bigger 20,000 to 25,000-strong force assembled by France and its allies.

This battle has been chronicled in such great detail over so many years that in the interest of conciseness the focus here will be exclusively on the role of the Genoese mercenary crossbowmen. It must be admitted that they did not distinguish themselves (nor did the French knights) in the battle of Crécy. To begin with, when the English army first landed in France southeast of Cherbourg, it met with very little French resistance, in part because a contingent of 500 Genoese crossbowmen had decamped from the French forces just a few days earlier: the French had failed to pay them, so they left.

Unfortunately, French financial records from the Crécy campaign have not survived, so it is difficult to know exactly how many Genoese crossbowmen were involved in it. Froissart claimed that there were 15,000 of them — surely a typical medieval exaggeration designed to astound the reader. Some modern historians believe there were 6,000 Genoese; others think that even this estimate is too high. They content themselves with the more modest guess of 2,000 to 6,000 crossbowmen.[2] What is clear is that, at Crécy, one French blunder followed another.

The French foolishly left their pavises (the big shields that protected the crossbowmen when they were reloading their crossbows) in their baggage train, rather than bringing them up to the front line where they were needed. Moreover, Philip VI, the French commander, stationed his Genoese crossbowmen in the front line, with the over-eager, glory-hungry, undisciplined French cavalry stationed immediately behind them. It is worthwhile to quote Froissart here at some length because his account is so dramatic and rings so true on most points.

Froissart writes:

You must realize that on the French side, the kings, dukes, counts and barons did not advance in any regular order, but one after another, as they pleased. As soon as King Philip came in sight of the English, his blood began to boil, such was his hatred. He cried out to his marshals: "Order the Genoese forward and let the battle begin, in the name of God and Saint Denis" [St. Denis was a Christian martyr who in the 3rd century was Bishop of Paris].

There were about fifteen thousand Genoese crossbowmen [sic]; but they were quite unready for battle, being very tired and having marched over fifteen miles in full armour, carrying their crossbows. They told the constable [their French commander] that they were in no condition to fight, and the Count of Alençon, when he heard of it, said, "This is what one gets for employing such rabble; they fail us in the hour of need!"

Meanwhile a violent storm broke from the heavens with tremendous thunder and lightning ... [This localized rain storm was important because the rain soaked the crossbow strings of the Genoese mercenaries, rendering their crossbows slack and ineffective. Crossbow strings could not be dismounted and restrung without tools. The English archers, on the other hand, could easily slip the strings off their longbows and kept the strings dry under their helmets.]

The storm soon passed, and the sun came out bright and clear, shining straight in the eyes of the French, whereas the English had it behind them. When the Genoese were in some kind of order, and were ready to attack the English, they began to shout extremely loud in order to dismay the English, who, however, held their ground and paid no attention. They cried out a second time, but the English did not move. A third time they shouted, extremely loud, and advanced, and aimed their crossbows and began to shoot. [At this point, they were some 164 yards from the English lines.[3]] The English then took a pace forward, and let fly their arrows in such unison that they were thick as snow.

The Genoese had never experienced such archery, and when they felt the arrows pierce their arms, heads, and coats of mail, they were much taken aback; some cut the cords of their crossbows [thus indicating that they surrendered and should be spared], others flung themselves to the ground, and all turned tail and fled.

The French had a large body of men-at-arms on horseback [this was the cavalry mentioned above] to supervise the Genoese. And when the latter tried to run away, they were prevented. For the King of France, seeing them turn back in disorder, cried out in a fury: "Kill this rabble, kill them! They are getting in our way [the French cavalrymen very much wanted to charge] and serve no purpose." Then you might have seen the men-at-arms laying all about them, killing all they could of the runaways. The English kept up their hail of arrows as strongly ever, shooting into the thick of the enemy; the arrows fell among the men-at-arms and their horses, bringing many of them down, horses and men together; once down, they were quite incapable of rising to their feet....

That day, the English archers brought a tremendous advantage to their side. Many people say that it was by their shooting that the day was won, although the knights achieved many noble deeds, fighting hand to hand, and rallying valiantly. But the archers certainly succeeded in one great achievement, for it was entirely by their fire that at the beginning the Genoese, and they were fifteen thousand in number [sic], were turned back. And a great number of French men-at-arms, well armed and mounted and richly appareled, were overthrown by the Genoese, who while running away, became entangled with them and brought them down so that they could not rise again.[4]

The ineffectiveness of the Genoese crossbowmen in this battle was also recorded by the Oxfordshire chronicler Geoffrey le Baker, who was writing about 1357 to 1360. He does not mention the thunderstorm which reportedly wet the crossbow strings, but it may have been only a local squall that did not affect the whole battlefield. What is clear is that Genoese crossbow bolts fell far short of the English lines. This is what is learned from Geoffrey:

So the troops stood drawn up in the field from mid-morning to mid-afternoon, while the threatening size of the French army was continually increased by new reinforcements. However, as the sun began to set, the first line of the army advanced, trumpets and cornets sounding, drums and kettledrums rolling; and the noise of the French troops seemed like thunder to the English. The French crossbowmen [i.e., the Genoese mercenary crossbowmen hired by the French] began the attack; their crossbow bolts did not reach the English, however, but fell a long way off [this may have been due to wet crossbow strings].

Much to the terror of the crossbowmen, the English archers began to pick off their closely-packed enemies with arrows, and they ended the hail of crossbow bolts with a rain of arrows. Realizing that the crossbowmen were not harming the English, the French men at arms, mounted on warhorses and agile charges, rode down seven thousand [sic] of the crossbowmen who were between them and the English, charging headlong into the English ranks in order to display their prowess.

So great a cry went up from the victims trampled by the French cavalry, which those in the rear of the French army took to be dying English troops. Every Frenchman strove to follow those who had already charged; foremost in such rashness and boldness were newly-made knights, all eager to gain the glory which they thought they would earn by fighting the English king....

Thus a great cry went up, as has been said, from the crossbowmen trampled by the cavalry and from the horses wounded by arrows, while the

French line of battle was badly disorganized by stumbling horses. When they attacked the well-armed English, they were cut down with swords and spears, and many were crushed to death, without a mark on them, in the middle of the French army, because the press was so great.[5]

In contrast to this major and world-famous battle, the Combat of the Thirty (1351) was a minor if long-remembered incident of the Breton civil war, which centered on a succession struggle in the Duchy of Brittany in France.[6] Despite its miniature scale when compared with major battles, this event was hailed by many medieval commentators as an example of the finest chivalry. The modern scholar A.H. Diverres wrote that "it won universal admiration as a feat of arms in France at the time."[7] Moreover, it can be said that it is a classic example of men loving to fight for the pure joy and fun of it. Such "voluntary combat" was one of the great pastimes of nobles in the Middle Ages and Renaissance. Indeed, it was what in the 19th century Alfred Lord Tennyson's fictional hero, Ulysses, would have called the "drunk delight of battle with my peers/Far on the ringing plains of windy Troy."

The Combat of the Thirty involved mercenaries as well as high-born knights. Here again, it is worth quoting Froissart at some length.

There took place in Brittany a most marvelous deed of arms which should never be forgotten but which one should hold up as an example to encourage all knights bachelor [the oldest form of English knighthood]... Messire Robert de Beaumanoir, a very valiant knight of a great family in Brittany, was the castellan [i.e., the officer in charge] of Castle Joselin, where he had a great many men-at-arms of his lineage and other mercenaries. And it so happened one day that he came to be roaming near the town and castle of Ploërmel, whose castellan was a German mercenary named Blandebourch [referred to by other sources as Robert Bramborough], who had with him a great many German, English, Breton and other mercenaries and who were all of the party of the Countess of Monfort. When Messire Robert saw that none of the garrison was coming out [to fight him], he went to the gate and called out this Blandebourch, under a guarantee of safety, and asked him whether he had any companion, or perhaps two or three, who wished to joust with steel lances against three others, for the love of their ladies. Blandebourch replied and said that their ladies would hardly wish that they should get themselves killed in a single joust, for this kind of venture would be over too soon. "But," he said, "I will tell you what I will do, if you like. We will choose twenty or thirty of our companions in the garrison and we will go to an

open field and there we will fight as long as we can endure it; and let God
give the victory to the better of us."
"By my faith," replied Messire Robert de Beaumanoir, "you speak very
well, and I vow we will do just what you say: now, pick a day."
An appointment was made for the following Wednesday and they each gave
each other a firm truce up to that day; and under its terms Robert and his
people departed. So they provided themselves with thirty companions,
knights, squires and others taken from the garrisons and Blandebourch
also chose thirty from all his companions.[8]

Beaumanoir had 30 Bretons on his side; his opponent had a mixed
force of 20 Englishmen, six German mercenaries, and four Breton partisans. They fought ferociously on foot with swords, daggers, bear-spears
and axes until four on the French side and two on the English side were
slain and a recess was called. When Beaumanoir himself was wounded
and called out for a drink of water, one of his colleagues famously
replied: "*Bois ton sang, Beaumanoir, la soif te passera*" ["Drink thy blood,
Beaumanoir; thy thirst will pass!"]. After a short rest, the combat ground
on until a warrior named Guillaume de Montauban suddenly mounted
his horse and rode down seven of his English enemies. By the end of the
fracas, the French side prevailed but all the fighters on either side were
either dead or seriously wounded.[9]

The Combat of the Thirty did not have any significant impact on
the succession issue, but its fame certainly lived on in prose, poetry, tapestry, sculpture, and painting. For example, a 14th century poem about
it opens with these words:

> Seigneurs, knights, barons, bannerets [a banneret was a senior knight
>   with the right to command troops and to display his unit's banner],
>   and bachelors I pray,
> Bishops and abbots, holy clerks [i.e. clergymen], heralds and minstrels
>   gay,
> Ye valiant men, of all degrees, give ear unto my lay.
> Attend, I say, and ye shall hear how Thirty Englishmen,
> As lions brave, did battle give to Bretons three times ten,
> And sith [since] the story of this fight I shall tell faithfully,
> A hundred years hereafter it shall remembered be,
> And warriors hoar [that is, warriors so old as to inspire veneration]
>   recount it to children on the knee.[10]

The Combat of the Thirty also became the subject of several paint-
ings; one of them is a scene from Pierre Le Baud's 1480 canvas, *Compi-*

lation des croniques et ystoires des Bretons (*Compilation of the chronicles and stories of the Bretons*).[11] More than 20 years after the Combat of the Thirty, Froissart noticed a scarred warrior seated at the table of Charles V. This man was honored above all others: he told Froissart that he owed his great favor with the king to the fact that he had been one of the Thirty. Another participant in that fight, a German mercenary captain named Croquart (or Crockart), was later offered a knighthood, a rich wife, and a sizeable annual income if he would enter the King's service. Preferring to remain a free agent, however, Croquart refused.[12] Interestingly, upon his return home he found that, despite the considerable wealth he had accumulated as a mercenary, the local nobles would not accept him as their social equal.[13]

To these engaging characters another and later arrival, namely, the mercenary chieftain Arnaud de Cervole (ca. 1320–1366), who was known as the Archpriest, must be added. He had entered the church and had risen to become the archpriest of Velines (i.e., the bishop's assistant) in the diocese of Perigueux in southwestern France. The archbishop of Bordeaux removed him from this clerical position, however, because he was mixing "with brigands and men of base extraction" in the pursuit of war.[14]

Arnaud subsequently lived an extremely active military life. He appears again in the early 1350s, when he led a band of 80 mercenaries in southwestern France. At that time he was already known for his skill at capturing walled cities and castles by *escalade* (climbing or scaling walls, e.g., by using ladders). In 1356 he was wounded and was captured after fighting in the forces of the Count of Alençon at the battle of Poitiers. In 1357–1358 he was mentioned both by Pope Innocent VI as leading a "large armed organization" (*magna societas armigerorum*) and by the treasurer of Dauphiné, through whose territory they passed, as being the chief of "the big company" (*la grand compaignie*).[15]

In 1358 he and his mercenaries laid siege to the papal city of Avignon and forced Pope Innocent VI to pay him thousands of golden florins to prevent him from attacking the city. (To give an idea of approximate purchasing power, in Florence in around 1400 one florin would buy two barrels of red wine or 110 pounds of meat. A florin and a ducat had roughly the same value.)[16] This is what Froissart says about the siege:

He [Arnaud] entered Avignon with most of his followers by friendly agreement [i.e., the city authorities did not try to oppose them by force], and was received with as much respect as if he had been the king of France's son, and dined several times with the Pope and the cardinals. All his sins were remitted him and when he left he was given forty thousand crowns [20,000 gold florins] to distribute to his companions. [In return for this ransom, however, Arnaud had to surrender all the castles he and his men had occupied in the papal territories, so his profit was much less that it seems at first glance.] The company left the district but still remained under the command of the Archpriest.[17]

In another version of this story, it is said that as soon as the Pope paid the ransom, Arnaud discharged all his troops, pocketed the money, and departed — leaving his men "ever more furious and dangerous."[18]

The French king John II, in a futile effort to suppress the mercenary companies, hired Arnaud in 1362 and sent him into the field with a small army led by the Count de Tancarwille and the Count de la Marche. However, this force was defeated at the battle of Brignais (1362) and Arnaud was captured but was later ransomed or otherwise released. In 1365 Pope Urban V invited him to lead a new crusade, ostensibly to the Holy Land but in reality to drive mercenaries out of the Pope's domains and at the same time to strike a blow against the Turks by helping Byzantium. Arnaud began to recruit mercenaries, but this would-be crusade was so badly organized that many of these men had disappeared by the end of the year. A new attempt at getting the crusade in gear was made in 1366 but with no better results. The end came for Arnaud himself when his own men — now unfed, unpaid, and angry — murdered him during an argument in 1366.

The battle of Poitiers (1356) was, as was noted earlier, the second of the three great English victories of the Hundred Years' War, namely, Crécy, Poitiers, and Agincourt. Like the battle of Crécy, the battle of Poitiers has been described so often that a thumbnail-sketch suffices here.

In essence, the English had decided to conduct a multi-pronged attack on France during the campaigning season of 1356. After various maneuvers by both sides, the French and English armies met to do battle near Poitiers. The French attack began early one morning in 1356 with a mounted charge by 300 elite knights under General Clermont, accompanied by a battalion of German mercenary pikemen. The task of these knights and of the pikemen was to charge and scatter the English archers and thus eliminate the great potential threat they posed to French forces. The knights and the pikemen, however, failed in their mission. Froissart has this to say about the course of the battle:

> The Prince [the Prince of Wales, i.e., the Black Prince, the eldest son of King Edward III of England] then charged the battalion of the Duke of Athens, the Constable of France. The encounter was very sharp, and many fell.... The Prince next met the German battalion, but they were soon overthrown. The English archers shot so quickly and so well that nobody dared come within range of them, and many were killed without getting a chance of being ransomed. The Counts of Nassau, Salzburg, and Neyde, who commanded the Germans, were all killed, and many other knights and squires that followed them.

Mercenary Scotsmen took part in the battle, too. According to the chronicler Geoffrey le Baker:

> There was with the French a Scotsman, William Douglas, a powerful man in Scotland, who had seen much campaigning in the Scottish wars. The usurper [this is Geoffrey le Baker's derogatory term for King John, who led the French forces] had knighted him again, because he knew that he had been a ferocious adversary of the English and had fought against them several times, he freely listened to his advice, and placed great trust in him. William led two hundred Scottish men at arms, whom he had brought from his own country. They were well aware that throughout the wars of the present king of England the English were mostly accustomed to fighting on foot, imitating the Scots.... So William preferred to follow his nation's style of fighting and attack on foot rather than on horseback, and he persuaded the usurper and the rest of the French to fight in similar fashion. The unlawful usurper, foolishly agreeing to the counsel of this busybody, sent his warhorses back to the city [Poitiers] lest anyone use them to take flight, retaining only five hundred horses clad in armour to protect them from arrows, whose commanders ordered them to attack the archers at the beginning of the battle, and ride them down under their horses' hooves; but this order was not carried out....
> [As the tide of battle turned decisively against the French,] William Douglas was wounded and fled, leading a handful of his company of Scots with his brother Archibald. Almost all of them were killed in the heat of battle, and the remainder forced either to meet an honest death or to flee, because ransoming was excluded.[19]

Jean de Venette (ca. 1307-ca. 1370) was a French chronicler and a Carmelite friar who wrote about the events around him during the Hundred Years' War. Jean vividly describes several battles of this war. After the battle of Poitiers, both the nobles and the mercenary companies had a free hand to do just as they pleased because there had been a general collapse of law and order. Jean says:

> Thus discord and all three estates[20] abandoned the task they had begun [i.e., to help France recover from the war]. From that time on, all went ill with the kingdom and the State was undone. Thieves and robbers rose up everywhere in the land. The Nobles despised and hated all others and took no thought for usefulness and profit of lord and men. They subjected and despoiled the peasants and the men of the villages. In no wise did they defend their country from its enemies; rather did they trample it under-foot, robbing and pillaging the peasants' goods. The regent, it appeared, clearly gave no thought to their plight. At that time the country and the whole of France began to put on confusion and mourning like a garment, because it had no defender or guardian....[21]

A modest but good example of post–Poitiers conditions in France is a note, written on the inside cover of his prayer book, by Hugh of Sens, the head of a small priory in Sens, Burgundy. He says that in 1358 pillaging English soldiers (they could well have been mercenaries of any non–French background) stripped his priory of all its goods, drank its wine, and carried off its oats, while he and his neighbors hid in the woods. Later the mercenaries stole all his clothes and ate all the priory's pigeons. The safe-conduct he had bought earlier from the captain of this band was of no use whatsoever because the captain had in the meantime been captured. Hugh thus had to pay for another safe-conduct to protect the priory's grain fields. Despairing, Hugh wrote:

> I am writing this out behind our barn on Wednesday, the festival of St. Martin, because I do not dare write elsewhere. Did you who live in cities and castles ever see trouble equal to my trouble? Farewell, Hugh.[22]

The prior's trouble was, alas, quite insignificant when compared to the *Jacquerie*, the peasant revolt which took place in northern France in the summer of 1358 during the Hundred Years' War. Its name comes from the padded surplice (the *jacque*) worn by French peasants as protection when fighting a war. They were collectively nicknamed "*Jacques Bonhomme*" (literally, "Jack Goodfellow"). The word *jacquerie* soon passed into both French and English to refer to any peasant uprising.

The peasants were reacting against the onerous treatment being accorded to them by the rich and powerful. In the wake of the shameful

French rout at Poitiers, they were forced to pay higher taxes; had to repair war-damaged properties without any payment for their labor; and to defend the *châteaux* (stately homes) of the aristocrats. Moreover — and this is the most important point here — the French government, such as it was, lacked any ability whatsoever to limit the rapes, looting, and pillaging inflicted on northern France by unemployed mercenaries and by unrestrained outlaws. Many peasants wondered why they should continue to tolerate a government which visibly could not protect its most productive citizens.

Although the mercenaries themselves kept out of sight and did not fight in the *Jacquerie* or overtly take the side of the peasants, their lawlessness contributed to the prevailing local instability. As in any rebellion, there was no shortage of atrocities. It is worth mentioning some of them here to give the reader a feel for these turbulent times. The contemporary French chronicler Jean Le Bel describes the fate of one particularly unfortunate aristocratic family in these words:

> I do not dare to write about or describe the horrors inflicted on women [by the rebellious peasants]. Among other things, they killed a knight, put him on a spit, and roasted him under the eyes of his wife and children. After ten or twelve of them raped the lady, they wished to force-feed his roasted flesh to her and to the children, and then made them die a miserable death.[23]

The peasants, armed only with staves and knives, were quite leaderless after their chief, Guillaume Cale, was captured, tortured, and beheaded by the well-trained and well-armed knights of the area. It is thought that the peasants may have killed a few hundred aristocrats during their rampages; in retaliation, however, once they got the upper hand, the nobles and their troops are thought to have killed many thousands of peasants. There is no record of any mercenaries being killed: it seems likely that they saw trouble coming and ran away before the retaliation began.

This is how Froissart, who is invariably on the side of the nobility and who is prone to exaggerate the number of combatants and casualties, describes one such massacre at a marketplace. "Villeins" were peasant farmers who were legally tied either to a lord of a manor or to the manor itself. Froissart says:

VII. *"Drink thy blood, Beaumanoir"*

The Count of Foix and the Captal de Buch [two prominent local aristocrats: "Captal," i.e., "captain" in Provençal, was a Gascon title accorded to
the five or six most important lords of Aquitaine in southwestern France]
and their men, who were ready-armed, formed up in the marketplace and
then moved to the gates of the market and flung them open. There they
faced the villeins, small and dark and very poorly armed, confronting them
with the banners of the Count of Foix and the Duke of Orleans and the
pennon of the Captal de Buch, and holding lances and swords in their
hands, fully prepared to defend themselves and to protect the marketplace
[where a number of noble ladies had in desperation taken refuge from the
villeins].
When these evil men [the villeins] saw them drawn up in this warlike
order — although their numbers were comparatively small — they became
less resolute than before. The foremost began to fall back as the noblemen
came after them, striking at them with their lances and swords and beating
them down. Those who felt the blows, or feared to feel them, turned back
in such panic that they fell over each other. Then men-at-arms of every
kind burst out of the gates and ran into the square to attack those evil men
of the town.
They mowed them down in heaps and slaughtered them like cattle; and
they drove all the rest out of the town, for none of the villeins attempted to
take up any sort of fighting order. They went on killing until they were stiff
and weary and flung many into the River Marne. In all, they exterminated
more than seven thousand Jacques [sic] that day. Not one would have
escaped if they had not grown tired of pursuing them. When the noblemen
returned, they set fire to the mutinous town of Meaux and burnt it to
ashes, together with all the villeins of the town whom they could pen up
inside.[24]

VIII

"They were bold and warlike fellows"

As mentioned earlier, mercenaries who lost their jobs as a result of the Treaty of Brétigny (1360) soon coalesced into the Great Companies. One of the most famous of these mercenary companies was the White Company, led by the English chieftain John Hawkwood. Chandos Herald tells how, in 1367, the Black Prince used mercenaries effectively in the civil war in Spain. The conversation between the colorful mercenary commander the Bascot de Mauléon and the chronicler Froissart in 1388, and the battles of Brignais (1362) and Grunwald/Tannenberg (1410) are also covered.

The Great Companies were newly-minted military units, drawn from the many thousands of experienced but out-of-work mercenaries who were trying to survive after the Treaty of Brétigny between the kings of England and France in 1360.[1] By the spring of 1362, the process of evacuating fortresses and transforming territories between England and France was nearly finished. However, the unforeseen result was that many of the disbanded forces quickly became independent companies under new captains. When they joined forces, they were sufficiently powerful not only to seize well-defended fortresses and towns, but also to undertake major engagements in the field.[2]

These companies would remain active in much of Western Europe until the renewal, in 1369, of the war between England and France. The modern French scholar Jean Favier defines such a mercenary unit as follows:

> A company consisted of from 50 to 200 men under the orders of a captain, who was both the organizer and executive officer of this military society and its leader in combat.[3]

116

One of the best summaries of how the companies arose is that offered by the modern Italian scholar Franco Cardini. In an article first written in Italian, then translated into French, and now quoted here in an edited free translation into English, Cardini explains that two factors were at play in this process:

> On the one hand, if businessmen, entrepreneurs, and bankers had now become the governing class, most notably in the urban communes of Italy, they did not have, despite all that, a style of life they found suitable to their new status. In fact, they remained fascinated by what could be called the "knightly-courtesy" manner of life and were eager to duplicate it in their own city palaces and country estates. On the other hand, however, they did have to tend to business and thus could not afford to throw themselves into the periodic military expeditions which were popular at that time. This state of affairs was the principal reason why companies of mercenaries multiplied in Europe in the 14th and 15th centuries. The leaders of these companies made all-inclusive offers to potential employers: they had their own weapons and their own equipment, which were immediately available and were more or less in good working order. But the fact that the mercenaries had to fight simply in order to live created real problems of its own. In the first place, it was in their own interest to prolong conflicts: for them, peace meant idleness and poverty. Thus the battles the mercenaries fought were never decisive. By mutual agreement, commanders tried to reduce their manpower losses and the expense of fighting. Finally, in times of peace, the mercenary companies became terrible bands of brigands. For these reasons, even when they had no military need to do so, governments preferred to prolong wars indefinitely and to pay the high price of hiring mercenaries: it was much better to pay this price rather than letting the mercenaries roam around freely without any money.[4]

There was no single overall organization or individual guiding the formation of the Great Companies, which were simply larger versions of existing mercenary companies. About 166 mercenary captains are known to have commanded companies operating in or from France during the decade after 1360; 91 of these men are referred to in contemporary sources as being the captains of one or another of the Great Companies. (Of these 91 commanders, eight are known to have died in battle, one was poisoned, and one was executed.[5]) Thus there were at least 91 Great Companies and may possibly have been even more.

The formation of these companies was a spontaneous, need-driven process. Mercenaries were of many "nationalities" (to use a modern term)—for example, Italian, German, Hungarian, Spanish, Greek, Albanian, French, Swiss, English, and Scottish. They enlisted under commanders who they hoped could win battles and who would pay them well. As the modern scholar Guido Guerri dall'Oro explains,

> The effectiveness of the mercenary companies was chiefly a function of their organizational skills, of their strict discipline, and of their military competence. These features made them superior in combat when compared to the heavy cavalry of the aristocrats, who in general aspired only for personal glory and who knew nothing at all about the rules, the tactics, and the techniques of war....
> Pay for the mercenaries: that was the essential thing. To hire mercenaries was not hard to do; to pay them regularly, whether one won or lost a given battle, was indeed hard to do. If an employer could not honor his contract with mercenaries, his problems began then and there....[6]

There is no single, definitive figure on the total strength of the Great Companies. Their numerical strength was in fact a function of the number of mercenary bands that could be recruited for a given operation, and on the size of each band. Contemporary sources, however, do give some rough indications about how many men could be involved.

We will soon meet, for example, a memorable Basque mercenary, the Bascot (or Bastot) de Mauléon. Both variants of this title mean "a soldier of fortune." In an interview in 1388 with Froissart, the Bascot indicated that 12,000 men had been available in 1360 after the conclusion of peace at Brétigny; of these, 3,000 to 4,000 were, he added, "really fine soldiers."[7] The rest, it must be assumed, were rank and file mercenaries with no special skills but were competent fighters nonetheless.

In 1363, the governor of the regions of Berry and Auvergne estimated the strength of the companies who congregated around the city of Brioude during the week after its capture at 2,000 lances (as indicated earlier, a "lance" was a three-man combat team), plus 1,000 mounted archers and infantrymen.[8] The mercenary companies sent into Spain by the French and the English in 1366–1367 probably included around 3,000 men-at-arms.[9] In a letter written in 1367 by King Peter IV of Aragon to the governor of Roussillon, the king said that a rival noble had recruited 13 captains of the companies then serving with the Black Prince; these captains commanded a total of 1,600 lances.[10]

Froissart says that when war between England and France broke out again in 1369, some 4,500 mercenaries joined the armies of these protagonists.[11]

Here is a sampling of what some contemporary observers had to say about the Companies:

- The author of the *Grandes Chroniques de France* says that "At that time [November 1360], there were great numbers of English and others in Brie and Champagne, who ravaged all the countryside, killing and ransoming men, and doing all the evil they could, of whom some called themselves the Great Company."[12]
- Froissart mentions gatherings of such men in Burgundy and Champagne, some of which were known as *les Tards-Venus* ("the Late-comers") because they were foraging in provinces that had already been stripped by other mercenaries.[13]
- The Carmelite friar Jean de Venette says that "these sons of Belial [i.e., these sons of lawlessness] and men of iniquity [were] warriors from various lands who assailed other men with no hope of right and no reason other than their own passions, iniquity and hope of gain, and yet were called the Great Company."[14]
- The monk Henry Knighton had this to say about the Anglo-German company commanded by Albert Sterz:

  At this time [late 1361] was organized a certain company of strong men called the Company of Fortune [*Societas fortunae*; later it became known as "the White Company" and is covered at greater length later], which some called the Great Company. It was composed of men from different parts, who, now that there was peace between the two kingdoms [England and France], had no means of livelihood other than through their own efforts. They were bold and warlike fellows, experienced and strenuous, who congregated together from different nations, and who lived by war, since in time of peace they had nothing."[15]

- An institution's own interests could strongly influence its views on mercenaries. For example, when the famous English mercenary John Hawkwood fought for Milan against the papal armies in 1371, the pope denounced him as being "a son of Belial." But, the next year, when Hawkwood sided with the pope and won several battles, he was praised as being "an athlete of God and a faithful Christian knight."[16]

119

It should not be a surprise to learn that being the commander of a Great Company could be a very hazardous calling. Consider, for example, what happened to a previously-successful mercenary leader named Guillaume Pot (also known as Guillemin Pot or Guillampot) in 1364. This account comes from a letter written by Guillaume de Clugny, the *bailli* of Auxois (a *bailli* was a local administrative officer in northern France), to the ducal council:

> Very dear and good friends, on Wednesday [18 September 1364] Guillemin Pot, who was lodged at Maisières, was passing by Beaune with 120 good lances and at least 100 other combatants, not counting the pillagers. As soon as they had passed we mounted our horses and pursued them until we took four or five of their men-at-arms and some 30 pillagers, who were killed, hung or taken prisoner, the others returning to their quarters.
> We then continued our journey to Dijon, as was our intention, and this Thursday morning the marshal [i.e., Gui de Pontallier, the marshal of Burgundy] sent 15 *glaives* [a *glaive* was a polearm, that is, a single-edged blade mounted on a pole, but the word is probably used here to mean "a well-armed soldier"] to form an ambush on the road they [Pot's mercenaries] would have to take, but it was discovered and the entire *route* [Pot's mercenaries] fell upon our men, who fled to Givrey, where they fought for a long time at the barriers...
> ...and while passing between Rouvres and Dijon we fell upon them [i.e., upon Pot's band] ... and with God's help they were defeated and either killed [in the engagement], taken prisoner or put to death. And Guillemin Pot and others of his *route* have been taken prisoner to Dijon.[17]

Pot was released under certain stringent conditions which required him not to act illegally, but he subsequently ignored them and returned to his old ways. He was recaptured by a Burgundian knight in October 1364 while raiding merchants who were attending a fair at Chalon. The knight handed him over to the duke's officers for a reward of 200 *livres* (the approximate price of a good sword]. Pot was then executed. His head was pilloried in the main square of the town, where it remained on pubic view for some eight months before being carried off by another mercenary company as a ghastly souvenir.[18]

Popes were concerned not only about the wanton destruction inflicted on the countryside by the Great Companies but also because these bands jeopardized papal supply lines and the constant flow of clergy, bankers, and courtiers going to and from Avignon, the current seat of papal power. (From 1309 to 1378, the years of the Avignon Papacy, the papacy was based in Avignon, not in Rome.) Urban V, for example, issued three bulls against the companies. The first was *Cogit nos* (27 February 1364), which provided spiritual support for the anti-mercenary forces of Languedoc. It stated in part:

> The wickedness of our age, in which the sons of iniquity have multiplied and, fired by the flames of their own greed, are dishonestly attempting to gorge themselves on the labour of others, and for that reason rage the more cruelly against the innocent peoples, compels us to draw on the resources of the apostolic power to counter their evil stratagems and to strive with even greater energy and effectiveness to organise the defense of these peoples, especially of those whom the wicked men have so far attacked, and are now attacking.[19]

This bull called on princes and other leaders to fight against the mercenaries, and offered a plenary indulgence for two years to those who were killed in such battles. (An indulgence is the full or partial remission of spiritual punishment for sins which have already been confessed and forgiven.)

The second bull, *Miserabilis nonnullorum* (27 May 1364), was also cast in terms designed to isolate the companies. The pope ordered them, under threat of excommunication, immediately (i.e., within one month) to disband their troops, to surrender the places they were occupying, and to repair the damage they had done. Clerics and laymen alike were forbidden to join them, hire them, or favor them in any way. Anyone who provided them with money, food, horses, arms, carts, boats, and any other provisions or merchandise, or who aided or advised them in any way whatsoever, would also be excommunicated. Bishops were ordered to report the names of the mercenaries and their accomplices so that action could be taken against them. A plenary indulgence was granted to anti-mercenary forces if they were killed in action.[20]

The third bull, *Clamat ad nos* (5 April 1365), focused on those who hired and led the mercenary companies, as well as on those who joined or supported them. It provided that all towns, villages, and individuals who negotiated with the companies and who paid protection money to them would be dealt with severely. It appears, however, that these bulls had little if any real impact on the ground, though some mercenary captains did take advantage of these opportunities to get absolution for their many sins.

Mercenary commanders were well-known and were often feared in their own times, but probably the most famous of the lot was the Englishman John Hawkwood (d. 1394). Variously said to have been the second son of an Essex tanner or the son of a tailor, Hawkwood served initially in the English army in France during the early stages of the Hundred Years' War. He reportedly fought in the battles of Crécy and/or Poitiers but was demobilized after the Treaty of Brétigny in 1360. Moving to Italy, he served with the White Company (discussed below)—a group English and German mercenaries under the command of Albert Sterz. In 1361 he joined the small mercenary groups known as the free companies and later served with the Great Company when it fought against papal troops near Avignon. By 1365, he had risen to become the commander of the White Company, a mercenary force so named either because of reflections from the men's brightly-polished plate armor or because the men originally wore white surcoats over their armor.

This job paid him very well. Income data for the 1360s are not readily available but an idea of wages then can be formed by looking at some of the comparable incomes in Florence in 1390. At a time when the estimated subsistence level for a man was 3 soldi per day, earnings were as follows:

Typical construction worker	9.4 soldi per day
Farm laborer roughly	9.4 soldi per day
Spinner of wool cloth	12.17 soldi per day
Master builder	17.1 soldi per day

In that year, Hawkwood's salary was 37,500 soldi per month—a sum 72 times greater than the wage of a master builder and more than 140 times greater than that of a construction worker. Most of his troops were paid adequately but not handsomely. For example, a lance unit, consisting of three men with three horses to maintain, earned a total of 44 soldi per day. Crossbowmen earned 9.7 soldi per day. However, common infantrymen with no special skills were paid only 3.8 soldi per day.[21]

The White Company was composed of many different nationalities, e.g., Germans, Italians, Englishmen, and Hungarians. At its high point in 1361, it could field about 3,500 cavalrymen and 2,000 infantrymen (the latter term also includes the archers); at its low point in 1388, it had shrunk down to a mere 250 men. In its glory days, it was based on the "lances" of three men: a man-at-arms, a squire, and an unarmed page. A group of lances, known as a contingent, was under the command of a corporal, who was frequently an independent sub-contractor. As befitting a tightly-run military organization, the White Company also had an effective administrative staff, consisting of Italian chancellors (men trained in law), Italian notaries, and an English treasurer.

The Florentine chronicler Filippo Villani remarked that if the Company had any military failings, it was only an "excessive boldness," i.e., aggressiveness, which made the men restless and encouraged them to set up camp "in poor order."[22] Villani makes it very clear that these men were not angels. The modern scholar William Caferro, quoting contemporary sources, says this:

> The band's first moves on Italian soil were intensely brutal. It entered the Piedmont region setting fires, looting, raping women, maiming non-combatants, and mistreating prisoners. Azario called them "better thieves than any others who have preyed on Lombardy." Villani said they were "young, hot and eager" and "accustomed to homicides and robbery, current in the use of iron [i.e., the use of swords and other metal weapons], having little personal cares." Azario describes how the band shut captives in boxes and threatened to drown them to hasten payment of ransoms, how the band systematically dismembered victims, beginning with the hands, then the nose, the ears; the trunks of the corpses were left in ditches outside the castles to be eaten by dogs.[23]

The White Company introduced into Italy a practice already common in France during the battles of the Hundred Years' War: sending dismounted men-at-arms into battle. When so doing, the Company fought dismounted and in close order, walking forward at a slow pace, often with two men-at-arms holding the same very long spear and bellowing battle cries. The archers followed close behind them. The Milanese writer Azario describes the Company's battle formation in these terms:

> [The soldiers had dismounted from their horses, which were held by pages during battles, and fought on foot.] They had very large lances with very long iron tips. Mostly two, sometimes three of them, handled a single lance so heavy and big that there was nothing it would not penetrate. Behind

them, toward the posterior of the formation, were the archers, with great bows which they held from their head to the ground [i.e., the bows were as long as a man is high] and from which they shot great and long arrows.[24]

The White Company would fight under many employers and would change sides whenever this seemed profitable. In 1369, Hawkwood fought for Perugia against the forces of the Pope; in 1370 he joined Bernabò Visconti, the Duke of Milan, in a war against an alliance of cities, including Pisa and Florence; in 1372 he fought for Visconti against his former master, the Marquis of Monferrato; then he resigned his command and the White Company served the Pope for a time.

The White Company distinguished itself as the best force in Italy. In 1363, when the city of Pisa was at war with Florence, its neighbor and rival, and needed more troops, the Florentines were unwilling to pay the very high price demanded by the White Company for its mercenaries, but Pisa was. The Florentine poet Antono Pucci captured this moment in verse to decide whether "the lion," i.e., Florence, knew more than "the fox," i.e., Pisa:

> In Lombardy there was a band
> that was called the White Company
> so cruel and with every vice
> that it had worn out all of Lombardy.
> Florence ... refused it [i.e., Florence refused to pay the White Company], and the fox embraced it.[25]

Mercenary bands like Hawkwood's could be accurately described as "traveling city-states." Hawkwood, for example, had to hire his own spies, informers, treasurers, chancellors to draw up papers, business managers, and different levels of employees to run his estates. Financially, he did extremely well. In 1376, for example, his mercenary army was paid 481,800 gold florins. An army does have considerable expenses but, even so, to understand the magnitude of this figure it must be noted that in 1377 the city of Siena, with approximately 50,000 people, had a total income of only 93,962 florins.[26]

Time does not stand still, however, and after 1370 most of the mercenary companies had ceased to operate under the name of the "Great Companies." The reasons were that many of the captains who had founded them were retired or dead, and many of their troops had been absorbed into the royal armies of England and France. While some of the descendants of the mercenary officers who had held most of France to ransom in the 1360s were still active in central and eastern France as late as the early 1390s, the glory-days of the Great Companies were by then in the past.[27] Hawkwood, however, still managed to prosper. His 500-florin salary had a great deal of purchasing power: in Florence in 1390, it was worth approximately 992 bushels of grain or about 401 barrels of wine.[28]

It is time now to look at an excellent first-hand account of the role of mercenary troops during the civil war in Spain in the 14th century.[29] This struggle pitted the legitimate ruler of Spain, Pedro I of Castile (1350–1369), supported by the mercenary and other forces of the Black Prince, against Pedro's illegitimate half-brother, Count Enrique of Trastámara. Since neither man could win the fight unaided, the civil war became internationalized: mercenary troops joined the fray in 1366.

The source for the following account is Chandos Herald (fl. 1360s–1380s), the author of a long poem about the life of the Black Prince. Chandos Herald is so-named because he was the herald of the English warlord John Chandos, the closest friend of the Black Prince. The following account, set in 1366–1367, shows how the Black Prince prepared for his foray into Spain with mercenary troops and how by the battle of Najera he restored Pedro of Castile to his throne.

The immediate background of this story is that, in the autumn of 1366, Pedro of Castile, an ally of Edward III, asked for the Black Prince's help in reclaiming his throne, which he had lost to his half-brother, Enrique of Trastámara. The Black Price saw this proposed expedition as a welcome change from the politics of Gascony, in which he was deeply embroiled, and persuaded his father to let him lead his troops and his mercenaries into Spain.[30] As Chandos Herald says,

> The prince returned to Bordeaux and got his men ready. He sent for many noble and valiant knights from all over his lands, leaving out neither great nor small; nor did Chandos stay idle, because he went to fetch men of the Great Company, as many as fourteen squadrons, not counting those who returned from Spain when they heard that the prince was going to the aid of king Pedro. They took leave of king Enrique, who let them go and paid them well, for he no longer needed them. He was then king of Castile, and was well content, because he did not think that anyone could overthrow him, since his power was so great....

...as soon as the Bastard [i.e., Enrique of Trastámara] learnt that the prince [with his troops] was hastening to the aid of king Pedro, he did his best to prevent them; he cut off the roads and every morning and evening laid ambushes for them, and got men at arms riding mules and other ruffians to attack them. But the Lord God brought them to the safety of the prince's lands, which pleased the prince greatly, because he was very keen to achieve his plan. And then he gathered gold, silver and coin to pay his men. All this took place three weeks before Christmas in the year 1366....

...The noble prince ordered payments [to his men] on a generous scale. Then the armourers at Bordeaux forged swords and daggers, coats of mail, helm, short swords, axes, gauntlets, in such number that it would have done for thirty kings....

The prince's army assembled at Dax [a town in Aquitaine in southwestern France], and all the barons and knights from the country around gathered there. All the companies encamped then in the Basque country [i.e., the traditional homeland of the Basque people, which is located in the western Pyrenees and which spans the border between France and Spain], in the mountains, and waited for two months, with much hardship, until the passes were clear and they could set out on their expedition. They waited all winter, until February [1367], until those from far off and nearby had all gathered.[31]

In April 1367, near Najera, in the province of La Rioja in Castile, the forces of the Black Prince, and their allies met and defeated the opposing army of Enrique of Trastámara, who had to seek shelter in Aragon and in Avignon. Froissart gives local color and sets the stage by telling about the participants in the battle:

Under the pennon [a triangular banner] of St. George, and attached to the banner of Sir John Chandos, were the free companies, who had in the whole twelve hundred streamers. Among them were good and hardy knights and squires, whose courage was proof: namely, Sir Robert Cheney, Sir Perducas d'Albret, Roger Briquet, Sir Garsis du Chastel, Sir Gaillard Viguier, Sir John Charnels, Nandon de Bagerant, Aymemon d'Ortige, Perrot de Savoye, le bourg [i.e., the illegitimate son of] Camus, le bourg de l'Esparre, le bourg de Breteuil, Espiote, and several others.[32]

Chandos Herald explains the battle in these words:

There was not a single man, however humble, in the prince's company who was not as bold and as brave as a lion.... The Spaniards turned and fled, all giving their horses their heads.... Then the slaughter began, and you could see foot soldiers being killed with daggers and swords....

The site of the battle was a pleasant plain, without a tree or a bush for a league around, beside a fine river, very swift and strong; and this river caused much harm to the Castilians that day, for the pursuit continued as far as the river. More than two thousand drowned there. On the bridge in front of Najera the pursuit was very fierce; you could see knights leaping into the water for fear, and dying one on top of each other. And the river ran crimson, to everyone's amazement, with the blood of dead men and horses. There was so much slaughter there that I do not think that anyone ever saw anything like it; the dead were so many that the total came to seven thousand seven hundred [almost certainly an inflated estimate] ... So the Spaniards were killed and taken, much to the joy of the prince, who waited on the battlefield, his standard raised, to rally his men.[33]

Froissart's account of how Sir John Chandos fared in this battle gives a vivid picture of medieval hand-to-hand combat:

Sir John Chandos showed exceptional bravery under his banner, and forged so far ahead into the fray that he was surrounded by the enemy and unhorsed. A huge man of Castile, Martin Ferrans by name, whose boldness and courage were far-famed, determined to kill him. But Sir John had not forgotten a knife that he had under his chain-mail; he now drew it and stabbed his attacker to death, when the latter was already on top of him. Sir John jumped up and his men rallied round him.[34]

The battle of Najera was a clear military success for the Black Prince but a clear failure in other terms. Pedro had promised the Black Prince huge sums of money for his help but, in the end, he was unable to provide them. This is not at all surprising, because it is estimated that the ultimate bill for the campaign came to a staggering total 2,720,000 florins—equal to nearly 22,000 pounds of gold.[35] While vainly waiting in hope of payment, the Black Prince caught some kind of dysentery which was to bedevil him for the rest of his life. Moreover, when he returned home to England, he faced discontent both from his own army, which had not been paid, and from the Gascons, whom he wanted to tax so that he could pay off his debts. The illness of the Black Price later became acute and although he would rise from his sick-bed to capture the city of Limoges in 1370, he eventually died at Westminster in 1376.[36]

Reversing usual chronological order, one of the most interesting mercenary leaders, the Bascot (or Bastot) de Mauléon, who is speaking with Froissart in 1388, can be introduced here. Bascot invokes the account, written by the Florentine chronicler Matteo Villani, of the battle of Brignais— a battle which had taken place 26 years earlier (in 1362) but one which the Bascot de Mauléon would still cite with pride as a fine example of mercenary prowess. At that battle, companies of mercenaries had inflicted a heavy defeat on a small French royal army.

The story begins in 1388, when Froissart visited the court of Gaston Phoebus, the Count of Foix, at Orthez in southwestern France. Orthez was an excellent place to collect information on the region. It was the chief town of Béarn, a viscounty located on the French side of the Pyrenees, and shared common frontiers with the kingdoms of Navarre and Aragon. Froissart stayed for 10 to 12 weeks and met many of the men-at-arms gathered there. One of them was the Basque mercenary chieftain Bascot de Mauléon.

This chance meeting would give the Bascot de Mauléon, who in reality was little more than a common highwayman, a modest but permanent niche in medieval history. He would admit candidly, "Sometimes I have been so thoroughly down on my luck that I hadn't even a horse to ride, and at other times I have been fairly rich, as luck came and went."[37] In any case, he gave Froissart an excellent and memorable interview. As Froissart puts it:

> I saw there [at the count's court] a Gascon squire, called le Bastot de Mauléon, an expert man at arms, and about fifty years old, according to his appearance. He arrived at the Hostelry of the Moon, where I lodged with Ernauton du Pin, in grand array, having packhorses with him which were being led, as in the case of a great baron, and he and his attendants were served on plate of gold and silver."[38]

During his meeting with Froissart, the Bastot de Mauléon said:

> This treaty of peace [the Treaty of Brétigny, 1360] being concluded, it was necessary for all men at arms and free companies, according to the words of the treaty, to evacuate the fortresses or castles they held. Great numbers collected together, with many poor companions who had learnt the art of war under different commanders, to hold councils as to what quarters they should march, and they said among themselves, that though the kings had made peace with each other, it was necessary for them to live.
> They marched into Burgundy, where they had captains of all nations, Germans, Scots, and people from every country. I was there also as a captain. Our numbers in Burgundy, above the river Loire, were upwards of twelve thousand, including all sorts; but I must say, that in this number, there were three or four thousand good men at arms, as able and understanding in war as any [that] could be found, whether to plan an engagement, to

seize a proper moment to fight, or to surprise and scale towns and castles, and well inured to war, which we showed at the battle of Brignais [see below], where we overpowered the constable of France, the count de Forêts, with full two thousand lances, knights, and squires.

This battle was of great advantage to the companies, for they were poor, and they enriched themselves by [capturing] good prisoners [who could then be ransomed], and by the towns and castles which they took in the archbishopric of Lyons on the river Rhone.[39]

More can be learned about the details of the battle of Brignais by reading a contemporary account by Matteo Villani (d. 1363), a chronicler from Florence. Petit Meschin, i.e., Meschin the Young, was a Gascon mercenary who would later (in 1369) be drowned in the Garonne River, along with his companion, on the orders of Louis, the duke of Anjou. Louis ordered their execution because they had conspired to hand him over to his enemies, the English.

Villani gives this report of the battle:

In March [1362], the king of France, affronted by the [mercenary] company of Petit Meschin of Auvergne, his fugitive little servant [i.e., his vassal] ... hastily assembled an army of around 6,000 cavalry, of French, Germans and others then in France, and having given command of it to Jacques de Bourbon, a prince of the blood, he sent him into Bourbonnais with 4,000 sergeants.

At this time, the company of Petit Meschin had taken one of the king's castles, called Brignais, and having garrisoned it with 300 men from his company, he raided the county of Forez with [5,000 mercenaries], the major part [being] Italians of his company. Meanwhile, Jacques de Bourbon arrived with his army, camped near Brignais, and believing he would rapidly secure it, besieged the place fearlessly. But, having nothing but contempt for his adversary, he took no proper precautions and was not on his guard.

Petit Meschin, who was experienced in matters of war and captain of a well-organized company which was spoiling for a fight, was a day and a half from Brignais. Having been informed of the disorder in the French camp, with the agreement of his company and tempted by the prospect of considerable booty, he hurriedly retraced his steps and, taking a short cut, arrived unexpectedly above the French camp several hours before daybreak and without any let-up attacked them with great noise and clamour.

Taken by surprise, and frightened by the terrible cries, the French lost heart and although they ran for their arms to repulse the enemy, the companies already pressed so hard upon them that they gave them no time to arm themselves. An army which included so many barons and valiant knights thus had the misfortune to be routed and put to flight, and many were killed and wounded. Those who were able to mount their horses and don their armour nearly all fell into the hands of that vassal of the king of France, Petit Meschin.

So great was the value of the ransoms and booty that all the company became rich. Their victory made them so confident and daring that the court of Rome [i.e., the papacy], which had experience being fleeced by the companies, feared that it would see them arrive at Avignon [then the seat of papal power].[40]

Mercenaries also played a role in 1410 in what the Polish call the battle of Grunwald and the Germans know as the battle of Tannenberg. In the interests of impartiality, both names, i.e., the battle of Grunwald/Tannenberg, are used here. This was a complicated struggle which involved many different units.[41] On one side, a total of 16,000 to 39,000 men came from various sources, e.g., from the Kingdom of Poland; from the Grand Duchy of Lithuania; and from various Polish-Lithuanian vassal, allied, and mercenary forces. On the other side were 11,000 to 27,000 men from the Teutonic Order, led by its Grand Master, Ulrich von Jungingen; its allies; guest crusaders; and mercenaries from Western Europe.

The Teutonic Order, whose formal name was the Order of the Brothers of the German House of Saint Mary in Jerusalem, was a German medieval military order formed in Acre at the end of the 12th century to help pilgrims in their travels to the Holy Land and to establish hospitals. It was also a crusading military order in the Middle Ages, consisting of a small military component which was strengthened by mercenaries as the need arose.

Because the Teutonic Knights had a strong economic base, they could afford to hire mercenaries throughout Europe to augment the troops they could raise via feudal levies. Reliance on mercenaries was sometimes a controversial policy, however. For example, the chronicler of the Teutonic order, Johann von Posilge, expressed dismay at the Polish king's policy of hiring mercenaries from Bohemia, Moravia, and elsewhere. He complained that such men "spurned honesty and God and went against the Christians to destroy the land of Prussia."[42]

The Teutonic Order arguably reached its high point in 1407, when it controlled many of the lands lying south and east of the Baltic Sea. Three years later, however, a combined Polish-Lithuanian army decisively defeated the Order at the battle of Grunwald/Tannenberg (1410). Grand Master Ulrich von Jungingen and 50 of the Order's 60 most senior officers died in this one fight. Polish and Lithuanian forces seized several thousand captives, keeping those who were rich enough or well-connected enough to pay ransom. The mercenary Holbracht von Loym, for example, had to pay the equivalent of 66 pounds of silver to secure his freedom.[43]

The precise number of soldiers involved in the battle of Grunwald/Tannenberg is not known. It is clear, however, that both sides used troops from several states and lands, plus numerous mercenaries. These mercenaries included two Banners of Czechs. (A Banner was not a flag or a standard but the basic military unit involved in this battle. Each Banner consisted of between 50 to 120 lances of two to five men each.) There was also a mercenary Moravian Banner and, in the Banner of St. George, a mixed contingent of Czechs and other mercenaries.

This battle broke the power of the once-mighty Order. The loss of 200 knights and thousands of foot soldiers weakened the Order's fighting ability so much that it had increasingly to rely on mercenaries. By the end of 1410, some 7,500 mercenaries had arrived in Prussia to strengthen the Order's forces. But mercenaries were always a mixed blessing for leaders: in 1411, for example, one group of mercenaries in Danzig seized a ship on a local river and turned pirate. In the long run, the Order's devastating losses in 1410 would prove to be fatal.[44]

IX

A Skeleton in Armor

Three thousand Genoese mercenaries were present on the French side at the battle of Agincourt in 1415, but they were stationed so far behind the front lines that they never had a chance to go into action. The kings of France valued the mercenary Scots Guard, which was formed in 1418. However, the impetuosity of the commander of Scottish mercenaries at the battle of the Herrings (1429) resulted in a French defeat. Rodrigo de Villandrando, a Spanish mercenary chieftain, had much better luck with the 10,000 mercenaries he led in France in 1433. The first step in the rise of standing armies in the Middle Ages was the decision of King Charles VII of France, in 1445, to give permanent jobs to the best troops of the mercenary companies he employed.

The battle of Agincourt (1415) between the military forces of England and France was the last of the three great English successes of the Hundred Years' War and forms the centerpiece of Shakespeare's play *Henry V*. In one of the most famous passages of this play, Henry V exhorts his troops in these moving words:

> We few, we happy few, we band of brothers;
> For he today that sheds his blood with me
> Shall be my brother.

Agincourt has been cited by the modern scholar Christopher Allmand as an excellent example of a small, well-disciplined, well-led, highly-motivated force with little to lose (i.e., the English) being able to defeat a much bigger force which lacked good discipline, competent leadership, and was too confident of victory (i.e., the French).[1]

There is no need to retrace here the full course of this battle but it should be noted that mercenaries were present at Agincourt — but only on the French side. The French regularly hired Genoese, Scottish, and other mercenaries. Ironically, 3,000 Genoese mercenary crossbowmen were deployed in the battle on the French side, but they proved to be totally useless. As the French cavalry charged headlong toward the English lines through the deep, churned-up mud of battlefield, the French knights were greeted with volley after volley of English arrows. The English archers shot so quickly and so well that the French believed — quite incorrectly, as it turned out — that Henry V had secretly stationed 200 archers in the surrounding woods to attack the French from the flanks, as well as head-on.

The modern historian Juliet Barker explains the French predicament at Agincourt:

> The accepted tactical response to [an arrow] bombardment of this kind was to return similar fire. This the French were unable to do. Most of their own crossbowmen and archers were at the rear of their ranks and therefore unable to get a clear sight line at the enemy or, indeed, to inflict a comparable mass volley without injuring and killing their own men, who stood between them and their targets. Those on the flanks were in a better position to do so, but they could not maintain the speed or the firepower of the English longbows.[2]

The English victory at Agincourt was overwhelming. Casualties for the battle are not precisely known, but a reasonable guess is that the French lost some 7,000 men; in addition, 1,500 French nobles were taken prisoner. English losses were very much less — perhaps only between 100 and 500 men killed.

An interesting historical footnote is that the French Duke of Bar, who was killed at Agincourt, is known to have hired English mercenaries as a matter of course. In fact, 100 English archers were still nominally on his payroll three weeks after the battle of Agincourt was over. There is no evidence, however, that they played any part in this fight.[3]

Scottish mercenaries, for their part, were often hired by and were valued by the French. One of the high points of this long-running bilateral military relationship came in 1418, when the Scots Guard (*la Garde Écossaise* in French) was founded by the Valois king of France, Charles II. This was an elite Scottish unit designed to provide personal bodyguards for the French monarchy. The steps by which it came about should be traced briefly.[4]

Scottish warriors are reported to have fought for Charlemagne (ca. 742–814) and then in the armies of Charles III (879–929). It was not until 1295, however, that the Scottish-French alliance known as the Auld (Old) Alliance was formed and documentary evidence of Scottish soldiers in France or of French soldiers in Scotland begins to be seen. From the beginning of the Hundred Years' War in 1337, Scottish companies were officially fighting for Philip IV of France. At the battle of Poitiers in 1356, the 1st Earl of Douglas and the future 3rd Earl of Douglas both fought for John II. In the 1360s, Scotsmen were to be found in the army of the French mercenary leader Bertrand du Guesclin. When Henry V invaded France in 1415, the Dauphin (the future Charles VII: the eldest son of the king of France, i.e., the heir apparent to the throne of France) looked for, and found, allies among the Scots and the Castilians.

In 1418 Robert Stewart (the Duke of Albany) appointed his son John Stewart (the Chamberlain of Scotland) to take command of the large Scottish expeditionary force (7,000 to 8,000 men) being sent to France. When they arrived at La Rochelle in 1419, the Dauphin showered expensive gifts, e.g., castles, on the Scottish leaders and persuaded them to go back to Scotland to recruit even more troops there. This they did, and returned to France in 1420 with an additional 4,000 to 5,000 soldiers. After the Scottish leaders returned to Scotland, the Dauphin incorporated the Scottish contingent into his armies and garrisons. He picked about 100 of the best of them to be his personal bodyguard.

The Scots fought with distinction throughout France and experienced both victories and defeats, e.g., the battle of Baugé in 1421 (a victory), the battle of Verneuil in 1424 (a major defeat: 6,000 men were lost), and the battle of the Herrings in 1429 (a loss discussed shortly). In 1429, too, some of Joan of Arc's troops were Scottish mercenaries. Contemporary French financial records, quoted verbatim (but in translation) here, reflect the following payments to some of them:

- To the Sheriff of Angus, from the land of Scotland, for the payment of 60 men-at-arms and 300 archers from the aforesaid land, 1,370 *livres-tournois* [approximately $17,399].
- To Michael Norwill, squire of the land of Scotland, for the payment of 20 men-at-arms and 25 projectile-troops [i.e. soldiers armed

either with bows and arrows or with primitive firearms], 130 *livres-tournois* [approximately $1,651].

- To Master John Chrichton, governor of Châtillon, for the payment of 8 men-at-arms and 16 archers from the aforesaid land of Scotland, 90 *livres-tournois* [approximately $1,143].
- To Jean Huberet, for seven bundles of arrows which he had purchased to give to some archers from the land of Scotland, who had used up their arrows against the English, 15 *livres-tournois* [approximately $190.50].

Most of the Scottish forces in France later either fragmented into mercenary companies whose depredations became a major problem for the French government, or were absorbed into the French army.

The king, however, kept his Scots Guard, which had protected him in a fracas in 1419, during which his companions had assassinated John the Fearless (i.e., John II, Duke of Burgundy) at a bridge. The flow of soldiers from Scotland into France continued for years to come. In 1450, for example, King James II sent a company of 24 Scots under the command of Patrick de Spens. By 1490, *la compagnie écossaise de la garde du roi* ("the king's Scottish bodyguard company") included 25 "bodyguards" (i.e., not individuals, but small military units) and 75 archers. The officer of each "bodyguard" had four men-at-arms under his command: a squire, an archer, a mounted crossbowman, and a servant.

Subsequently, over the years as more Frenchmen were recruited, the Scottish element gradually died out. The Scots Guard was eventually disbanded in 1791. Reestablished in 1814, it was dissolved for the second and last time in 1830. Even then, the remaining troops still bore their French title: "*les fiers Écossais*" ("the proud Scots").

Pride was of great importance in upper class medieval life, but so was a good sense of humor. One of the later battles of the Hundred Years' War bears a most remarkable name: it is known as the battle of the Herrings (1429). This name was applied jokingly to begin with, but over the years it stuck fast.

The English were besieging Orléans and needed more supplies.[5] A famous English military leader — Sir John Fastolf, who would be immortalized by Shakespeare as "Sir John Falstaff" — began assembling a convoy at Paris. In the convoy's 300 wagons were supplies of artillery, cannon balls, crossbow bolts—and numerous barrels of herring. The season of Lent was approaching; when it arrived, the army would be prohibited, on religious grounds, from eating meat. The fish were therefore very important because soldiers needed a good deal of protein to stay healthy and to fight well.

Fastolf left Paris with a force of about 1,000 mounted archers and began moving south towards Orléans. The French commander, Charles of Bourbon, soon learned of the English approach. Advancing with 3,000 to 4,000 men, including about 400 Scotts led by Constable Sir John Stewart of Darnley, Charles tried to intercept the convoy and thus prevent the re-supply of the English at Orléans. When the two armies met, Charles brought forward several light cannon and began to bombard the English lines. These caused havoc among Fastolf's men, who were not within longbow range of the French position and who could not attack the French artillery because they were outnumbered on the ground.

If Stewart had not been so impatient, the French probably would not have been defeated. As it was, he ordered his Scottish troops to dismount and to form up into battle lines. Contrary to Charles's orders, however, Stewart's men then charged forward and attacked the English lines. This forced a premature halt to the artillery barrage: the French were afraid of hitting their own men. But as soon as the Scots came within range of Fastolf's deadly archers, the Scots began to suffer very heavy losses. Their advance faltered. Fastolf immediately ordered an English counterattack, which forced the French to retreat from the field.

During this battle, Stewart was killed and Charles was wounded. Fastolf and his men advanced to Orléans. Many of Fastolf's supply wagons had been overturned and casks of herring were strewn around the battlefield. This French defeat marked a low point in their campaign to defend Orléans.

The Scottish soldiers mentioned above are a good example of the problem of "mercenary identity" flagged in the Preface. It can reasonably be asked: should these Scottish be considered mercenaries? John France, an expert on medieval mercenaries, gives this answer:

> Scotland was an ally of France but the French were paying for these soldiers. I would say that they were not "pure" mercenaries, that is, they were

not in this fight simply for the money and only for the money. So, the answer is a qualified "yes," they were mercenaries.[6]

If there were not huge numbers of mercenaries present at the battle of the Herrings, the reverse was certainly true in southwestern France a few years later. In 1433, for example, at the height of his power the Spanish mercenary chieftain Rodrigo de Villandrando led around 10,000 mercenaries, mostly Englishmen, on forays throughout southwestern France. In this process, his men extracted ransoms from the petty lords; demanded "protection money" (*patis*) from the local people to "protect them" from mercenary attacks, i.e., from the mercenaries themselves; and sacked the lovely fortified villages (*bastides*) of the region. Rodrigo's story is worth briefly recounting here.[7]

Rodrigo was so famous for the pillaging his forces inflicted on Gascony that he was known as the "Emperor of Pillagers" (*Empereur des Brigands*) and as "The Skinner" (*L'Écorcheur*). His mercenary career was such a whirlwind of violent activity that it would take too much time and space here to spell it out in precise detail and to explain the circumstances of each attack. Instead, the most important events are mentioned.[8]

Rodrigo arrived in France from Spain in around 1410 and joined the mercenary company led by Amaury de Séverac. Rising to become captain of that band, he entered the service of Charles VII of France when his protector Amaury died in 1427. Early in his career he pillaged Treignac, Meymac, and Tulle. In 1430 he fought at the battle of Anthon, leading around 400 men who were variously armed with billhooks, sledge hammers, and spades. At that battle, his enemies (the Burgundians) scattered in panic but were cut down as they fled. One timid Burgundian man-at-arms, however, hid in a hollow tree. He was wedged fast there by his armor: his skeleton was not discovered until the tree was cut down in 1672.[9]

Later Rodrigo fought against Louis II, who was a vassal of Philip the Good. In 1431 he was rewarded by John II of Aragon, who gave him the county of Ribadeo and accorded him the right to dine at John's table once a year. In that year he also pillaged Saint-Clémont-de-Régnat and was hired to put down a peasant rebellion. In 1432 his men were hired by Georges de la Trémole and defended Les Ponts-de-Cé against the attacks of Jean V de Bueil. In around 1433 Rodrigo was at the peak of his power. He had under his command some 10,000 mercenaries, most of whom were English and who were known as "Rodrigoys." In short, he seems to have been the dominant power in the Médoc region of France.

That same year, he seized and held for a very high ransom the castle of Lagarde Viaur. By the late 1430s he was pillaging Bor-et-Bor, Salers, and Laparade. In 1436, his troops pillaged Cordes and, in 1437, the furriers (fur dealers) of Charles VII at Hérisson. The next year he joined the French forces of Albret and Ponton de Xaintrailles and set off on a quick, violent raid on horseback (a tactic known a *chevauchée*[10]) in the Bordelais and Médoc, finally being stopped only by the walls of Bordeaux itself. In 1440 he sided with Charles of Bourbon against Charles VII in the revolt known as the Praguerie. In 1441 he pillaged Changy and Pavie; in 1442 he again had French royal support for further depredations in northern Gascony. Later that year he threatened Bazas and then, in 1443, upper Languedoc and the Lauragais on his way to Spain. As a result of this last foray, Rodrigo was banned from France and became marshal of Castile in Spain. Willing his worldly goods to a monastery, he died there in about 1457.

Important and useful as mercenaries were, late medieval rulers slowly began to see the clear merits of the standing army, i.e., a professional and permanent force composed of full-time career soldiers who were not disbanded during times of peace. Standing armies (this term dates in English only from 1603, although the concept itself is of course much older) tend to have companies of equal size, which are armed, equipped, and trained according to some overall master plan. The officers and soldiers of standing armies are directly employed by the state and are responsible to it, not to private magnates or to regional authorities. They are usually better equipped and are better prepared than part-time soldiers. What is perhaps most important is that they are usually more disciplined and more reliable, e.g., they are not prone to leave *en masse*, unlike feudal or mercenary troops, as soon as their contracts expire or when conditions in the field become unfavorable.

The army of ancient Rome was a standing army during much of the Imperial period and for some time thereafter. The Janissaries of the Ottoman Empire constituted standing armies, beginning in the 14th century: by 1472 there were about 10,000 Janissaries in Sultan Mehmed's forces.[11] By stretching the point a bit, even some of the best-organized mercenary bands in Western Europe can be thought of as mini-standing armies. The mercenary company of Micheletto degli Attendoli, for example, survived for at least 25 years (1425–1449), serving successively Florence, the kingdom of Naples, Venice, and the papacy. Between contracts it remained intact and even had a permanent administrative structure, e.g., a chancellor and a treasurer. By means of contracts for a year or two years on average, noticeably longer than those which captains of adventuring companies had been used to in the previous century, and with insignificant breaks in continuity, Micheletto was able to maintain his company in the best possible conditions.[12]

If an employer was very pleased by the performance of a mercenary, he could be hired again and again. Milan kept the German captain Michael Colm on its payroll for 10 consecutive years; Florence kept Heinrich Paer for 16 years; and, setting a record that probably was never beaten, the Papacy kept Huglin von Schöneck for 23 years.[13] It is less clear what an employer could really do if a mercenary, once employed, made unreasonable demands. The answer seems to be that in such a case the employer could do very little except to protest or, in a worst-case scenario, fire the mercenary.

In 1441, Filippo Maria Visconti, the Duke of Milan, was appalled to learn that the mercenary Niccolò Piccinino refused to attack a Venetian army unless he was first given the northern Italian city of Piacenza as a fief, i.e., as a present. The Duke protested that

> these condottieri have now reached the stage when if they are defeated we pay for their failures, and if victors we must satisfy their demands and throw ourselves at their feet — even more than if they were our enemies. Must the Duke of Milan bargain for the victory of his own troops, and strip himself to receive favours from them?[14]

Mercenary forces could easily become brigands when peace broke out. Standing armies would eventually resolve this problem. The first "formal" standing army in Western Europe, however, was not established until 1445, when Charles VII of France, rather than disbanding his whole army during a truce with the English, appointed royal captains to keep in his employment the best troops from the mercenary companies then in his pay.[15] When not needed in war, these men could be assigned to garrisons or taught how to transport and operate the cannons which were increasingly coming into use on the battlefield.[16] Moreover, such men came with one enormous advantage over their less-experienced colleagues. Since during the Middle Ages and Renaissance the only way to learn war thoroughly was to experience it in person, they already knew what they were doing.[17]

It must be noted that as the modern scholar Maurice Keen has pointed out, Charles VII did not intend by this move to create a new kind of force, but merely to use this truce to bring under royal control the most voracious of the mercenary companies then pillaging the countryside, e.g., either by suppressing them or by hiring them.[18] There was no clear expectation that the troops retained on duty would remain in service indefinitely, or that the taxes imposed to generate the money needed to pay would continue for years to come if there was no military emergency.

Indeed, as might be expected, these taxes were very unpopular. The contemporary writer and diplomat Philippe de Commines (1447–1511) tells that what citizens had against the concept of a standing army was not its permanence but its cost, which led to hardships and a dramatic rise in the level of taxation in the third quarter of the 15th century.[19] In practice, however, the new troops were not disbanded, and the taxes continued to be collected. As a result, France acquired a standing army. (That said, it must be stressed that almost all 16th and 17th century armies also used a great many mercenaries.)

The first French standing army was an impressive but not a huge force. Charles VII's order of 1445 set up 15 military companies (*compaignies d'ordonnance*); a second order the next year added five more. Each company totaled approximately 700 men, e.g., about 100 "lances." A lance was in this case a unit of six mounted men, namely, a man-at-arms; a *coutillier* (literally, a "knifeman"), who was armed with a sword and a knife; a page; two archers; and a servant. The commanding officer was paid by the king and was expected to field the right number of men and to make sure they would obey his orders. In 1448 these mounted troops were buttressed by a new volunteer force of part-time unmounted militia (the *francs-archers*). Since the standards of equipment and training of these militiamen were not very high, however, they were not much use as a combat force.

In England, the system of a permanent army dates only from the founding of the New Model Army in 1645. This army was formed by the Parliamentarians during the English Civil War and was disbanded in 1660 after the Restoration. It differed from earlier English forces because it was designed for service anywhere in the country, including Scotland and Ireland, rather than being limited to a single theater of operations. Its men were full-time professionals, not part-time militia or mercenaries called up only in time of need.

X

"The Light of Italy"

Under King Matthias Corvinus of Hungary (r. 1458–1490), the Black Army was a highly skilled mercenary force but it became too expensive for the country to support. Federico da Montefeltro was not only one of the most successful mercenaries of the Italian Renaissance but was also a famous patron of the arts: his study, finished in 1476, is now in the Metropolitan Museum of Art. The success of Swiss mercenaries at the battle of Nancy (1477) encouraged more European leaders to hire them. The failure of other mercenaries, during the Pazzi conspiracy of 1478, to kill Lorenzo de Medici led to their own deaths. The Holy Roman Emperor Maximilian I formed the mercenary Landsknecht regiments in 1487; they would eventually displace Swiss mercenaries on the battlefield.

The term "Black Army," coined after the death of King Matthias Corvinus of Hungary (1443–1490), refers to his foreign mercenary forces, which consisted chiefly of Bohemians, Poles, and Germans.[1] There are various theories about the origin of this unusual name. The first recorded references to a "black army" appear in memoranda written immediately after Matthias died. His death occurred when his soldiers were pillaging Hungarian and Austrian villages because they had not been paid; they may have sewed a black stripe on their uniforms as a sign of mourning. If so, it is not clear today whether they were mourning their lost leader, their lost pay, or both.

The foundations of this highly skilled mercenary army were laid by the father of Matthias in the early 1440s. The concept of *a professional standing army of mercenaries*, however, is said to have come to young Matthias himself—when he was reading about the life of Julius Caesar. The eventual result of this creative idea was that the soldiers of the Black Army would be well-paid, full-time mercenaries who were devoted to perfecting their military skills. At its peak strength in 1487, this army could field some 28,000 men, i.e., 20,000 horsemen and 8,000 infantrymen. Moreover, as noted earlier in this book, every fifth soldier in the infantry had an arquebus—an unusually high ratio at the time.

As Matthias' income increased, he was able to hire more and more mercenaries. Contemporary records differ on the numbers involved because these changed from one battle to another and because some soldiers were employed only for the duration of a given campaign. Nevertheless, if all the nobility's Banners (military units), all the mercenaries, all the soldiers of conquered Moravia and Silesia, and all the troops of allied Moldavia and Wallachia are added up, Matthias might have had as many as 90,000 men at his disposal.

Managing this force was not child's play. The major disadvantage of having troops who were paid periodically or only rarely was that if they did not receive their pay, they would simply leave the battlefield or even, in some cases, they would revolt. Such revolts had to be put down by the king, but since these rebels were well-trained, disciplined, men-at-arms they were very hard to suppress.

The good news, from the king's point of view, was that since only a relatively small number of his troops revolted at any given time, their captains could often be encouraged to return to the fold simply by offering them lands and castles, which they could then mortgage and use the proceeds to pay their troops. If this ploy did not work, however, Matthias would resort to military force, tempered by mercy. In 1467, for example, his troops captured a rebel garrison. After the captured men had watched some other prisoners being hung, they begged for mercy—which Matthias kindly granted. He even made one captured rebel officer a captain in the Black Guard because he was such a good fighter.

In 1481, Matthias himself summed up the battlefield duties of his infantry in a letter to Gabriele Rangoni, bishop of Eger. The description, disposition, and tactics of this unit follow closely the actual practices of the Italian mercenary armies. Matthias writes:

> The third force of the army is the infantry, which divides into various orders: the common infantry, the armored infantry, and the shield-bearers.... The armored infantry and shield-bearers cannot carry their armor and shields without pages and servants, and since it is necessary to

provide them with pages, each one of them requires one page per shield and armor....

Then there are handgunners [i.e., soldiers carrying primitive hand-held firearms known as hand cannons] ... They are very practical, set behind the shield-bearers at the start of the battle, before the enemies engage, and in defense. Nearly all of the infantry and the handgunners are surrounded by armored soldiers and shield-bearers, as if they were standing behind a bastion. The large shields set together in a circle present the appearance of a fort and are similar to a wall in whose defense the infantry and all those among them fight almost as if from behind bastion walls or ramparts and at a given moment break out from it.[2]

Before Matthias died in 1490, he had asked his officers to support his son, John Corvinus, as the new king, but Hungary soon collapsed into rival factions struggling for power. Moreover, in about 1492, because some Black Army mercenaries had not been paid they switched sides and joined the army of the Holy Roman Empire, which was then invading Hungary. Another Black Army unit was not paid, either, so it survived by looting the nearest monasteries, churches, villages, and manors.

The failure to pay mercenaries arose because the king simply could not afford to support such a large number of hired troops. Indeed, it has been calculated that out of an annual income of about 900,000 ducats, the king had to set aside 400,000 ducats to pay these men.[3] Revolts by the mercenaries finally led the Black Army itself being disbanded in 1494. Its surviving members were either integrated into local garrisons or, as in the case of some who had turned traitor, were arrested for treason, were locked up, and were quietly allowed to starve to death.

Federico da Montefeltro (1422–1482), the Duke of Urbino (a small city located in central-eastern Italy), was famous both as a successful mercenary leader and as a patron of the arts. He began his career as a mercenary at the age of 16 and only three years later, in 1441, distinguished himself by capturing the castle of St. Leo. He also may have been involved in the assassination of his half-brother, who had been named by Pope Eugene IV as the Duke of Urbino. What is clear is that Federico seized the city after his half-brother's death and succeeded him as lord of Urbino until he later became Duke in 1474.

The city was not rich, however, so Federico signed up as a mercenary with Francesco I Sforza and was the leader of 300 knights. Remarkably, in an age of conspiracy and treachery, Federico was one of the very few mercenaries who was able to inspire loyalty among his troops. Moreover, he was one of the mercenary chieftains who inspired Machiavelli to write *The Prince*, which is discussed later.

Federico lost his right eye during a tournament and bore a scar there which was so disfiguring that portraits of him always show the "good" (i.e., the unscarred) side of his face. The bridge of his nose was also severely injured, but he had surgeons remove the bridge so that his field of vision was not impaired. These wounds did not inhibit his prowess as a mercenary captain, however, and he continued to ply this trade with great success until his death in 1482, when he was defending the city of Ferrara as the Commander of the Italic League. He was extremely popular with his men (he took care of the killed or wounded and provided dowries for their daughters); never lost a war; and earned almost every possible military honor, including being made, by Edward IV of England, a Knight of the Most Noble Order of the Garter.

In our opinion, however, Federico's greatest and most last lasting achievements lie not in warfare but in the humanities. Nicknamed "The Light of Italy," he was interested in the classics, especially history and philosophy, and hired the best copyists and editors to create the finest library outside of the Vatican. Remarkably, his "studiolo" ("small study," which was completed in 1476 and was the most private and most luxurious room in his palace), is now on permanent display at the Metropolitan Museum of Art. It is world-famous for its *trompe-l'oeil* decoration executed in wood marquetry.[4] (*Trompe-l'oeil* means "deceive-the-eye" in French. This is an artistic technique using realistic images to create the optical illusion that the objects thus depicted exist in three dimensions. Marquetry is the art and craft of applying pieces of veneer to a structure to form decorative patterns, designs, or pictures.)

During the Burgundian Wars (1474–1477) in France, Charles the Bold, the expansionist and ambitious Duke of Burgundy, who had already been defeated three times in battle, came to a sorry end.[5] These wars were a struggle between the Dukes of Burgundy and the Kings of France. They showed that cavalry was not of much use against well-trained formations of pikemen or against infantrymen armed with the new firearms. The wars took place in Lorraine and northwest Switzerland

and involved the Swiss Confederacy, which played a decisive role thanks to the very high quality mercenaries it provided.

The result was the death of Charles the Bold in the final, decisive battle of the Burgundian Wars (the battle of Nancy in 1477) and was a Franco-Swiss victory. The Duchy of Burgundy and some other Burgundian lands then became part of France. What is more important for present purposes is that the Burgundian Wars highlight the growing importance of Swiss mercenaries on the battlefields of Europe.

At the battle of Nancy, Charles the Bold had only between 2,000 and 4,000 men (including some Italian mercenaries), in contrast to the 10,000–12,000 soldiers from Lorraine and the Lower Union of the Rhine — plus 10,000 Swiss mercenaries — led by René, Duke of Lorraine. When Charles' army began to crumble under the assault of René's forces, Charles and his staff tried in vain to halt the rout but they were caught up in it instead. They were swept along until his party was surrounded by Swiss mercenaries. A halberdier swung his battle axe at Charles' head and landed a heavy blow on his helmet. Charles tumbled off his horse; the tide of battle flowed over and around him; his disfigured body was not discovered for three days. The stellar performance of the Swiss mercenaries in this battle increased their already-high reputation and led to their more frequent employment across Europe.

Not all mercenaries were trustworthy. Conspiracies, betrayals, and political assassinations — often involving mercenaries — were frequent events in the Middle Ages and Renaissance. The Pazzi conspiracy of 1478 is a good case in point.[6]

When young Lorenzo de Medici was the *de facto* ruler of Florence, some of his most outspoken and most violent opponents were the members of the Pazzi family, whose main trade was banking. The ins-and-outs of the Italian political and financial situation at that time are too complicated to discuss here and are not essential to the story.[7] What is important is that the Pazzi family and their backers received the tacit support of Pope Sixtus IV (who wanted to enrich the sons of his sister, not the Medicis) and the support of the archbishop of Pisa, Francesco Salviati, to have Lorenzo, his brother Giuliano, and other Medici supporters murdered in a surprise attack.

The site of this attack was the Duoumo, the great cathedral of Florence. The plotters recruited Gian Battista da Montesecco, a noted *condottiere* (Italian mercenary) who was the commander of a company of mercenaries in Perugia and who agreed to help them — on the condition that he not be asked to kill Lorenzo himself because he did not want to spill blood on holy ground.

The conspiracy swung into action when Lorenzo and Giuliano were at High Mass at the cathedral, together with 10,000 other worshipers. Gian Battista and his men seized a strategic gate, while at the same time the ambush was triggered in the cathedral itself. Four mercenaries attacked Lorenzo and Giuliano. One of them was Francesco de Pazzi, who was so overwhelmed with rage and adrenaline that, when he struck out with his knife, he stabbed himself in the thigh. The assassins stabbed Giuliano 19 times and killed him, but Lorenzo's would-be assailants (two disgruntled priests) failed in their own attempt and, though wounded in the shoulder, Lorenzo managed to escape.

In the meantime, Archbishop Salviati led some of the Perugian mercenaries to the Palazzo della Signoria (the seat of government in Florence) with the intention of seizing civic power. When they arrived, they were politely ushered into a room — but one which had secret catches on the doors to prevent them from being opened from inside. They were therefore trapped. Medici supporters then rushed into the room, clubbed the archbishop to the ground, and took him prisoner.

Lorenzo's revenge was quick, brutal, and thorough. The trapped mercenaries were killed by Medici supporters. The leading conspirators were tortured and executed. Francesco de Pazzi and Archbishop Salviati were hanged from the windows of the Pallazo della Signoria. Other members of the Pazzi family were executed, too. Gian Battista was tortured; he confessed and was beheaded. His confession is still in the archives of Florence and provides many of the details given above. Ironically, if Gian Battista himself had not had such qualms about killing Lorenzo, the Pazzi conspiracy might well have succeeded.

It is interesting to note in passing that, even as late as the Pazzi conspiracy, organizing and directing Italian armies was still a very difficult business. In the Pazzi era, for example, when Milanese and Venetian troops were sent to Tuscany to support the Florentines, the administration of their combined army left a great deal to be desired. Gian Jacopo

Trivulzio, a Milanese commander, gives this graphic account of the chaos he witnessed:

> These Florentine troops are so badly organized that it disgusts me; the men-at-arms are spread out in confusion, often with squadrons mixed up together in a way which seems to conform to no plan, and squadrons as much as half a mile apart. The soldiers are billeted all over the place without any provision for pioneers [support troops] or other essential auxiliaries; there are very few infantry, about 700, of which 150 only are properly armed although I have made constant protests about this.... The Florentine officials sell victuals [foodstuffs] at the dearest price possible without any concern for the regulations of prices and quality; the money is debased so that it buys very little; and if provisions are sent from Lombardy or elsewhere these Florentines make us pay duty on them, or even keep them for themselves.[8]

The Pazzi conspiracy itself involved only a small number of mercenaries but the new regiments of mercenaries, known in English as Landsknechts and founded by Maximilian I in 1487, could consist of up to 12,000 men.[9] In German, *Landsknechte* (plural) and *Landsknecht* (singular) were terms coined from the words for "land," i.e., country, and for "servant," so their name meant "servant of the country."

The Landsknechts were thus European (initially predominately German) pikemen and infantrymen who flourished from the late 15th to the late 16th century and who won the reputation of being some of the very best mercenaries in Western Europe. They fought in almost every 16th century military campaign — sometimes on both sides of the same battle. They had learned their skills from Swiss mercenaries, e.g., the use of very long pikes (up to 18 feet long) and the deployment of the nearly-impervious "pike square" formations.

Landsknecht regiments could swell in size, e.g., from 4,000 up to 12,000 men, as the military need arose. Their regiments were accompanied by numerous camp followers and by a baggage train carrying heavy equipment, food, and the personal belongings of the mercenaries. Their wives and children formed part of this cavalcade, too. The female camp followers filled many roles: mothers, nurses, cooks, cleaners, and sexual companions. Other participants on these journeys included common laborers, merchants and their families, animals for food, thieves, and scavengers.[10]

If on the battlefield an experienced Landsknecht was not using a pike, he might be seen swinging a 6-to-8-foot-long halberd, or perhaps wielding a double-edged sword 6 feet long known as a *Zweihänder* (literally, a "two-hander" sword), which weighed between 7 and 14 pounds. Its purpose was to knock aside the enemy's pikes, thus sowing disorder in the enemy's tightly-packed ranks and creating openings for opposing infantrymen to break in and attack them. These swords were also used to guard the mercenaries who were entrusted with carrying their unit's flag: the swords were so big and so lethal that a few soldiers armed with them could stop many other soldiers who were only lightly armed.

A Landsknecht was thus a powerful man equipped with powerful weapons. He had to provide his own weapons and armor and had to be physically fit: recruits had to prove their fitness by jumping over a barrier made of three pikes or halberds. As a result of this careful selection process, such a man was likely to be very effective in battle. In 1502, for example, the Landsknecht Paul Dolstein described a siege during which he was fighting on the side of the King of Denmark. He wrote: "We were 1,800 Germans and we were attacked by 15,000 Swedish farmers ... we struck most of them dead."[11]

Landsknecht warriors posed a considerable threat to civilians as well as to the enemy. The *Oxford Companion to Military History* makes these telling points:

> The very epitome of the 16th-century military freebooter and vagabond, the landsknechts were rightly feared wherever they went. Their garish, ripped, and rakishly padded costume and improbably large weaponry, meant that the landsknechts presented an awe-inspiring sight to friend and foe alike. An unwholesome appetite for plunder and strong drink, and blood-curdling cries of "Beware, farmer: I'm coming!" made them feared by the civilian population in the regions where they campaigned. And indeed they fought in almost every campaign in every region of Europe from 1486 to their decline at the end of the 16th century.[12]

The "costume" mentioned above came about because they sometimes wore colorful clothing stripped from fallen opponents and because they always delighted in dressing flamboyantly. Maximilian I had exempted them from the sumptuary laws of the time (these were laws intended to restrain the expenditure of citizens on luxurious apparel), so the Landsknechts wore doublets deliberately slashed at the front, back, and sleeves—with shirts or other wear pulled through the cuts to form puffs of different-colored fabric (a style known as "puffed and slashed"). They also wore multi-colored hose; jerkins (short sleeveless jackets, usually made of light leather); broad beret-type hats with tall feathers; and broad, flat shoes. Needless to say, a band of these men would certainly stand out in a crowd.[13]

Briefly and to end this chapter, the now somewhat shadowy and elusive Black Bands must be addressed.[14] These were formations of 16th century mercenaries serving as Landsknechts. One Black Band fought in the French army for 10 years, had a strength of 4,000 to 5,000 men, and took part in some notable battles. It was created in 1514 by George, Duke of Saxony to fight for his claims in East Frisia during what was known as the Saxon feud. Whether this Black Band was a new creation, or whether it was somehow part of the "Black Guard" (also known as the "Great Guard") founded in 1488 by unemployed Landsknechts, is not entirely clear now. What is clear is that a Black Guard fought in East Frisia in 1514 and devastated large parts of it in the process.

When the Saxon feud ended in 1515, Duke George abandoned the men of the Black Guard, who were then reduced to living off the land as brigands. Charles of Geldern hired them, however, and led them in the Italian wars, covered in the next chapter. The Black Bands of Guelders, one of the most prestigious Landsknecht contingents, had 12,000 pikemen, 2,000 arquebisiers, 2,000 swordsmen, and 1,000 halberdiers in about 1515. In 1525 the captain of one of the Black Bands was Georg Langenmanel, a German, but this Black Band was sometimes, as in the battle of Pavia (which took place in present-day Italy in 1525 between Spain and France), put under the command of a French officer.

In this battle, the Black Band was greatly outnumbered: it found itself facing two blocks of Landsknechts totaling some 12,000 men. The result was predictable: the Black Band, with a strength of only about 5,000 men, was hacked to pieces and was virtually destroyed. It therefore ceased to exist as a combat force, although it would be reconstituted later on.

XI

"Mercenaries and auxiliaries are useless and dangerous"

Mercenaries were used very frequently in the eight Italian Wars (1494 to 1559): the core of the French infantry consisted of Swiss mercenaries, while the Italian cities hired both native and German mercenaries. Although many leaders were eager to hire mercenaries, in his famous work The Prince *(1532) Niccolò Machiavelli strongly warned them not to do so. As might be expected, however, his advice fell on deaf ears: during the Thirty Years' War (1618–1648), marauding bands of mercenaries would lay waste to entire regions of Central Europe.*

Edna St. Vincent Millay (1892–1950), the first woman to receive the Pulitzer Prize for Poetry, famously said: "It's not that life is one damn thing after another; it's just one damn thing over and over." The 64-year period of the Italian Wars is an excellent case in point here.[1]

These wars initially arose from dynastic squabbles but soon evolved into a more general and very repetitive struggle for power and territory. They have many different names: the Great Italian Wars, the Great Wars of Italy, the Habsburg-Valois Wars, and the Renaissance Wars. Whatever name is preferred, however, it basically refers to the same thing, namely, the complicated series of conflicts between 1494 and 1559 that involved, at various times, France, the Holy Roman Empire, the city-states of Italy, England, Scotland, Spain, the Ottoman Empire, the Swiss, Saxony, and other players.

Taking place in southern and Western Europe, the wars finally ended in a Habsburg victory, with Spain emerging as the dominant European power. However, they are such a confusing kaleidoscope of military and political factors, ambitious leaders (mercenaries, nobles, and kings), alliances, counter-alliances, and betrayals they are not described here in great detail. Instead, the focus is very selective, only on those parts of some campaigns where mercenaries were used in a significant way.

The Italian War of 1494–1498: In an earlier chapter, the First Italian War pitted Charles VIII of France against the Holy Roman Empire, Spain, and an alliance of Italian powers under the leadership of Pope Alexander VI. In the opening stages of that war, Charles VIII invaded Italy with an army that included 8,000 Swiss mercenaries. At first his forces moved through Italy without much opposition: the *condottieri* (mercenary) armies of the Italian city-states were much too weak to stop the French forces.

The French reached Naples in February 1495 and captured it without a siege or a pitched battle. The Italian city-states, however, realizing that a foreign monarchy in their midst could endanger their own autonomy, created the League of Venice. This new institution pulled together an army under the leadership of the *condottiero* (mercenary chieftain) Francesco II Gonzaga. Charles VIII, not wanting to be trapped in Naples, marched north to Lombardy, where he fought the League at the battle of Fornovo (July 1495), using artillery and 3,000 of his own mercenaries. The outcome was both a success and a failure for him: he managed to retreat to France with most of his army intact, but he had to leave behind nearly all the booty he had seized in Italy.

The Italian War of 1499–1504: In 1499, Louis XII of France, having made an alliance with the Republic of Venice and with Swiss mercenaries, invaded the Duchy of Milan. Ludovico Sforza of Milan hired an army of Swiss mercenaries himself. The Swiss mercenaries, however, did not want to fight each other and Ludovico was defeated by Gian Giacomo Trivulzio, a noted Italian mercenary who held several military commands during the Italian Wars. (Trivulzio had abandoned Ludovico and, switching sides, had joined Charles VIII.) Ludovico himself was handed over to the French in 1500 and spent the rest of his life jailed in miserable conditions in an underground dungeon in France.

The War of the League of Cambrai (1508–1516): The War of the League of Cambrai, also known as the War of the Holy League and by other names, too, was a major conflict during the Italian Wars. The chief participants were at varying times: France; the Papal States; the Republic of Venice; Spain; the Holy Roman Empire; England; Scotland; the Duchy of Milan; Florence; the Duchy of Ferrara; and, last but by no means least, the redoubtable Swiss mercenaries. The final victors were the French and Venetians.

Pope Julius II had wanted to curb the territorial ambitions of the Republic of Venice, so in 1508 he formed the League of Cambrai for this purpose. By focusing only on the role of mercenaries, one can note that in 1509 Louis XII of France left Milan at the head of a French army and invaded Venetian territory. To oppose him, Venice hired a mercenary army under two cousins— Bartolomeo d'Alviano and Nicolo di Pitigaliano. Unfortunately, however, they could not agree how to oppose the French.

As a result, when Louis XII crossed the Adda River, Bartolomeo advanced to attack him. Nicolo, on the other hand, saw no virtue in a pitched battle, so he moved away to the south. When Bartolomeo fought the French at the battle of Agnandello, he found that he was outnumbered and he urgently asked his cousin to send him reinforcements. Nicolo, however, simply ordered Bartolomeo to break off the battle and he then continued on his own way. Bartolomeo, disregarding these orders, kept on fighting until his army was surrounded and was destroyed. Nicolo, for his part, managed to steer clear of the victorious French forces but when his mercenary troops heard of Bartolomeo's defeat, they deserted in large numbers, forcing Nicolo to retreat with the remnants of his army. The Venetian collapse was complete but Nicolo soldiered on.

In 1509 the citizens of Padua, aided by detachments of Venetian cavalry under the command of the "proveditor" Andrea Gritti, revolted. (A proveditor was a civilian official charged with overseeing the actions of the mercenary captains hired by the Republic of Venice.) Padua was guarded by some Landsknechts but they were too few in number to resist the revolt effectively, so Padua reverted to Venetian control. Relief forces were sent toward Padua but Nicolo had enough time to concentrate his remaining troops there. At the siege of Padua, although enemy artillery fire breached the city's walls, Nicolo and his men were able to stand fast: the city did not fall. When Nicolo died of natural causes in 1510, Andrea Gritti took his place as proveditor.

Pope Julius II was increasingly worried by the growing French military presence in Italy, so he hired an army of Swiss mercenaries to attack the French in Milan and he formed an alliance with the Venetians, who also feared the French invaders.

The Italian War of 1521–1526: Francis I of France had wanted to become Holy Roman Emperor. When Charles V of Spain got the job instead, this gave Francis the pretext to start a general war. The war, fought in Italy, France, and Spain, pitted Francis and the Republic of Venice against the Holy Roman Emperor Charles V, Henry VIII of England, and the Papal States. The result was a Spanish and Imperial (Holy Roman Empire) victory. From what might be called a "pro-mercenary" point of view (in the sense that many of the advantages of mercenaries, at least as seen by their employers, have been recounted), the most interesting action of this war was the rout of Swiss mercenaries at the battle of Bicocca in 1522.

In this battle, a combined French and Venetian force, led by Odet de Foix, the Vicomte de Lautrec, was decisively defeated, north of Milan, by a Spanish-Imperial and Papal army commanded by Prospero Colonna. Lautrec had wanted to attack Colonna's lines of communication but his (Lautrec's) Swiss mercenaries complained that they had not been paid since their arrival in Lombardy. They demanded an immediate battle, threatening to abandon the French and return to their cantons if Lautrec refused to attack. Their demand forced him, against his will, to assault Colonna's well-fortified position. Lautrec's Swiss pikemen moved forward over open fields under a fierce artillery bombardment, suffering heavy losses, and had to stop at a sunken road backed up by earthworks. There they encountered the concentrated fire of Spanish arquebusiers and were forced to retreat. Their total losses were more than 3,000 dead.

The net result was that, a few days later, the Swiss mercenaries marched back to their cantons, while Lautrec had to retreat into Venetian territory with the remnants of his army. The significance of this battle is three-fold: it marked the end of Swiss pike-dominance among the infantry units of the Italian Wars; it forced the Swiss to change their policy of attacking with only massed columns of pikemen, i.e., without the support of other troops; and it was one of the first engagements where firearms played a decisive role in the outcome. The Italian historian and statesman Francesco Guicciardini (1483–1540) remarked on how this battle changed the military attitude of the Swiss. He wrote:

They went back to their mountains diminished in numbers, but more diminished in audacity; for it is certain that the losses which they suffered at Bicocca so affected them in coming years that they no longer displayed their wonted vigour.[2]

The really decisive engagement of the Italian War of 1521–1526, however, was the battle of Pavia (1525), in which a Spanish-Imperial army under Charles de Lannoy, working together with a garrison of Pavia under Antonio de Leyva, attacked the French army, which was under the personal command of Francis I of France.[3] The end result was that the French army was soundly defeated: in fact, Francis himself was captured by Spanish troops when his horse was killed from under him by Caesare Herocolani, an Italian mercenary. Francis was then imprisoned by Charles V and was forced to sign the humiliating Treaty of Madrid.

Mercenaries played significant roles in the battle of Pavia but rather than trying to recount their exploits here in exhaustive detail, it is better to look briefly at a few of the highlights. Examples include the following:

- A mass of French troops arrived at Pavia in October 1524 to besiege the city. Inside the city were about 9,000 men, mainly mercenaries, whom the Spanish commander Antonio de Leyva was able to pay only by melting down the gold and silver plate of the local churches.
- Confusingly, two different mercenary Black Bands were involved at the battle of Pavia. One, headed by Giovanni de' Medici, consisted of Italian mercenary arquebusiers who had just entered French service. The other, led by François de Lorraine, consisted of renegade Landsknecht pikemen.
- Antonio de Leyva overran 3,000 Swiss mercenaries who had been manning the siege lines. Survivors tried to flee across a river but suffered massive causalities as they did so.

After his decisive defeat in the battle of Pavia, Francis wrote these famous lines in a letter to his mother, Louise of Savoy:

To inform you of how my ill-fortune is proceeding, all is lost to me save honour and life, which remain safe....[4]

The War of the League of Cognac (1526–1530): This war was fought between the Habsburg lands of Charles V (e.g., Spain and the Holy

Roman Empire) and the League of Cognac (an alliance of France, Pope Clement VII, the Republic of Venice, England, the Duchy of Milan, and the Republic of Florence). The result was a decisive Spanish-Imperial victory.

The most interesting mercenary involved in this war was the Genoese admiral Andrea Doria (1466–1560). Orphaned at an early age, when he grew up he became a soldier of fortune, first serving in the Papal guard and then under different Italian princes. In 1503, when fighting in Corsica in the service of Genoa, which was then ruled by the French, he took part in the revolt of Genoa against the French, and forced the French to evacuate the city. This made his name as a mercenary commander.

His next assignment, as chief of the Genoese fleet, was to wage war against the Turks and the Barbary pirates. While he was doing this, the French recaptured Genoa, which was later seized by the armies of the Holy Roman Emperor. Doria, however, sided with the French and entered the service of King Francis I of France, who promoted him to captain-general. In 1524 he relieved Marseille, which was under attack by the Holy Roman Empire, and later helped the French return to power in Genoa.

Later, Francis sent an army to Genoa, where Doria, still on the French side, seized much of the Genoese fleet. Doria, however, then turned his back on the French and sided with Charles in 1528. Doria's subsequent offensive against Genoa ended any remaining hopes Francis had of keeping his hold on Italy. Much later, in 1543, Doria transported a relief army to Nice during the siege of that city by the Ottoman leader Hayreddin Barbarossa. After the Peace of Crépy in 1544, however, he wanted to end his days in peace and quiet in Genoa. His great wealth and power, coupled with the arrogance of his family, had made him many enemies there. In 1550, at the age of 84, he went to sea again to face the Barbary pirates, but without much success. He returned to Genoa for good in 1555 and died there five years later.

The Italian War of 1536–1538: This war between Holy Roman Emperor Charles V and Francis I of France was triggered by the death of Francesco Maria Sforza, the Duke of Milan, and by their conflicting claims to the Duchy of Milan. The Truce of Nice (1538), which ended the war, made no significant change in the map of Italy and left divisive matters unresolved. In fact, this settlement is remembered chiefly because Charles and Francis hated each other so much that they refused to sit in the same room together. Their enmity forced the mediator, Pope Paul III, to shuttle from room to room to work out an agreement. Mercenaries do not appear to have played any significant role in this short war.

The Italian War of 1542–1546: This ruinously expensive war — basically a contest pitting Francis I of France and Suleiman I of the Ottoman Empire, on the one hand, against the Holy Roman Emperor Charles V and Henry VII of England, on the other — was inconclusive. All the players used mercenaries at one time or another: at the battle of Serravalle in 1544, for example, the troops of Alfonso d'Avalos, fighting on behalf of Charles V and his allies, defeated an Italian mercenary army in French service.

A battle worth looking at here is the battle of Ceresole (1544), which took place near Turin, Italy and which is remembered by military historians as "the great slaughter" because of the heavy losses which occurred when columns of arquebusiers and pikemen clashed in the middle of the battlefield.

The belligerents were France, whose forces were led by the Count of Enghien, and the Holy Roman Empire (including Spain) under Charles V, whose troops were commanded by Alfonso d'Avalos. On the ground, a wide range of forces of differing backgrounds, i.e., both mercenary and regular, were engaged in this battle. The major combat units were:

On the French side

- 4,000   Swiss troops
- 4,000   Gascon infantrymen
- 3,000   French infantry recruits
- 2,000   Italian infantrymen

On the Spanish-Imperial side

- 7,000   Landsknechts
- 6,000   Italian infantrymen
- 5,000   Spanish and German infantrymen

What made this particular battle so horrific (the French lost up to 2,000 men dead and wounded; the Holy Roman Empire, up to 6,000 dead or wounded, with more than 3,000 other men captured) was that the columns of each side contained both men with firearms and men with pikes, arranged in a new type of formation. A French nobleman, Blaise de Lasseran-Massencôme, the lord of Montluc, took credit for devising this novel strategy. His idea was to put his firearms men very far forward and in a row, i.e., in the second rank of a column, just behind the leading row of pikemen. Presumably on command, the first row of pikemen would kneel down and would place the butts of their pikes in the earth with the points facing the enemy. The firearms men would then fire over the tops of the pikemens' heads.

Blaise candidly tells what happened when this system was actually tried at Ceresole. He had confidently expected that

> in this way we should kill all their captains in the front rank. But we found that they were as ingenious as ourselves, for behind their first line of pikes they had put pistoleers [i.e., men armed with handguns: long-barreled arquebuses would have been too unwieldy at such close quarters]. Neither side fired till we were touching — and then there was a wholesale slaughter: every shot told; the whole front rank on each side went down.[5]

The losses in this battle were so heavy that the ill-fated concept of alternating rows of firearms men and pikemen was never tried again. Instead, in later battles when firearms (generally arquebuses) were used, they were not fired at point-blank range but only from the relatively greater safety of the flanks of large formations of pikemen or they were used for skirmishing.

The Italian War of 1551–1559: In 1551, Henry II of France declared war on Charles V with the twin goals of recapturing Italy and of establishing French domination of European affairs. However, to make a long and complex story very short, the French failed to change the balance of power in Italy or to break Habsburg control. In terms of mercenary involvement, the most interesting aspect of this war was the battle of Marciana (also known as the battle of Scannagallo), which took place in Tuscany in 1554 and was a decisive Florentine and Spanish-Imperial victory.

Here the belligerents were the Duchy of Florence, Spain, and the Holy Roman Empire, on one side, and the Republic of Siena and France, on the other. Large numbers of troops were involved: 17,000 infantrymen and 1,500 cavalrymen for the Duchy of Florence and its allies; and 14,000, infantrymen and 1,000 cavalrymen for Siena and France. Many of the fighters were mercenaries. For example, the mercenary chieftain Ascanio della Cornia provided 6,000 infantrymen and 300 cavalrymen; Landsknechts were much in evidence; and at one point a corps of 1,300 hungry mercenaries was killed when trying to collect food to eat. As a result of this battle, Siena lost its independence and was absorbed into the Grand Duchy of Tuscany.

The modern scholar Michael Mallett summarized the Italian Wars in these words:

> It was the scale of the Italian Wars which created their enormous impact on European warfare. The emphasis on size and permanence of armies produced not only more disciplined and extensive use of known weapons and techniques, but also placed a premium on co-ordination between arms. The day had passed when a single arm — whether it was the French heavy cavalry or the Swiss pikes—could dominate the battlefield.... The Italian Wars were a vast melting pot; the heat and flames were new; the ingredients were not. Italy had contributed significantly to these ingredients even though she herself was to be consumed in the flames.[6]

Niccolò Machiavelli (1469–1527), the Italian Renaissance figure whose name is still cited frequently today by scholars, politicians, and debaters alike, had negative views on mercenaries.[7]

The son of a legal official, Machiavelli had a good grasp of Latin and the Italian classics when he entered government service in 1494 as a clerk. After the Florentine Republic was proclaimed four years later, he rose to prominence as secretary of the 10-man council which conducted Florence's diplomatic negotiations and military operations. It was during his diplomatic missions that he became familiar with the political tactics of many Italian leaders. In 1502 and 1503, Machiavelli also became familiar, at first hand, with the state-building methods of Cesare Borgia, the Duke of Romagna, who was expanding his holdings in central Italy through a mixture of military prowess, audacity, prudence, self-reliance, firmness, and cruelty. His army was essentially a mercenary army, heavy with contingents of French and Spanish troops. When he faced a revolt by his own mercenaries in 1502, he crushed it brilliantly and ruthlessly. Machiavelli studied closely the methods Cesare employed to trick the rebellious mercenaries and then magnified his achievements in *The Prince*.[8]

From 1503 to 1506 Machiavelli was put in charge of reorganizing the military defense of Florence. At that time, condottieri bands (i.e. mercenary armies) were common in Italy, but Machiavelli did not think they could ever be relied on to remain loyal to their employers. He therefore argued in favor of citizen armies which, being native to a given state and thus having a personal stake in its fortunes, were much more likely to be loyal. Machiavelli's thinking here was largely inspired by the citizen armies of ancient Rome.

In 1512, as a result of the rivalry between Spain and France (see the previous section on the Italian Wars), the Medici family returned to power in Florence. The republic was dissolved and, as a key figure in the former anti-Medici government, Machiavelli was placed on the torture rack because he was suspected of conspiracy. After his release, he retired to his estate near Florence, where he wrote his most important books. He tried hard to win the favor of the Medicis but was unsuccessful in this effort and was never given another government position.

Machiavelli's best-known book — *The Prince* (*Il Principe*) — was not printed until 1532, five years after his death, although an earlier version was first circulated in 1513 under the Latin title of *De Principatibus* (*About Principalities*). The basic and most famous teaching of *The Prince* is that a leader, in order to survive, let alone to win glory, is fully justified in using immoral means to achieve these objectives. Here the focus is on the two chapters of *The Prince* that have the most to say about mercenaries. It is worth quoting them at some length to get the full impact of Machiavelli's thought.

His Chapter XII ("How Many Kinds of Soldiery There Are, And Concerning Mercenaries"), for example makes these forceful points:

> I say, therefore, that the arms with which a prince defends his state are either his own, or they are mercenaries, auxiliaries, or mixed.
> Mercenaries and auxiliaries are useless and dangerous; and if one holds his state based on these arms, he will stand neither firm nor safe; for they are disunited, ambitious and without discipline, unfaithful, valiant before friends, cowardly before enemies; they have neither the fear of God nor fidelity to men, and [one's own] destruction is deferred only so long as the attack is; for in peace one is robbed by them, and in war by the enemy. The fact is, that they have no other attraction or reason for keeping the field than a trifle of stipend, which is not sufficient to make them willing to die

for you. They are ready enough to be your soldiers whilst you do not make war, but if war comes they take themselves off or run from the foe....
I wish to demonstrate further the infelicity of these arms [i.e., mercenaries]. The mercenary captains are either capable men or they are not; if they are, you cannot trust them, because they always aspire to their own greatness, either by oppressing you, who are their master, or others contrary to your intentions; but if the captain [i.e., the leader of the mercenaries] is not skillful, you are ruined in the usual way [i.e., you will lose the war]. And if it be urged [i.e., argued] that whoever is armed will act in the same way, whether mercenary or not, I reply that when arms have to be resorted to, either by a prince or a republic, the prince ought to do in person and perform the duty of captain.... And experience has shown princes and republics, single-handed, making the greatest progress, and mercenaries doing nothing but damage; and it is more difficult to bring a republic, armed with its own arms, under the sway of one of its citizens than it is to bring one armed with foreign arms. Rome and Sparta stood for many ages armed and free. The Switzers are completely armed and quite free.[9]

In his Chapter XIII ("Concerning Auxiliaries, Mixed Soldiers, And One's Own"), Machiavelli provides his considered findings on this subject:

And if the first disaster to the Roman Empire should be examined, it will be found to have commenced only with the enlisting of the Goths [as mercenaries]; because from that time the vigour of the Roman Empire began to decline, and all that valour which had raised it passed to others.
I conclude, therefore, that no principality is secure without having its own forces; on the contrary, it is entirely dependent on good fortune, not having the valour which in adversity would defend it. And it has always been the opinion and judgment of a wise man that nothing is so uncertain or unstable as fame or power which is not founded on its own strength. And one's own forces are those which are composed either of subjects, citizens, or dependents; all others are mercenaries or auxiliaries.[10]

In making these such statements, however, Machiavelli was certainly not a disinterested scholar. He very much wanted to get another high-level position with the government of Florence, and the only way to do so was to win the support of the ruling Medici family. A letter written by Machiavelli and discovered only in 1810 reveals that he wrote *The Prince* to impress the Medicis. However, since they were not prepared to pay the very high fees demanded by the best warriors of the time—namely, the Swiss mercenaries—in *The Prince* he had to fall back on a less-effective but more feasible solution, namely, a rural militia composed of Florentine citizens. Such a force, he argued, would be much cheaper and much more reliable than mercenaries.

Machiavelli clearly hoped that this proposal, coupled with his related ideas on the merits of a strong indigenous government (which was badly needed, in his view, to keep Florence free from foreign domination), would commend itself to the Medicis. It is clear, however, that it did not: Machiavelli never got another job, and mercenaries continued to be widely used by Italian city-states and by other employers.

The Thirty Years' War (1618–1648) can be the final example of the continuing importance of mercenaries. Much of the enormous damage of this war was inflicted by mercenaries, who plundered every area they crossed. The modern scholar Peter Wilson gives this good summary of an epic struggle:

> The Thirty Years' War was one of the longest and most devastating conflicts in European history. Nearly all the major European powers were drawn into this violent religious and political crisis, which raged across the continent.... It killed around a quarter of all Germans, with marauding bands of mercenaries laying waste to entire towns and regions across Central Europe, some of which never recovered.[11]

It must be noted here that these "marauding bands" were not the same as the earlier mercenary companies as were seen in Italy. During the Thirty Years' War, the regimental units that made up each army were not, strictly speaking, mercenary regiments themselves. That is to say, these units were not well-organized "swords for hire" that could readily change sides from one battle to another, according to the decisions of their commanders. The individual soldiers in a given regiment, however, were very often mercenaries. Disciplining them was nearly impossible because 17th century armies were expected by their governments to be largely self-financing and self-sufficient. This meant that they were literally forced to live off the land — by extracting food, drink, shelter, valuables, sex, and other pleasures from the local inhabitants— by force if necessary.

Count Ernst von Mansfeld (1580–1626), a German military commander, was the most famous mercenary leader of the early period of the Thirty Years' War.[12] At that time, governments did not have the money or the administrative skills necessary to pursue their military ambitions. As a result, they often hired, on a contract basis, successful men who were able to undertake such difficult tasks for them as levying taxes; transferring money from one city or country to another; leading overseas expeditions; conducting maritime warfare; or — as military entrepreneurs, (i.e., as mercenary captains) — recruiting, organizing, training, commanding armies, and putting down local rebellions,. These men were very good at what they did but they were also very expensive. More than 300 of them were active in Germany alone during the Thirty Years' War.[13]

Ernst von Mansfeld helped Frederick V, who was King of Bohemia from 1619 to 1620, by defending the Upper and Rhine Palatinate, a historic state of the Holy Roman Empire. Because of his close ties with Frederick, who provided the cash and troops, Mansfield had 15,000 to 20,000 men under his command. He was an excellent organizer, thanks in large part to his network of experienced recruiting officers. Although he was a good strategist and a fine tactician, he was also quite ruthless and was willing to risk his men's lives. If defeated, he would sometimes retreat so quickly that his own forces would disintegrate. This made him rather expensive to employ because new forces would then have to be recruited in the wake of his retreat.[14]

Like other mercenary captains, Mansfeld had his share of military successes and of military failures, but unlike the vast majority of other captains he also understood the propaganda value of the written word. At his direction, for example, in 1622 his administrative staff produced a wide-ranging "apologia" — that is, a formal defense of his opinions, positions, or actions — which was designed to uphold his reputation and to impress prospective employers with his military expertise and knowledge. In the words of the modern Dutch scholar Aart Brouwer (with light editing), the essence of Mansfeld's apologia is as follows:

> The tone of the apologia is that of a soldier, a cool professional who speaks in a succinct manner and with a degree of sarcasm, even of a superficial rationality, about battles past and his own and often bloody part in them. What is most remarkable about the apologia is Mansfeld's cynical but pragmatic view of mercenary soldiers, whose loyalty, he says, depends solely on regular payments. As soon as these are withheld, they will "take their income where they find it, and once the doors have been opened they will run on and on at the same level of lawlessness. The Germans, Dutch, French, Italians and Hungarians each add their own national vices and mis-

chief to the mix, so that there is no form or shape of fraud or ruse which they will not practice."[15]

The Dutch hired Mansfeld in 1622 because Spain was preparing to attack the strategically-important Dutch town of Bergen-op-Zoom and they needed his expertise. To get to Bergen-op-Zoom, however, Mansfeld and his men had to march through Lorraine and Habsburg territory — while being pursued by the army of the Spanish general Córdoba. When Mansfeld reached the town of Fleurus in the Spanish Netherlands (present-day Belgium), he found to his great surprise that Córboda had got there first by marching through Luxembourg and the Ardennes.

The resulting battle of Fleurus seems to have been something of a draw. On the one hand, Córdoba claimed victory and sent a set of captured Mansfeld colors, e.g., battle flags, to the Infanta Isabella in Brussels. (Infanta Isabella of Spain was, together with her husband Albert of Austria, the joint sovereign of the Spanish holdings in the Low Countries and in the north of France.) On the other hand, much of Mansfeld's ragtag mercenary army, with only two field guns, had managed to push the veteran Spanish troops aside and to force its way into the Netherlands, where it regrouped and fought on. The Dutch appreciated what Mansfeld had accomplished but, on balance, they considered his troops to be *goet volck maer buyten discipline* ("good people but without discipline") and ordered him to seek quarters outside their own country.[16]

After many more adventures, Mansfeld died of natural causes in 1626 in what is now Bosnia. Wild rumors immediately spread upon his death, e.g., that he had died standing up in full armor with his sword drawn; that he had expired in the arms of his most loyal servants; or that he had left behind many valuable hidden treasures. In reality, however, his death was much less romantic and less eventful than his life. According to a modern biographer, Mansfeld had repeatedly broken the law, had used violence and subterfuge to steal the possessions of other people or to destroy their livelihood, and had undermined every kind of moral or worldly authority as he saw fit.[17]

Another famous mercenary chieftain of the Thirty Years' War was Albrecht von Wallenstein (1583–1634), the last of the great mercenary captains who sprang from the Italian Renaissance. He was variously a Bohemian soldier, a statesman, and the commanding general of the armies of the Holy Roman Emperor Ferdinand II.[18] During the Thirty Years' War, he offered his services—backed up by an army of 30,000 to 100,000 men—to Ferdinand. He already had a string of mercenary successes to his credit. In 1617, for example, he used his inherited wealth to recruit and lead 200 cavalrymen during Ferdinand's war with Venice, thereby relieving the fortress of Gradisca during a Venetian siege.

After the Thirty Years' War began in 1618, Wallenstein raised a regiment of cuirassiers (mounted cavalry soldiers equipped with armor and firearms) and in 1619–1621 won great distinction under Charles Bonaventure de Longueval, the Count of Bucquoy, in clashes with Ernst von Mansfeld and Gabriel Bethlen. Then, in order to help Ferdinand, Wallenstein offered to raise an army of 24,000 men for the imperial service, following the principle of *bellum se ipsum alet*. (In Latin, this means "the war will feed itself"—in other words, both the food and the money needed to support an invading army would be seized from the people being attacked.)

Wallenstein received his commission for this war in 1625 and was remarkably successful. His achievements in the field brought him the former estates of conquered Bohemian nobles. He also loaned money to Ferdinand, who repaid him with lands and titles. Over time, however, Ferdinand decided that Wallenstein had become too ambitious, was fundamentally untrustworthy, and was therefore such a potential threat that he had to be removed by force. The final result was that one night in 1634 an Irish mercenary captain named Walter Devereux and a few of his companions broke into the house where Wallenstein was staying and kicked open his bedroom door. Roused from sleep and unarmed, Wallenstein asked for quarter but instead Devereux ran him through with a halberd. After this assassination, Ferdinand rewarded the murderers with honors and riches.

The Thirty Years' War ground on for another 14 years after Wallenstein's death. The famous "tree of battle" depicted by J. Christoph Grimmelshausen (ca. 1621–1676), who saw military service in the last dozen years of the Thirty Years' War can be usefully cited. His remarkable work, entitled *Simplicissimus the Vagabond*, was written in 1668 and has no parallel.

The roots of Grimmelshausen's "tree of battle" are the peasants, who give it strength. Its lower branches are full of common soldiers, known as "hen roost-robbers" and as "coat-beaters" (that is to say thieves and brawlers: i.e., by extension, mercenaries), and who are insolent, swaggering, and vile. On the uppermost branches of the "tree," however, perch in great comfort the "higher" folk who fill their pockets from the fattest and best pieces of the "tree," which are cut from its roots. These dignitaries are permanently separated from the teeming hoards in the lower branches by a very smooth place on the trunk of the tree, which is "greased with all manner of ointments and curious soap of disfavour, so that no man save of noble birth could scale it."[19]

The most important point here is that mercenaries continued to be very widely used in this era. Christian IV, the king of Denmark-Norway, for example, raised an army of 20,000 mercenaries, plus a national army of 15,000 men. Gustavus II Adolphus, the king of Sweden, recruited large numbers of German and Scottish mercenaries. The revolting excesses of the mercenaries (see below), however, contributed to the rise of better-disciplined professional standing armies later on.

Perhaps the Thirty Years' War can be summarized by noting that it continued for 30 years; that it involved at various times some 17 states, i.e., political entities of one kind or another; and that it generated about eight million casualties, both military and civilian. Mercenaries and other marauders were responsible for much of the sufferings and deaths experienced by the civilian populations in their paths. One method of torture and execution, known as the *Schwedentrunk*, a German word meaning "Swedish Drink," is perhaps the most interesting.

This phrase was coined by the German victims of Swedish troops during the Thirty Years' War. The techniques it connoted were widely used by other soldiers and especially by the civilians who followed the Swedish baggage train, who received no pay. This translation of a con-temporary German description of this process describes what happened:

> They [the torturers] laid the bound servant [the victim] on the ground, stuck a wooden wedge in his mouth, and poured [using a funnel] into his belly a bucket full of foul manure water, which they call a Swedish Drink.[20]

The *Schwedentrunk* was used throughout the occupied towns of southern Germany to force peasants or townspeople to surrender their hidden money, food, or animals, or to extort sex from women. There were vari-ations on this theme but the basic idea was to make a tied and gagging victim swallow a large amount of urine, excrement, liquid manure, or sullage ("gray water," i.e., wastewater from a household). Because such items are liquid, they cannot be compressed. As a result, the victim's stomach and bowels were forced to expand to painful proportions. The torturers then either used wooden boards to squeeze the belly or simply trampled the victim underfoot. Like "waterboarding" in present times, this process must have worked very well: the victims had no choice, if they wished to live, but to give in to their torturers' demands.

Conclusion

The mercenaries discussed in this book were the highly-skilled products of many generations of endemic warfare in Western Europe. They flourished in regions where political and therefore military authority was weak or non-existent and where, as a result, they had a good chance of finding jobs as soldiers. When there was a formal peace or merely a long lull in the fighting, they had no choice but to become brigands in order to survive. Mercenaries included fighters of many different kinds. Some were knights; others were men-of-war; still others were sergeants or squires; most, however, were simply very tough foot soldiers. In all cases, however, they had to be able to master new skills, e.g., how handle, safely and effectively, many different types of lethal weapons.

The Merovingians, for example, favored a throwing axe known as the francisca. The English excelled at the use of the longbow. The Genoese were famous for their skill with the crossbow. The long pikes and the ferocity of the Swiss made them the most sought-after mercenary troops of their age. Welsh and Cornish knifemen ran up behind the advancing line of their own side's men-at-arms and, with rondel daggers, dispatched any fallen but still living soldiers who seemed too poor to pay ransom. Sappers dug tunnels to undermine castles and fortifications. Genoese galley-hands fought at the naval battle of Sluys in 1340.

Going back to the two fundamental questions raised in the Preface of this book, a third needs to be added. These three questions are:

- Who were the medieval and Renaissance mercenaries?
- What did they do?
- Why did mercenaries continue to flourish even after the rise of standing armies?

Partial answers to these questions are already scattered throughout the text, but it may be useful to pull them together, very briefly, in this final chapter.

Regarding the first question above, many young men, especially those who were living in violence-prone, chronically-impoverished regions and who were not married, had very little to lose — and potentially a great deal to gain — by becoming mercenaries. As the English philosopher Thomas Hobbes put it in *Leviathan* (1651),

> Whatsoever therefore is consequent to a time of Warre, where every man is Enemy to every man; the same is consequent to the time, wherein men live without other security, than that their own strength, and their own invention, shall furnish them withall. In such condition ... the life of man [is] solitary, poore, nasty, brutish, and short.[1]

If faced with such depressing prospects in life, it is no wonder that some of the most adventuresome — or the most desperate — young men decided to put the plow aside and take up the sword instead.

Kings and princes had the right and the power to summon all able-bodied men to arms at times of great danger — say, when facing an invasion — but these potentates had no interest in arming their whole populations. To do so would not only be expensive and administratively difficult, but it might also encourage armed revolts against the established order. Scholars today are not entirely sure how infantrymen were recruited in the earliest days of the Middle Ages but as the money economy of Europe gradually became stronger, there are more and more mentions of paid men; indeed, such men came to represent a major element in most armies by the mid–12th century.[2] Thus *pay*, rather than national need, coercion, or feudal obligation, increasingly became the best way to recruit young men and to replace them when they were killed or injured.

It bears repeating here, however, that the military profession in medieval and Renaissance Europe was never a simple or straightforward calling. A traditional agricultural economy was usually not rich enough to pay for a permanent army staffed with large numbers of men well-equipped with expensive horses, armor, and weapons. The net result was that rulers relied on short-term armies instead. These were more affordable than standing armies but were not without their own problems. As John France explains,

Short-term armies were made up of many different kinds of people enjoying complicated relationships with their commanders. We may talk of the army of this king or that, but most soldiers probably saw themselves as being the men of a whole host of lesser captains and lords. The greater army was a composite of retinues and hirelings [i.e., mercenaries], and though the overall commander's money held the whole thing together like cement, it was less a monolith than a network of complicated relationships.[3]

Regarding the second question listed above, mercenaries could do, or could be trained to do, virtually any job a regular (non-mercenary) medieval or Renaissance soldier in an army could do. However, mercenaries were expensive, so they probably were not normally assigned to low-level support duties—e.g., transporting supplies, handling livestock, cooking, etc.—where cheaper unskilled labor would have been available and where their own hard-won combat skills would have been wasted entirely.

Since rank-and-file mercenaries were almost always illiterate and never wrote about their wartime experiences, there is not much information on what they really did on a day-by-day basis. Fortunately, however, the more than 100 miniature illustrations in Froissart's *Chroniques* are available. These give the modern reader an accurate picture of the heat of battle in late medieval times—and, by extension—a picture of what mercenaries had to endure in order to earn their wages. So, as promised earlier in this book, the reader's attention is now directed to one of the best of these manuscripts—i.e., BNF (Bibliothèque de France) FR 2643—because it contains such exceptionally useful and colorful pictures of medieval warfare. Some of the illustrations are described here, with their Bibliothèque de France reference numbers so interested readers can find them relatively easily.[4]

Illustration BNF (Ms FR 2643 f 207), for example, depicts the battle of Poitiers in 1356: in the course of this fight, some 300 French knights, accompanied by a battalion of German mercenary pikemen, were defeated by English archers. This illustration shows some of the French knights in action but does not show the German pikemen in action. They are seen standing in the French line of battle under the French flag and have not lowered their pikes to charge the English. One can easily imagine, however, that if the English archers had not prevailed, the pikemen might well have made short work of the English troops because few if any of them wore heavy armor.

The illustration shows the two armies facing each other — the French on the viewer's right, and the English on his or her left. In some places these armies, both bristling with weapons, are only two or three paces apart. Looking at them though a magnifying glass (useful because the illustrations are miniatures and the enlargements available on the Internet are rather fuzzy), one is immediately struck by the carnage so graphically displayed here. The French are clearly having a bad time of it:

- In the right foreground, a French knight in armor, facing away from the English and wounded himself, reels forward, trying hard to keep his seat in the saddle of his badly-wounded horse, which has two arrows sticking in its rump and is already down on its knees.
- Directly behind him, a second French knight in armor, also facing away from the English, has an arrow sticking out of his back; his horse has an arrow in its rump and another in a rear leg.
- Behind this second French knight, a third French knight in armor has turned in his saddle and defies the English with his drawn sword — while trying to control his terrified horse, which is plunging away from the English line of battle and which has three arrows in its rump and leg.
- At the same time, on the left side of the illustration, one can see that an English archer has just released an arrow at the third French knight (his arrow is shown in mid-flight and at such close range it is certain to hit the knight), while another English archer has his bow at full-draw and is just about to release yet another arrow at the same French knight, also at very close range.

Another Froissart illustration — BNF (Ms FR 2643 f 272) — records the battle of Brignais in 1362. This battle was a fine example of mercenary prowess: during it the free companies soundly defeated the French army.

The illustration is centered on a road rising uphill through some mountains. On the upper left, a group of mercenaries is attacking a large French army, shown on the right. Remarkably, the mercenaries are attacking the French by hurling big rocks at them. Half way up the road, i.e., between the mercenaries and the army, four French knights, afoot and wearing armor, are vainly trying to protect themselves, using their shields, from this barrage of rocks. They are surrounded by dead French soldiers, however, so the mercenaries clearly seem to have the upper hand.

The short answer to the third question — why did mercenaries continue to flourish even after the rise of standing armies?— is that there still remained a need for them. What rulers learned during the Thirty Years' War was that it could be very difficult to control mercenary forces. This fact, coupled with the increasing prosperity of Western Europe, encouraged kings to raise and to fund their own centrally-controlled national standing armies. Nevertheless, there were often times and places where an experienced body of professional soldiers, who fought only for pay and who could be used or discarded at the will of their employer, could be a very useful asset indeed.

In summary, this book on medieval and Renaissance mercenaries looks at history from a new and different perspective. Most readers are accustomed to learning about historical events as if these events were full-stage productions directed by Shakespeare. In that case, it is easy enough to focus on the main actors of the drama —for example, on the mightiest kings, the greatest Popes, the cleverest usurpers of power — and on the rise and fall of dynasties.

The stage, however, as Shakespeare well knew, has its own limitations. What can physically be shown on stage is of necessity shunted off-stage. Such scenes may be alluded to and perhaps even described but they will always remain in the shadows. This is the case with the countless but nameless rank-and-file mercenaries alluded to in this book. This book has tried to cast some light on these shadowy back-stage players, as well as on their more-visible commanders. To the extent that it has succeeded, the reader gets a better understanding of these men, who were the backbone of an evolving world marked more by brutality and violence than by chivalry and pious prayer.

Appendix 1: Armor

Good armor was expensive, but not prohibitively so. The price of armor varied considerably over the years. In Genoa, in about 1250 it would have cost some 1,400 grams of silver, i.e., a knight's wages for between a month and a month and a half, to provide armor for a knight and his squire. In the beginning of the 14th century in England, however, the same equipment would have only cost about £1, representing perhaps 10 days' wages for a knight.[1]

Protection for the Head

Mail coif. A mail hood, usually worn with a hauberk, i.e., a knee-length shirt of mail made of up to 15,000 interlocking iron rings.

Great helm. A stereotypical knight's helm from the Crusader period. Often removed at a tournament after the initial "clash of lances" because it hindered sight and breathing and was very hot.

Cervelliere. A steel skullcap worn underneath a great helm.

Bassinet. Replaced the great helm by the mid–14th century; much used by infantry and also by cavalry.

Armet. A stereotypical knight's helm, favored in Italy.

Sallet. A favored helm in England and Western Europe; may have influenced the design of German helmets in World War II.

Close helm. A bowl helmet with a visor.

Close helmet. An early form of a helmet with a moveable visor.

Barbute. Close-fitting helmet reminiscent of ancient Greek helmets.

Burgonet. Open-face bowl-shaped helmet.

Protection for the Neck

Aventail or camail. Detachable mail hung from a helmet to protect the neck and shoulders.

Gorget. Steel collar to protect the neck.

Bevor. A piece of plate armor, worn with a sallet to cover the jaw and throat.

Protection for the Torso

Brigantine. Cloth, canvas or leather garment lined with small steel plates.

Hauberk or haubergeon. Mail shirt with sleeves reaching to the mid-thigh.

Cuirass. A breastplate.

Pixane. A mail collar.

Plackart. Extra layer of armor to cover the belly.

Fauld. Bands to protect the front waist and hips.

Culet. Small horizontal lames, i.e., bands of steel plate, which protect the small of the back or the buttocks.

Cowter. Plate that guards the elbow.

Spaulder. Bands of plate that cover the shoulder and part of upper arm.

Pauldron. Covers the shoulder, armpit, and sometimes the back and chest.

Gardbrace. Extra plate that covers the front of the shoulder.

Rerebrace or brassart. Plate that covers the section of upper arm from elbow to area covered by shoulder armor.

Besagew. Circular plate that covers the armpit.

Vambrace. Forearm guard.

Gauntlet. Gloves that cover from the fingers to the forearms.

Guard of vambrace. An additional layer of armor.

Protection for the Legs

Chausses. Mail hose, either knee-high or covering the whole leg.

Poleyn. Plate that covers the knee.

Schynbald. Plate that covers only the shins.

Greave. Covers the lower leg, back and front.

Cuisse. Plate that covers the thighs.

Sabaton or solleret. Covers the foot.

Tassete or tuille. Bands hanging from faulds or breastplate to protect the upper legs.

Protection for Other Parts of the Body

Gousset. Mail that protects areas not covered by plate.

Lame. Bands of steel plate.

Doublet or arming doublet. Padded cloth worn under armor.

Rondel. Any circular plate.[2]

Appendix 2: Swiss Mercenaries

In *Hamlet* Act IV, Scene 5, Shakespeare has the king call out: "Where are my Switzers? Let them guard the door."[1] Here Shakespeare is referring to the famous Swiss mercenaries, whose courage, reliability, and battlefield skills made them the most sought-after mercenaries during the Late Middle Ages. Their discipline and training even allowed them to withstand cavalry charges. Because they were so good at their work, it is worth saying something here, very briefly, about their abilities.

The modern scholars Michael Mallett and Christine Shaw tell us this about the Swiss mercenaries:

> The French could boast the finest heavy cavalry in Europe in the *companies d'ordonnance*, permanent units raised and paid for by the Crown, in which the French competed to serve. For infantry, the French had come to rely heavily on Swiss mercenaries. In the 1490s, the reputation of the Swiss stood very high. They were a different kind of "national" army. A well-established system of training, organized by the governments of the cantons, resulted in a high proportion of able-bodied men having the strength and ability to handle pikes, halberds and two-handed swords, and the discipline to execute complex manoeuvres in formations of several thousand men.[2]

Employers hired these men not only for their military skills but also because entire contingents could be recruited simply by contacting the Swiss cantons. Young men there were required to serve in the militia system, were willing and well-prepared to do so, and welcomed the chance to serve abroad. Alternatively, Swiss men could also hire themselves out individually or in small groups. It is clear that the Swiss were hard fighters and hard-headed businessmen as well. Their motto was: *pas d'argent, pas de Swisse* (no money, no Swiss).

Appendix 2: Swiss Mercenaries

Swiss mercenaries were highly valued through late medieval Europe because of the power of their determined mass attacks, in deep columns, with pikes and halberds. They specialized in sending large columns of soldiers into battle in "pike squares." These were well-trained, well-disciplined bands of men armed with long steel-tipped poles and were grouped into 100-man formations that were 10 men wide and 10 men deep. On command, pike squares could wheel and maneuver so quickly that it was nearly suicidal for horsemen or infantrymen to attack them. As they came at their enemy with leveled pikes and hoarse battle cries, they were almost invincible.

These Swiss soldiers were equally proficient in the use of crossbows, early firearms, swords, and halberds. A halberd is an axe blade topped with a spike and mounted on a long shaft. If the need arose, they could easily lay their pikes aside and take up other weapons instead. They were so effective that between about 1450 and 1500 every major leader in Europe either hired Swiss pikemen or hired fighters like the German Landsknecht who copied Swiss tactics. The extensive and continuous demand for these specialist Swiss and landsknecht pike companies may well have given them the illusion of permanency. In any case, what it did show was that medieval and Renaissance warfare was becoming better disciplined, more organized, and more professional.

Swiss fighters were responding to several interrelated factors: limited economic opportunities in their home mountains; pride in themselves and their colleagues as world-class soldiers; and, last but not least, by a love of adventure and combat. In fact, they were such good fighters that the Swiss enjoyed a near-monopoly on pike-armed military service for many years. One of their successes was the battle of Novara in northern Italy 1513 between France and the Republic of Venice, on the one hand, and the Swiss Confederation and the Duchy of Milan, on the other. The story runs as follows.

A French army, said by some sources to total 1,200 cavalrymen and about 20,000 Landsknechts, Gascons, and other troops, was camped near and was besieging Novara. This city was being held by some of the Duke of Milan's Swiss mercenaries. A Swiss relief army of some 13,000 Swiss troops unexpectedly fell upon the French camp. The pike-armed Landsknechts managed to form up into their combat squares; the Landsknecht infantrymen took up their proper positions; and the French were able to get some of their cannons into action. The Swiss, however, surrounded the French camp, captured the cannons, broke up the Landsknecht pike squares, and forced back the Landsknecht infantry regiments.

The fight was very bloody: the Swiss executed hundreds of the Landsknechts they had captured, and 700 men were killed in three minutes by heavy artillery fire alone. To use a later English naval term from the days of sail, the "butcher's bill" (the list of those killed in action) was somewhere between 5,000 and 10,000 men. Despite this Swiss success, however, the days of their supremacy as the world's best mercenaries were numbered. In about 1515, the Swiss pledged themselves to neutrality, with the exception of Swiss soldiers serving in the ranks of the royal French army. The Landsknechts, on the other hand, would continue to serve any paymaster and would even fight each other if need be. Moreover, since the rigid battle formations of the Swiss were increasingly vulnerable to arquebus and artillery fire, employers were more inclined to hire the Landsknechts instead.

In retrospect, it is clear that the successes of Swiss soldiers in the 15th and early 16th centuries were due to three factors:

- Their courage was extraordinary. No Swiss force ever broke in battle, surrendered, or ran away. In several instances, the Swiss literally fought to the last man. When they were forced to retreat in the face of overwhelming odds, they did so in good order while defending themselves against attack.
- Their training was excellent. Swiss soldiers relied on a simple system of tactics, practiced until it became second nature to every man. They were held to the mark by a committee-leadership of experienced old soldiers.
- They were ferocious and gave no quarter, not even for ransom, and sometimes violated terms of surrender already given to garrisons and pillaged towns that had capitulated. These qualities inspired fear in their opponents.[3]

Chronology

Late 4th century	Vegetius writes *De re militari* (*On Military Matters*), a handbook still very popular in the Middle Ages.
476	The western portion of the Roman Empire ceases to exist (the eastern portion will endure until 1453).
ca. 752	Some of the Merovingians are probably the first medieval mercenaries. Their dynasty ends in 752, when their last ruler is deposed.
832	The Duke of Naples is said to hire Saracen (Muslim) mercenaries in southern Italy.
839	When civil war breaks out in Sicily, the two princes struggling for power both hire Saracen mercenaries.
911	Varangians first serve as mercenaries for the Byzantines.
988	The Varangian Guard will become one of the most famous mercenary corps of history.
991	The battle of Conquereuil: Count Fulk Nerra of Anjou uses mercenaries against Count Conan of Brittany.
999	Norman pilgrims help defend the city of Salerno against a Muslim attack. This experience prepares the ground for Norman mercenaries to flock to Italy.
1015–1066	Harald Hardrada leads mercenaries for the Byzantine Empire and then for the Normans in Sicily.
ca. 1024	Violence is deeply rooted in medieval social structure and mentality: Bishop Burchard deplores the many murders committed by his own parishioners.
1046–1085	The Norman adventurer Robert Guiscard plays a key role in the Norman conquest of southern Italy.
1066	William the Conqueror uses mercenaries when he launches his

181

conquest of England and relies on them to help keep him in power thereafter.

1071   The Norman adventurer Roussel de Bailleul refuses to send his mercenaries into the battle of Manzikert, foreseeing that it will be a disaster for his Byzantine employers.

1083–1163   Anna Comnena (Greek princess, scholar, doctor, hospital administrator, and daughter of the Byzantine Emperor) describes the Varangian Guardsmen in favorable terms.

1094   The Spanish hero El Cid, having served as a mercenary captain for both Christian and Muslim leaders, carves out his own fiefdom in Valencia.

After 1140   Following the failure of the Second Crusade, unemployed mercenaries and common criminals jeopardize law and order in France.

1141   The high point of the career of the mercenary leader William of Ypres was probably the Rout of Winchester.

1140s–   The troubadour Bertrand de Born extolls warfare as an excit-
ca. 1215   ing adventure but has a low opinion of mercenaries.

1167   Henry II of England brilliantly uses Welsh mercenaries when attacking the French town of Chaumont.

1173   Henry II of England relies on mercenaries to bring his rebellious family into line.

1199   Mercadier, a French mercenary captain, avenges King Richard's death by flaying alive the young crossbowman who shot the king.

1204   Lupescar, another famous French mercenary commander, is blamed for England's loss of Normandy to France.

1215   Magna Carta, the great charter of English liberties, calls for the expulsion of all foreign mercenaries from England.

1217   English sailors capture and behead the French mercenary-sailor Eustache the Monk.

1224   Holy Roman Emperor Frederick II decides to resettle Sicilian Muslims on the mainland in Lucera.

1266   At the battle of Benevento, two rival factions—the Guelfs and the Ghibellines—use French, German, and Italian mercenaries.

1290–late   Three groups of Irish mercenaries—the galloglas, the kerns,
1500s   and the redshanks—are sequentially active in Ireland

1292	The term "chivalry" makes its first appearance in English.
1303	The Italian adventurer Roger de Flor founds a mercenary unit known as the Catalan Company. He is considered to have been the first great Italian *condottiere* (mercenary captain).
1337–1453	Mercenaries find ready employment during the Hundred Years' War.
1340	The battle of Sluys took place between a French fleet (staffed with mercenary Genoese galleys and crossbowmen) and an English fleet.
1342	The mercenary leader Werner von Urslingen founds the first Great Company of mercenaries.
1346	Neither the mercenary Genoese crossbowmen nor the French knights fight well at the battle of Crécy.
1346–1347	The major use of ships in medieval warfare is to carry troops: 738 ships are needed to transport Edward III's troops across the English Channel to France.
1351	The Combat of the Thirty, which involve both mercenaries and knights, is long hailed as an example of the finest chivalry.
1356	German mercenary pikemen and Scottish mercenaries see action at the battle of Poitiers.
1358	The Jacquerie, a peasant revolt in northern France, is caused in part by the government's inability to control unemployed mercenaries and common outlaws.
1360	The Treaty of Brétigny encourages some unemployed mercenaries to coalesce into the Great Companies.
1362	The battle of Brignais enriches mercenaries.
1364–1365	Papal bulls are issued denouncing the mercenary companies.
ca. 1365– *ca.* 1430	Christine de Pisan writes both poetry and a book on chivalry.
1366	The civil war in Spain attracts mercenary troops.
1367	Battle of Najera: the Black Prince and his mercenaries defeat Enrique of Trastámara and restore Pedro I to his throne.
1394	Death of the famous English mercenary commander John Hawkwood.
1410	In the battle of Grunwald/Tannenberg, the power of the Teutonic Order is broken for once and for all.

1415	Battle of Agincourt.
1418	The mercenary Scotts Guard is formed and becomes valued by the kings of France.
1424	The mercenary captain La Hire establishes his reputation by a daring raid on a Burgundian town.
1429	Battle of the Herrings.
1433	Rodrigo de Villandrando leads 10,000 mercenaries in France.
1445	King Charles VII of France takes the first step toward a standing army.
ca. 1450	Technological advances make firearms more effective on the battlefield.
ca. 1466	Jean V de Bueil writes *Le Jouvencel*, a military primer for young noblemen.
ca. 1471	Death of Sir Thomas Malory, author of *Le Morte d'Arthur*.
1476	The "studiolo" ("small study") of the mercenary leader Federico da Montefeltro is still considered a masterpiece today.
1477	The stunning success of the Swiss mercenaries at the battle of Nancy encourages more European leaders to hire them.
1478	During the Pazzi conspiracy, the failure of mercenaries to kill Lorenzo de Medici leads to their own deaths.
1487	At its peak strength, the mercenary Black Army of Hungary could field some 28,000 men. In that same year, Maximilian I founds the Landsknecht mercenaries.
1495–1559	The eight Italian wars.
1520s	The father of modern Sweden, Gustav Vasa, hires mercenaries to seize power for him.
1532	Publication of Machiavelli's *The Prince*.
1618–1648	Thirty Years' War.
d. 1626	Ernst von Mansfeld is the most famous mercenary leader of the early period of the Thirty Years' War.
d. 1634	Albrecht von Wallenstein is the last of the great mercenary captains who sprang from the Italian Renaissance.
1645	The New Model Army is founded in England.
1668	Grimmelshausen's "tree of battle" summarizes the last dozen years of the Thirty Years' War.

Chapter Notes

Preface

1. See France, "Mercenaries and Paid Men: The Mercenary Identity in the Middle Ages."

2. After Mallett, *Mercenaries and Their Masters*, p. 116.

Introduction

1. There are five versions of what the Pope allegedly said at the Council of Clermont. These accounts, all of which were written after Jerusalem had been captured by the Crusaders, differ so substantially that we do not know precisely what the Pope said there.

2. Verbruggen, *The Art of Warfare in Western Europe During the Middle Ages*, p. 124.

3. Wikipedia, "First Crusade," pp. 10–11, citing Nicolle, *The First Crusade*, pp. 21, 32.

4. Mallet, *Mercenaries and Their Masters*, p. 258.

5. After Kreutz, *Before the Invaders*, p. 20.

6. This paragraph is drawn from France, "An Account of the Battle of Hattin Referring to the Frankish mercenaries in Oriental Muslim States," pp. 172–173.

7. Mallett, "Mercenaries," p. 228.

8. Some of these comments are drawn from a private communication from Dr. John France of 29 January 2012.

9. Nicholson, *Medieval Warfare*, p. 53.

10. Quoted by Verbruggen, *The Art of Warfare in Western Europe During the Middle Ages*, p. 69.

11. Quoted in "Squires," p. 1.

12. After Morillo, *Warfare under the Anglo-Norman Kings*, pp. 74–77.

13. After Morillo, *Warfare under the Anglo-Norman Kings*, pp. 55, 76.

14. After Rice, "Mercenaries of the Angevin Empire," p. 3.

15. Some of these points are drawn from a private communication of 30 December 2011 from Dr. William Caferro.

16. Caferro, *John Hawkwood*, p. 91.

17. Medieval war, however, did not aim at the complete destruction or the unconditional surrender of an enemy. Lack of resources, coupled with the class and religious ethics of the time, often resulted in indecisive campaigns, battles, and peace agreements. (Adapted from Morillo, *Warfare under the Anglo-Norman Kings, 1066–1135*, p. 28.)

18. Cited by Contamine, *War in the Middle Ages*, p. 308.

19. After Prestwich, "The Gunpowder Revolution, 1300–1500," p. 184.

20. After Morillo, *Warfare Under the Anglo-Norman Kings, 1066–1135*, pp. 14–15.

21. Quoted by Verbruggen, *The Art of Warfare During the Middle Ages*, p. 37.

22. After Barker, *Conquest*, pp. 76–77.

23. Quoted by Wright, *Knights and Peasants*, p. 26.

24. Quoted by Verbruggen, *The Art of Warfare in Western Europe in the Middle Ages*, p. 38.

25. Quoted by Wright, *Knights and Peasants*, p. 40, citing *Le Jouvencel*, i, pp. 95–96 and ii, p. 83.

26. Quoted by Murphy, *Condottiere 1300–1500*, p. 44.

27. After Nicholson, *Medieval Warfare*, pp. 45–46.

28. Some of these comments are drawn from private communications with Dr. John France.

29. After Contamine, *War in the Middle Ages*, p. 117.

30. Caferro, *John Hawkwood*, p. 68.

31. Caferro, *John Hawkwood*, p. 68.

32. After Keen, pp. 228–229.

33. Bloch, *Feudal Society*, Vol. II, p. 411. Italics added.

34. Reuter, "Carolingian and Ottonian Warfare," p. 13.

35. After Bloch, *Feudal Society*, II, pp. 411–412.

36. After Janin, *Medieval Justice*, pp. 13–16.

37. Bloch, *Feudal Society*, Vol. II, pp. 411–412.

38. Malory, *Le Morte d'Arthur*, Vol. II, p. 458.

39. Malory, *Le Morte d'Arthur*, Vol. II, pp. 462–463,

40. Nicholson, *Medieval Warfare*, p. 17.

41. The 9 x 19mm Parabellum pistol cartridge was designed by Georg Luger and introduced in 1902 by the German weapons manufacturer Deutsche Waffen-und Munitionsfabriken (DMW) for its Luger semi-automatic pistol. For this reason, the cartridge is often called the 9 mm Luger cartridge.

42. The modern historian Helen Nicholson notes that while there is an obvious similarity between these late Roman federates and the great mercenary companies of the fourteenth century (we shall discuss these companies later on), the men of the companies came from within the fold of Western European Roman Catholicism, not from outside it. The Germanic tribesmen employed as federates were either pagans or Arian Christians. After Nicholson, *Medieval Warfare*, pp. 42–43.

43. After McKitterick, *The Early Middle Ages*, p. 61.

44. Flavius Vegetius Renatus, *On Roman Military Matters*, p. 33. This passage has been broken up for ease of reading.

45. Wikipedia, "Chivalry," p. 1.

46. Quoted by Pernoud, *Lumière du Moyen Age*, p. 263.

47. Some of the observations in this section are drawn from Nicholson, *Medieval Warfare*, pp. 148–163.

48. After France, "Mercenaries and Paid Men: The Mercenary Identity in the Middle Ages," p. 4.

49. "Angevin" refers to the Angevin Empire, a collection of states ruled by the Angevin Plantagenet dynasty. The Plantagenets controlled an area extending from the Pyrenees to Ireland during the 12th and early 13th century. This empire included about half of medieval France, all of England, and part of Ireland.

50. After Pryor, "Soldiers of Fortune in the Fleets of Charles I of Anjou," p. 137.

51. After Prestwich, "The Challenge to Chivalry: Longbow and Pike, 1275–1475," pp. 180–181.

Chapter I

1. After Latzko, "The Market for Mercenaries," p. 3.

2. The best candidates for ransom were men of high social and therefore financial status. Prisoners of much lower standing were not good candidates for ransom. How they were treated depended on a number of factors which defy generalization. For example, William I's lieutenants mutilated and exiled the Flemish mercenaries they captured in 1075 and confiscated their possessions. On the other hand, that same year the Breton mercenaries captured by the English were granted their lives and were spared mutilation when they swore to leave England within 30 days and never to return without the king's permission. After Morillo, *Warfare Under the Anglo-Norman Kings 1066–1135*, p. 178.

3. Wright, *Knights and Peasants*, p. 53,

4. The quotation and facts of this section are drawn from Wikipedia, "Jean Froissart," pp. 2–6.

5. Quoted by Wright, *Knights and Peasants*, pp. 13–14, citing Froissart, *Chroniques*, ed. Luce, i, p. 1.

6. Favier, *La Guerre de Cent Ans*, p. 303. Translated by Hunt Janin.

7. Adapted from Wright, *Knights and Peasants*, p. 57.

8. After Mallett, *Mercenaries and Their Masters*, p. 15.

9. France, "Crusading warfare and its adaptation to eastern conditions in the twelfth century," p. 58.

10. An interesting fact is that paid soldiers, whether they were paid in cash or in kind, played an important role in England throughout the Anglo-Saxon period but, as a general statement, mercenaries did not. The lack of mercenaries in pre-Viking England was due to (1) an aristocratic ethos which emphasized reciprocal loyalty between lord and man, and (2) an economy in which commercial exchange played only a modest role. After Abels, "Household Men, Mercenaries and Vikings," pp. 160–161.

11. Some of the comments in this section are drawn from France, "Mercenaries and Paid Men. The Mercenary Identity in the Middle Ages," pp. 1, 11–12.

12. After Allmand, *The Hundred Years War*, p. 48.

13. Adapted from France, "Mercenaries, and Paid Men. The Mercenary Identity in the Middle Ages," p. 18.

14. After France, "Mercenaries and Ca-puchins in Southern France in the Late Twelfth Century," pp. 296, 311–312. This movement seems to have achieved a good deal in a short time but it petered out when senior clerics realized that princely power was sus-tained by the mercenaries. The Capuchins dis-cussed here must not be confused with the later Order of Capuchin Friars Minor.

15. After France, "Mercenaries and Paid Men," p. 6.

16. Quoted by Crouch, "William Marshal and the Mercenariat," p. 18.

17. After Nicholson, *Medieval Warfare*, p. 49.

18. After Verbruggen, *The Art of Warfare in Western Europe During the Middle Ages*, p. 51.

19. Brigandage in medieval times is a sub-ject that resists easy definition. On the one hand, some brigands were simply criminals who took advantage of chaotic local conditions to rob, rape, pillage, and kidnap simply in order to survive and to line their own pockets.. Other brigands, particularly those active during France's wars with En-gland, have been hailed by some modern his-torians as comprising a kind of medieval French Resistance against the English invaders. See Barker, *Conquest*, p. 65.

20. France, "Mercenaries and Paid Men. The Mercenary Identify in the Middle Ages," pp. 11–12.

21. After "Knighthood Training," pp. 1–2.

22. After Hosler, "Revisiting Mercenaries under Henry Fitz Empress, 1167–1188," pp. 37–38.

23. After Verbruggen, *The Art of Warfare in Western Europe During the Middle Ages*, p. 127.

24. Quoted in Prestwich, "The Gunpowder Revolution, 1300–1500," p. 201.

25. This and the following examples are taken from Verbruggen, *The Art of Warfare in Western Europe During the Middle Ages*, pp. 129–144.

26. Wishful thinking had always played a big role in the *chansons de geste* and continued to attract later medieval audiences. In 1378, for example, Owain Lawgoch (a Welsh mer-cenary who claimed the title of Prince of Wales), was, on the orders of the English, as-sassinated at the siege of Mortagne-sur-mer in France. After his death, however, Welsh poets spread the message that he was merely asleep in a cave, awaiting his day of destiny. Jenkins, *A Concise History of Wales*, pp. 109–110.

27. Private communication of 23 October 2012 from Dr. John France.

28. Quoted by Wright, *Knights and Peas-ants*, p. 6.

29. This section draws heavily on "Me-dieval Weapons & Armour," pp. 1–47, and "Medieval Warfare," pp. 1–17.

30. Arms and Armor of the Late Middle Ages and Early Renaissance, "Training with Weapons: Weapons as Part of the Daily Life of the Warrior," pp. 5–7.

31. After Wikipedia, "Matter of France," p. 1.

32. After Goodrich, *Medieval Myths*, p. 89.

33. After Turnbull, *Tannenberg 1410*," p. 25.

34. Latzko, "The Market for Mercenaries," p. 8.

35. After Early Modern England, "Sports scientists examine the medieval archers of the Mary Rose," p. 1. Evidence from the wreck of the *Mary Rose* suggests that the commonest draw-weight of a medieval English longbow was between 150 and 160 pounds and that it was able to fire a 4-ounce arrow some 240 yards. Source: Barker, *Agincourt*, pp. 89–90.

36. Quoted in "Medieval Weapons & Ar-mour," p. 19. The author of this quote was not identified in the article.

37. The oak door may well have been split or otherwise weakened during the siege, mak-ing it possible for the arrows to penetrate it. Both these accounts are taken from Ver-bruggen, *The Art of Warfare in Western Europe During the Middle Ages*, p. 118.

38. Some of the information on crossbows is drawn from "Medieval Crossbow," pp. 1–4.

39. After Mallett, *Mercenaries and Their Masters*, p. 154.

40. Quoted by Contamine, *War in the Mid-dle Ages*, p. 71.

41. After Hardy, *Longbow*, pp. 44–46.

42. After Hardy, *Longbow*, p. 69.

43. After Prestwich, "The Gunpowder Revolution, 1300–1500," p. 203.

44. Quoted in Prestwich, "The Gunpowder Revolution, 1300–1500," p. 194. Italics added.

45. "Medieval Weapons & Armour," p. 34.

46. After Nicholson, *Medieval Warfare*, p. 116.

47. "Christine de Pisan," pp. 1–2.

48. After Nicholson, *Medieval Warfare*, pp. 88–89, and Contamine, *War in the Middle Ages*, pp. 141–142.

49. After Contamine, *War in the Middle Ages*, p. 143.

50. After Contamine, *War in the Middle Ages*, p. 96.

51. "Medieval Warfare," p. 1.
52. After Verbruggen, *The Art of Warfare in Western Europe During the Middle Ages*, pp. 188–189.

Chapter II

1. This account draws from Bachrach, *Merovingian Military Organization*, pp. 3–4.
2. Quoted by Norman, *The Medieval Soldier*, p. 11.
3. After "Merovingians," p. 1.
4. Medieval Warfare, "Throwing Axes— Franciscas," p. 17.
5. Quoted by Bachrach, *Merovingian Military Organization 481–751*, p. 132.
6. After Verbruggen, *The Art of Warfare in Western Europe During the Middle Ages*, p. 68.
7. Adapted from Bachrach, "Merovingian Mercenaries and Paid Soldiers in Imperial Perspective," pp. 183–184.
8. Parts of the following account are drawn from Wikipedia, "Antrustion."
9. Verbruggen, *The Art of Warfare in Western Europe During the Middle Ages*, p. 67.
10. After Loud, *The Age of Robert Guiscard*, p. 16.
11. After Kreutz, *Before the Normans*, p. 168, n28.
12. After Loud, *The Age of Robert Guiscard*, p. 16.
13. After Loud, *The Age of Robert Guiscard*, p. 50.
14. Kreutz, *Before the Normans*, p. 169, n47.
15. Some of the following information on Lucera is drawn from Wikipedia, "Muslim Settlement of Lucera," pp. 1–5.
16. Quoted by Tuchman, *A Distant Mirror*, pp. 320–321.
17. After Keen, *Medieval Warfare*, p. 214.
18. After Matthews, "Lucera, a Muslim Colony in Modern Italy," p. 2.
19. Sources used in this chapter include Wikipedia, "Byzantine Empire," "Byzantine Army," "Decline of the Byzantine Empire," and "Varangian Guard," and Soldiers of Misfortune, "The Varangian Guard: The Vikings in Byzantium."
20. Soldiers of Misfortune, "The Varangian Guard," p. 2. This quotation has been edited for ease of reading.
21. Quoted by Heath, *The Vikings*, p. 22.
22. Wikipedia, "Siege of Constantinople (1204)," quoting Angold, Michael, *The Byzantine Empire 1025–1204*, pp. 327–328.

23. The following information is drawn from D'Amato, *The Varangian Guard 988– 1453*, pp. 5–6, 12.

Chapter III

1. This process is well-described by G.A. Loud in *The Age of Robert Guiscard: Southern Italy and the Norman Conquest.*
2. Loud, *The Age of Robert Guiscard*, p. 60. This chapter also draws on other sections of Loud's book, e.g., pp. 61, 66.
3. Wikipedia, "Rainulf Drengot," p. 1, quoting Amatus of Montecassino, *History of the Normans*, Book I.
4. Quoted by Loud, *The Age of Robert Guiscard*, p. 2. No in-line citation is given for this quote.
5. Anna Comnena, *The Alexiad*, Book 1, p. 1.
6. Quoted by Loud, *The Age of Robert Guiscard*, p. 75.
7. Quoted by Holland, *Millennium*, p. 272.
8. Quoted by Loud, *The Age of Robert Guiscard*, p. 130.
9. Morillo, *Warfare Under the Anglo-Norman Kings 1066–1135*, pp. 17–18.
10. After Latzko, "The Market for Mercenaries," p. 2.
11. After Stenton, *Anglo-Saxon England*, pp. 585–586.
12. After Douglas, *William the Conqueror*, p. 191.
13. Quoted by Douglas, *William the Conqueror*, p. 192.
14. Drawn from a private communication of 19 May 2012 from Dr. John France.
15. After Oksanen, "The Anglo-Flemish Treaties and Flemish Soldiers in England, 1101–1163," p. 263.
16. After Douglas, *William the Conqueror*, p. 202.
17. Quoted by Verbruggen, *The Art of Warfare in Western Europe During the Middle Ages*, p. 281.
18. After Douglas, *William the Conqueror*, p. 279.
19. After Douglas, *William the Conqueror*, pp. 279, 280.
20. At the head of the *familia regis* we find the senior officers and commanders who administered the military system. The most important men were the military officers of the *domus regis*, which lay, as it were, in the exact center of the spider web of the entire govern-

ment. Its members included the chancellor, chamberlain, constables, master-marshal, and the deputy marshals. After Morillo, *Warfare Under the Anglo-Norman Kings, 1066–1135*, p. 61.

21. After Douglas, *William the Conqueror*, p. 280.

22. Adapted from the abstract of "Responses to the Threat of Invasion, 1085," p. 1.

23. Quoted by Douglas, *William the Conqueror*, p. 348.

24. Quoted by Morillo, *Warfare Under the Anglo-Norman Kings*, p. 52.

25. Sources used in this section on the Battle of Manzikert include the Latin Library's "Battle of Manzikert (1071 A.D.)"; Paul Markham's "Manzikert"; and Wikipedia's "Battle of Manzikert" and "Roussel de Bailleul."

26. From Anna Comnena, *The Alexiad*, Book 1, sections 7–8.

27. Quoted in the "Battle of Manzikert (1071 A.D.)," p. 4.

28. Private communication of 23 October 2012 from Dr. John France.

29. After the "Battle of Manzikert (1071 A.D.)," pp. 4–5, 6.

30. Sources used for this section on El Cid include Wikipedia, "El Cid" and "Cantar de Mio Cid"; New World Encyclopedia, "El Cid"; and Barton and Fletcher, *The World of El Cid*.

31. Ross, "The Story of the Poem of the Cid," p. 1.

32. See Barton and Fletcher's chapter, "*Historia Roderici*," in their *The World of El Cid*, pp. 90–147.

33. Quoted by Barton and Fletcher, *The World of El Cid*, p. 137.

34. Quoted by Barton and Fletcher, *The World of El Cid*, p. 146.

Chapter IV

1. Following Lindholm and Nicolle, *Medieval Scandinavian Armies (1)*, and after private communications of 1 September 2012 from Martin Rundkvist and of 13 September 2012 and 8 October 2012 from Thomas Roth.

2. After Norman, *The Medieval Soldier*, pp. 89–90.

3. Stenton, *Anglo-Saxon England*, p. 412.

4. After Heath, *The Vikings*, p. 49.

5. After Lindholm and Nicolle, *Medieval Scandinavian Armies (2)*, p. 21.

6. *Anglo-Saxon Chronicle*, "The Reign of King Stephen," pp. 2–3.

7. Verbruggen, *The Art of Warfare in Western Europe During the Middle Ages*, p. 129.

8. Quoted by Verbruggen, *The Art of Warfare in Western Europe During the Middle Ages*, p. 129.

9. Many of the following points come from Norgate, "William of Ypres," p. 3.

10. After Verbruggen, *The Art of Warfare in Western Europe During the Middle Ages*, pp. 129–130.

11. The crusader was at the same time both a pilgrim and a soldier, being bound by a solemn vow to visit the Holy Sepulcher as part of an organized and armed expedition. This vow was shown, proudly and publicly, by wearing a cross sewn to one's clothes. The vow was a permanent obligation which could be enforced by legal sanctions. As a practical matter, the sewn cross also made it much more difficult for a crusader to desert his unit when combat threatened. This fact helped officers to keep crusader armies intact under stressful conditions.

12. Sources used on the Second Crusade include Géraud, "Les Routiers au douzième siècle;" The ORB, "The Second Crusade"; and Wikipedia, "Second Crusade."

13. As is customary for papal bulls, this bull has become known by its first two words, "Quantum praedecessores," i.e., "How much our predecessors...."

14. After Wikipedia, "Second Crusade," p. 12.

15. This is adapted and translated from Géraud, "Les Routiers au douzième siècle," pp. 126–128.

16. After Gérard, "Les Routiers au douzième siècle," p. 128.

17. Quoted by France, "Mercenaries and Capuchins in Southern France in the Late Twelfth Century," p. 1.

18. After Hosler, "Revisiting Mercenaries Under Henry Fitz Empress, 1167–1188," p. 33.

19. Quoted by Verbruggen, *The Art of Warfare in Western Europe During the Middle Ages*, p. 28.

20. In this era, there was certainly no shortage of mercenaries. In southern France alone, in addition to the Basques the chronicler Godfrey of Breuil lists the following fighters-for-hire, not all of which can be identified today: *Brabançons, Hannuyers, Asperes, Pailler, Navar, Turlannales, Roma, Cotarel, Catalans,* and *Aragones.* After Verbruggen, *The Art of Warfare During the Middle Ages,* p. 134. The "Cotarel" were probably also known as the "Cotteraux." These two names are

thought to come either from the very low social status of the men — a "cotter" was a peasant farmer in the Scottish Highlands—or from their use of the lowly dagger (*couteau* in French) rather than the knightly sword. After Keen, *Medieval Warfare*, p. 213.

21. Medieval Sourcebook: Robert of Hoveden, p. 2.

22. Quoted by Verbruggen, *The Art of Warfare in Western Europe During the Middle Ages*, p. 141.

Chapter V

1. Sources used here include Wikipedia, "Mercadier," p. 1; Rice, "Mercenaries of the Angevin Empire," p. 5; Verbruggen, *The Art of Warfare in Western Europe During the Middle Ages*, pp. 136–137; France, *Mercenaries and Paid Men*, pp. 16–18; and Géraud, "Mercadier."

2. After Verbruggen, *The Art of Warfare in Western Europe During the Middle Ages*, p. 136.

3. Verbruggen, *The Art of Warfare in Western Europe During the Middle Ages*, pp. 136–137.

4. Quoted by Contamine, *Warfare in the Middle Ages*, p. 247.

5. After Verbruggen, *The Art of Warfare in Western Europe During the Middle Ages*, p. 137.

6. Quoted by France, *Mercenaries and Paid Men*, p. 3.

7. Quoted by Crouch, "William Marshal and the Mercenariat," p. 17.

8. After Crouch, "William Marshal and the Mercenariat," pp. 17–18.

9. Cited by Verbruggen, *The Art of Warfare in Western Europe During the Middle Ages*, p. 137.

10. Fordham University, "The Text of Magna Carta," clause 51, p. 5

11. Wikipedia, "First Barons' War," p. 5.

12. Much of this account is drawn from Ohlgren, *A Book of Medieval Outlaws*, p. xviii, and from Kelly, "Eustache the Monk," pp. 61–98.

13. In criminal cases in the Middle Ages, trial by combat was usually fought to the death of one of the parties. Champions could be hired if the principals were too old or otherwise prohibited from fighting. Eustache probably chose a champion because as a monk he was not allowed to shed blood. Hainfrois may have chosen one because he was too old. In any case, this fight is one the very rare —

and perhaps the only — recorded example of an innocent party losing a trial by combat. The outcome of such trials was believed to reflect the will of God. (Source: Kelly, "Eustache the Monk," notes 11 and 12, p. 300.

14. Quoted by Kelly, "Eustache the Monk," p. 92.

15. After Wikipedia, "Eustace the Monk," p. 2.

Chapter VI

1. Froissart, *Chronicles*, p. 363.

2. This section draws heavily on Marsden, *Galloglas*.

3. Quoted by Marsden, *Galloglas*, p. 2.

4. Dymmok, "A Treatice [sic] of Ireland," p. 2.

5. Quoted by Marsden, *Galloglas*, p. 81.

6. After Marsden, *Galloglas*, p. 107.

7. Quoted by Marsden, *Galloglas*, p. 110, and by McCullough, *Wars of the Irish Kings*, p. 243.

8. Quoted by Marsden, *Galloglas*, p. 79.

9. Quoted by Marsden, *Galloglas*, p. 115.

10. Prendergast, "Scots Mercenary Forces in Sixteenth Century Ireland," pp. 368, 378.

11. After Mallett, *Mercenaries and Their Masters*, pp. 207–108.

12. After U.S. Naval Academy, "Fourteenth-Century Mercenaries," p. 1.

13. Early Catalan mercenaries included William della Torre, who first appeared in Sienese service in 1277 as an undistinguished member of a band of 19 mercenaries and who was later noted for garrisoning Tuscan castles; and Diego de Rat, who was lent to Florence with his group of mercenaries by the Duke of Calabria and who eventually had 200 to 300 cavalrymen and as many as 500 infantrymen under his command. Mallett, *Mercenaries and their Masters*, pp. 25–26.

14. The Catalan chronicler Bernat Desclot described the Almogavars as follows: "The men whom we call Almogavars live exclusively by their arms and dwell neither in towns or villages, but only in forests and mountains. They fight daily against the Saracens, penetrating a day or two's march into Saracen territory, pillaging the collecting booty and bringing back with them numerous prisoners and many goods. They live off this booty...They are a very strong, quick and agile people eager in pursuit and difficult to follow." Quoted by Contamine, *War in the Middle Ages*, p. 73.

15. After Caffero, *John Hawkwood*, p. 64.

16. Medieval commentators tended to exaggerate the size of Western European armies but this must not obscure the fact that big armies did exist in other parts of Europe. The central imperial budget of the Ottoman Empire in 1528, for example, numbered some 120,000 to 150,000 members of regular military units, plus 47,000 mercenaries. After Bennett, *The Medieval World at War*, p. 221.

17. A French scholar, Y. Renouard, writing in 1968, gives us a good explanation of the *condotta* system. The businessmen of the Renaissance, he tells us,

knew that at certain moments war was necessary to advance the development of business and the prosperity of the [city-state]; they did not hesitate to declare it on occasion. But they did not fight themselves. Continual appeals to arms disturbed too much the good management of those [business] companies, those societies with world-wide connections, where everyone's talents found employment...Was it not reasonable and economical to avoid mobilizing the most efficient citizens and to pay mercenaries who could fight while merchants, active in their counting houses, earned the money to pay for them? This was the *condotta* system [Quoted by Contamine, *War in the Middle Ages*, p. 157, citing Y. Renouard, *Les hommes d'affaires italiens du Moyen Age*, Paris, 1968, p. 237].

18. After Mallett, *Mercenaries and Their Masters*, p. 107.

19. Contamine, *War in the Middle Ages*, p. 248.

20. Contamine, *War in the Middle Ages*, p. 248.

21. Some of these comments are drawn from Wikipedia, "The Duchy of Athens," pp. 1–5.

22. After Wikipedia, "Battle of Cephissus," pp. 1–2.

23. *The Chronicles of Sir John Froissart*, Chapter L, "The naval engagement between the king of England and the French before Sluys," p. 2.

24. "The Battle of Sluys," p. 3.

25. After Fowler, *Medieval Mercenaries*, p. 2.

26. Quoted by Paz, *The Role of Mercenary Troops in Spain in the Fourteenth Century: The Civil War*, p. 337.

27. After Mallett and Shaw, *The Italian Wars*, p. 2.

28. After Keen, *Medieval Warfare*, p. 218.

29. After Caffero, *John Hawkwood*, p. 64.

30. Quoted by Caffero, *John Hawkwood*, p. 62.

31. As Lieutenant-General of the King, the Constable of France outranked all the nobles and was second-in-command only to the King.

Chapter VII

1. Quoted by Contamine, *War in the Middle Ages*, citing Froissart, *Chroniques*.

2. After Nicolle, "The Failure of an Elite — The Genoese at Crécy," p. 2.

3. After Nicolle, "The Failure of an Elite — The Genoese at Crécy," p. 2.

4. Froissart, *Chronicles*, pp. 144–145, 149. These citations have been broken up for ease of reading.

5. Barber, "Life and Campaigns of the Black Prince," pp. 43–44.

6. After Wikipedia, "Combat of the Thirty," pp. 1–3.

7. Diverres, *Froissart: Voyage en Béarn*, p. 118.

8. Muhlberger, "Deeds of Arms," pp. 1–2.

9. Parts of this account of the Combat of the Thirty are drawn from Tuchman, *A Distant Mirror*, pp. 131–132.

10. From Jeanne d'Arc, p. 1.

11. For a small but good color reproduction of a detail of this canvas, see Wikipedia, "Combat of the Thirty," p. 1.

12. After Tuchman, *A Distant Mirror*, pp. 164–165.

13. After Allmand, *The Hundred Years War*, p. 135.

14. This section draws heavily from the U.S. Naval Academy article on "Fourteenth-Century Mercenaries."

15. After Fowler, *Medieval Mercenaries*, p. 2.

16. After Mallett, *Mercenaries and Their Masters*, p. 136.

17. Quoted by U.S. Naval Academy, "Fourteenth-Century Mercenaries," p. 2.

18. After Wikipedia, "Arnaud de Cervole," p. 1. This section draws on other parts of the article, too.

19. Barber, *Life and Campaigns of the Black Prince*, pp. 73, 77.

20. Most Medieval men and women believed that their society, when properly organized, should consist of three "estates," i.e., the clergy, the nobility, and the commoners. As Bishop Adalbero of Laon put it, "Here below, some pray, others fight, still others work..." Of the three estates, the clergy was the most important, having been ordained by God. Next came the nobility (the knights), whose

job it was to protect the realm. Traditionally holding down the bottom of the list were the commoners, who had to labor incessantly so that all might eat. With the gradual rise of the bourgeoisie, however, the more prosperous commoners (known as burghers), tended to displace the commoners in this idealized outline of the social order. The rich burghers thus took over the third-place position; the poor commoners slipped even further down the scale and became known as the Fourth Estate.

21. Wikipedia, quoting *The Chronicles of Jean de Venette*, Jean Birdsall, trans., and Richard A. Newhall, ed. (New York: Columbia University Press, 1953), p. 43.

22. Quoted by Wright, *Knights and Peasants*, p. 66.

23. After "La Jaquerie, révolte paysanne d'après Jean Le Bel (1358)," p. 2. Translation by Hunt Janin.

24. After Kreis, "Jean Froissart on the *Jacquerie*, p. 3.

Chapter VIII

1. One of best modern sources on the Great Companies is Kenneth Fowler's *Medieval Mercenaries—Volume I: The Great Companies*, which has been used extensively here. We can only regret the fact that the second volume was never written. Fowler said that it would focus on the activities of the English, Breton, and Gascon mercenaries in Italy from 1361 to 1394 and that particular attention would be given to the career of John Hawkwood. Fortunately, a more recent book—William Caferro's *John Hawkwood* (2006)—provides full information on Hawkwood. It, too, has been used extensively here.

2. After Fowler, *Medieval Mercenaries*, pp. 42–43.

3. Adapted from Favier, *La Guerre de Cent Ans*," p. 301. Translated by Hunt Janin.

4. Adapted from Cardini, "Guerre et Croisade," pp. 446–447.

5. After Fowler, *Medieval Mercenaries*, pp. 6, 21.

6. This is a free translation by Hunt Janin from Guido Guerri dall'Oro's article, "Les Mercenaires dans les Compagnes Napolitaines de Louis le Grand, Roi de Hongrie, 1347–1350," pp. 69, 70.

7. Froissart, *Chroniques*, xii, p. 98, quoted by Fowler, *Medieval Mercenaries*, p. 6.

8. Kervyn de Lettenhove in Froissart, *Oeuvres*, xx, p. 234, quoted by Fowler, *Medieval Mercenaries*, p. 6.

9. After Fowler, *Medieval Mercenaries*, p. 6.

10. After Fowler, *Medieval Mercenaries*, p. 329.

11. Froissart, *Chroniques*, vii, p. 336, quoted by Fowler, *Medieval Mercenaries*, p. 6.

12. *Chron. Jean II et Charles V*, I, pp. 327–8, quoted by Fowler, *Medieval Mercenaries*, p. 2.

13. Froissart, *Chroniques*, vi, pp. 61, 257, quoted by Fowler, *Medieval Mercenaries*, p. 2.

14. The Carmelite friar Jean de Venette, *Chronicle*, p. 93, quoted by Fowler, *Medieval Mercenaries*, pp. 2–3.

15. Knighton, *Chronicon*, ii, pp. 114–115, quoted by Fowler, *Medieval Mercenaries*, p. 3.

16. After Caferro, *John Hawkwood*, p. 24.

17. After Fowler, *Medieval Mercenaries*, p. 106.

18. After Fowler, *Medieval Mercenaries*, p. 106.

19. Quoted by Fowler, *Medieval Mercenaries*, p. 119.

20. After Fowler, *Medieval Mercenaries*, p. 120.

21. After Caferro, *John Hawkwood*, p. 75.

22. After Caferro, *John Hawkwood*, p. 50.

23. Caferro, *John Hawkwood*, p. 48.

24. After Caferro, *John Hawkwood*, p. 48.

25. Adapted from a quotation by used by Caferro, *John Hawkwood*, pp. 60–61.

26. After Caferro, *John Hawkwood*, pp. 338–340.

27. After Fowler, *Medieval Mercenaries*, pp. 297, 301.

28. After Caferro, *John Hawkwood*, p. 75.

29. Some of these points have been drawn from Paz, "The Role of Mercenary Troops in Spain in the Fourteenth Century: The Civil War."

30. After Barber, *Life and Campaigns of the Black Prince*, p. 10.

31. Quoted by Barber, *Life and Campaigns of the Black Prince*, pp. 110–111.

32. Quoted by Wikipedia in "The Battle of Nájera," p. 1.

33. Quoted by Barber, *Life and Campaigns of the Black Prince*, pp. 128- 129.

34. Froissart's *Chronicles*, p. 201.

35. After Fowler, *Medieval Mercenaries*, p. 196.

36. After Barber, *Life and Campaigns of the Black Prince*, pp. 10–11.

37. Lightly edited; quoted by Caferro, *John Hawkwood*, p. 68.

38. Quoted by Muhlberger, "Tales from Froissart," p. 1. This quote has been lightly edited to improve readability.

39. Quoted by Muhlberger, "Tales from Froissart," p. 2.

40. Villani, *Istorie*, lib. x, cap. xcv, cols. 680–1, quoted by Fowler, *Medieval Mercenaries*, p. 48.

41. The order of battle given here follows Wikipedia, "Battle of Grunwald."

42. Adapted from Turnbull, *Tannenberg 1410*, p. 26.

43. Wikipedia, "Battle of Grunwald," p. 4.

44. After Turnbull, *Tannenberg*, pp. 25, 26, 92.

Chapter IX

1. After Holmes, ed., *The Oxford Companion to Military History*, p. 9, citing Christopher Allmand, *Henry V* (London, 1998).

2. Barker, *Agincourt*, p. 296.

3. After Barker, *Agincourt*, p. 411, n37.

4. Sources used in this section include Wikipedia's "Garde Écossaise" and "Auld Alliance," and the Historical Academy for Joan of Arc Studies' "Royal Financial Records Concerning Payments for Twenty-Seven Contingents of Joan of Arc's Army Which Arrived at Orléans on 4 May 1429."

5. This account is drawn from "Hundred Years' War: Battle of the Herrings," p. 1, and from Wikipedia, "Battle of the Herrings."

6. A lightly-edited private communication of 5 November 2012 from Dr. John France.

7. Sources used in this section include the Wikipedia articles in French and in English on Rodrigo de Villandrando.

8. The Wikipedia article cited in the bibliography lists Rodrigo's exploits but it appears from this article that the most detailed source on Rodrigo de Villandrando's mercenary exploits is J.E.J. Quicherat's *Rodrigue de Vellandrando, l'un des combattants pour l'indépendance française au Xve siècle* (Paris: Hachette, 1879).

9. After Barker, *Conquest*, p. 152.

10. A *chevauchée* (literally a "horse charge") was a short, sharp raid designed to weaken an opponent by wreaking havoc, burning, and pillaging enemy territory in order to reduce the productivity of a region; to terrify the population; and to discredit the enemy's government. The English used the *chevauchée* many times: e.g., in the major battles of the period (Crécy, Poitiers, and Agincourt). This tactic

fell out of use at the end of the 14th century due to the rise of siege warfare.

11. After Keen, *Medieval Warfare*, pp. 280–281.

12. Quoted by Contamine, *War in the Middle Ages*, p. 165.

13. After Caferro, *John Hawkwood*, pp. 72–73.

14. Quoted by Mallett, *Mercenaries and Their Masters*, p. 105.

15. Traditional historiography suggests that in 1445 Charles VII issued a single *Grande Ordonnance* and thereby established a standing army but it seems more likely that two dozen or more directives along these lines were published in France nearly simultaneously.

16. After Allmand, *The Hundred Years War*, p. 166.

17. After Nicholson, *Medieval Warfare*, p. 122.

18. This account follows Keen, "The Changing Scene: Guns, Gunpowder, and Permanent Armies" in Keene, *Medieval Warfare*, pp. 283–291.

19. After Allmand, *The Hundred Years War*, p. 169.

Chapter X

1. Not much information on the Black Army of Hungary is available in English or in French on the Internet. Sources used here include Wikipedia, "Black Army of Hungary"; Oxford Reference, "Black Army of Hungary"; Haywood, "Hungarian Armies 1300 to 1492"; and Keen, *Medieval Warfare*, pp. 281, 283.

2. Quoted by Rogers, "Black Army of Hungary," p. 2.

3. After Keen, *Medieval Warfare*, p. 281. As noted earlier, a ducat and a florin had roughly the same value.

4. After Hicks, "The Urbino Studiolo," pp. 3–8.

5. Sources used in this section include Wikipedia, "Burgundian Wars" and "Battle of Nancy"; About.com military history, "Burgundian Wars: Battle of Nancy"; Medieval Times, "Battle of Nancy (1477)"; Keen, *Medieval Warfare*, pp. 287, 288; Contamine, *War in the Middle Ages*, pp. 218, 298N, 300–301; Verbruggen, *The Art of Warfare in Western Europe During the Middle Ages*, p. 148; and Nicholson, *Medieval Warfare*, pp. 51–52, 129.

6. Numerous sources tell the story of the Pazzi plot. We have used here the simplest and clearest one we know of, i.e., Murphy, "The

Pazzi Plot," in *Condottiere 1300–1500*, pp. 48–50.

7. A summary of the complicated political and financial situation can be found in Mediateca di Palazzo Medici Riccardi, "1478—The Pazzi Conspiracy," pp. 1–3.

8. Quoted by Mallett, *Mercenaries and Their Masters*, pp. 130–131.

9. Sources used in this section include Wikipedia, "Landsknecht"; Oxford Companion to Military History: landsknecht; landsknecht.com, "History"; and Keen, *Medieval Warfare*, pp. 228, 229, 271.

10. After landsknecht.com, "History," p. 1.

11. Quoted in Wikipedia, "Landsknecht," p. 4, citing John Richards, *Landsknecht Soldier*," p. 51.

12. Adapted from Oxford Companion to Military History, "landsknecht," p. 1.

13. These comments are drawn from Wikipedia, "Landsknecht."

14. After Wikipedia, "Black Band (landsknechts)," and Mallett and Shaw, *The Italian Wars*, p. 179.

Chapter XI

1. Some of our comments on the Italian Wars are drawn from the more than 70 pages of Wikipedia articles on this subject; see the lead Wikipedia article on "Italian Wars."

2. Guicciardina, *History of Italy*, p. 335, quoted by Wikipedia, "Battle of Biocca," p. 3.

3. Some of the points made in this section are drawn from Wikipedia, "Battle of Pavia."

4. Quoted by Wikipedia, "Battle of Pavia," p. 5.

5. Quoted by Wikipedia, "Battle of Ceresole," p. 4.

6. Mallett, *Mercenaries and Their Masters*, pp. 259–260.

7. Sources used in this section include "Biography of Niccolo Machiavelli"; *The Prince* (Chapters XII and XIII); and Wikipedia, "The Prince."

8. After Machiavelli, *The Prince*, pp. 87–88.

9. Machiavelli, *The Prince*, Chapter XII. This quotation has been divided for ease of reading.

10. Machiavelli, *The Prince*, Chapter XIII.

11. Wilson, *Europe's Tragedy*, back cover.

12. After Krüssmann, English review of *Ernst von Mansfeld*, pp. 1–2.

13. After Brouwer, "Book Review: *Ernst von Mansfeld*," p. 6.

14. After Wilson, *Europe's Tragedy*, p. 326.

15. Brouwer, "Book Review: *Ernst von Mansfeld (1580–1626)*," p. 19.

16. After Brouwer, "Book Review: *Ernst von Mansfield (1580–1626)*," pp. 22–23.

17. After Brouwer (quoting Krüssmann), "Book Review: *Ernst von Mansfeld (1580–1626)*, p. 26.

18. Sources used in this section include Wilson, *Europe's Tragedy*; Wikipedia, "Albrecht von Wallenstein"; and Britannica Online Encyclopedia, "Albrecht von Wallenstein."

19. Adapted from Wright, *Knights and Peasants*, pp. 9–10.

20. Quoted by Wikipedia, "Schwedentrunk." Other parts of this article have been used in our description.

Conclusion

1. Hobbes, *Leviathan*. Italics added.

2. After France, "Mercenaries and Paid Men," p. 11.

3. France, "Mercenaries and Paid Men," p. 12.

4. Readers can contact the Bibliothèque nationale de France website (manuscrits@bnf.fr) and ask, in English or French, for assistance.

Appendix 1

1. After Contamine, *War in the Middle Ages*, p. 95, N72.

2. This list is drawn from Wikipedia, "Components of medieval armour," pp. 1–7, and from Nicolson, *Medieval Warfare*, pp. 103–109.

Appendix 2

1. This appendix draws heavily from Wikipedia, "Swiss Mercenaries, " pp. 1–3.

2. Mallett and Shaw, *The Italian Wars*, p. 4.

3. These points are drawn from Gush, "Renaissance Warfare. Part 9: Swiss," p. 1.

Bibliography

Abels, Richard. "Household Men, Mercenaries and Vikings in Anglo-Saxon England" in John French. *Mercenaries and Paid Men: The Mercenary Identity in the Middle Ages.* Leiden: Brill, 2008, pp. 143–165.

_____. "Practical Chivalry in the Twelfth Century: William Marshal." http://usna.edu/Users/history/abels/hh315/William%20Marshal%20chivalry.htm. Accessed 26 May 2011.

Ainsworth, William Harrison, trans. 1859; ed. Steve Muhlberger 2001. "The Combat of the Thirty." http://www.jeanne-darc.info/p_war/O_battles/combat_thirty.html. Accessed 1 August 2012.

Allmond, Christopher. *The Hundred Years War: England and France at War, c. 1300-c. 1450.* Cambridge: Cambridge University Press, 1989.

Anglo-Saxon Chronicle. http://www.google.fr/search?q=anglo+saxon+chronicle+when+christ+and+his+saints+were... Accessed 4 September 2012.

Arnow, Chad. "The Battle of Poitiers." http://www.myarmoury.com/feature_battle_poitiers.html. Accessed 25 October 2012.

Bachrach, Bernard S. "Merovingian Mercenaries and Paid Soldiers in Imperial Perspective" in John France, ed., *Mercenaries and Paid Men: The Mercenary Identity in the Middle Ages.* Leiden: Brill, 2008, pp. 167–192.

_____. *Merovingian Military Organization 481–751.* Minneapolis: University of Minnesota Press, 1972.

Barber, Richard, ed. and trans. *The Life and Campaigns of the Black Prince.* Woodbridge: Boydell, 1997.

Barker, Juliet. *Agincourt: The King, the Campaign, the Battle.* London: Abacus, 2006.

_____. *Conquest: The English Kingdom of France in the Hundred Years War.* London: Abacus, 2010.

Bartlett, Robert, ed. *Medieval Panorama.* London: Thames & Hudson, 2001.

Barton, Simon, and Richard Fletcher. *The World of El Cid: Chronicles of the Spanish Reconquest.* Manchester: Manchester University Press, 2000.

"Battle of Conquereuil." http://home.eckerd.edu/~oberhot/conquereuil.htm. Accessed 8 May 2012.

"Battle of Manzikert (1071 A.D.)." http://www.thelatinlibrary.com/imperialism/notes/manzikert.html. Accessed 1 September 2012.

"The Battle of Grunwald—1410: lst Battle of Tannenberg." http://www.imperialteutonicorder.com/id41.html. Accessed 30 October 2012.

"The Battle of Sluys. 24 June 1340." http://www.maisonclaire.org/resources/battles/sluys.html. Accessed 20 April 2012.

Bennett, Matthew, ed. *The Medieval World at War.* London: Thames & Hudson, 2009.

"Biography of Niccolo Machiavelli—The Prince." http://www.age-of-the-sage.org/historical/biography/niccol o_machiavelli.html. Accessed 23 August 2012.

Bloch, Marc, trans. L.A. Manyon. *Feudal Society. Volume 1— The Growth of Ties of Dependence.* Chicago: University of Chicago Press, 1961.

_____. *Volume II—Social Classes and Political Organization.* Padstow: Routledge, 1995.

Borrill, Keira, trans. "Jean Froissart, Chronicles" in "The Online Froissart," Peter Ainsworth and Godfried Croenen, eds. Version 1.2 (May 2011). http ://www.hrionlline.ac.uk/onlinefrois sart. Accessed 9 May 2012.

Boylan, Kevin. "Medieval Irish (1300– 1487 A.D.)." http://fanaticus.org/DBA /armies/dba164.html. Accessed 6 January 2012.

Britannica Online Encyclopedia. "Albrecht von Wallenstein." http://www .britannica.com/print/topic/634857. Accessed 17 December 20012.

Brouwer, Aart. "Book Review: *Ernst von Mansfeld (1580–1626),* by Walter Krüssmann." http://crossfireamersfoort.wo rdpress.com/2012/07/14/book-review-ernst-von-mansfelt-1580–1626 by... Accessed 9 December 2012.

Caferro, William. *John Hawkwood: An English Mercenary in Fourteenth-Century Italy.* Baltimore: Johns Hopkins Press, 2006.

Cardini, Franco. "Guerre et Croisade" in Jacques Le Goff and Jean-Claude Schmitt, *Dictionnaire Raisonné de l'Occident Médiéval.* Paris: Fayard, 1999, pp. 435–449.

Central European University. "Arms and Armor in the Late Middle Ages and Early Renaissance: Training with weapons as part of the daily life of the warrior." http://web.ceu.hu/medstud /manual/SRM/training.htm. Accessed 20 August 2012.

Chaucer, Geoffrey. *The Canterbury Tales: A Selection.* London: Penguin, 1996.

"Christine de Pisan." http://www.them iddleages.net/people/christine_pisan.h tml. Accessed 2 May 2012.

"Chronicle of the Counts of Anjou, c. 1100." *Medieval Sourcebook,* from Louis Halphen and René Poupardin, *Chroniques des Comtes d'Anjou et des Seigneurs d'Amboise.* Paris: Picard, 1913, trans. Stephen Lane. http://www .fordham.edu/halsall/source/Anjou.as p. Accessed 10 May 2012.

The Chronicles of Sir John Froissart, Chapter L, "The Naval Engagement Between the King of England and the French Before Sluys." http://www. maisonstclaire.org/resources/chronicl es/froissart/book_1ch_026–050/fc_ bl_ch. Accessed 21 April 2012.

The "Companions" of Jeanne d'Arc. "Bueil, Jean V de." http://xenophon-group.com/montjoie/compgns.html. Accessed 18 August 2012.

Comnena, Anna, ed. and trans. Elizabeth A. Dawes. *The Alexiad.* London: Routledge, Kegan, Paul, 1928. Internet History Sourcebooks. http://www.ford ham.edu/halsall/basis/AnnaComnena-Alexiad01.asp. Accessed 2 September 2012.

Crouch, David. "William Marshal and the Mercenariat" in John France, ed. *Mercenaries and Paid Men: The Mercenary Identity in the Middle Ages.* Leiden: Brill, 2009, pp. 14–32.

Contamine, Philippe, trans. Michael Jones. *War in the Middle Ages.* Oxford: Basil Blackwell, 1986.

Dall'Oro, Guido Guerri. "Les Mercenaires dans les Campagnes Napolitaines de Louis le Grand, Roi de Hongrie" in John France. *Mercenaries and Paid Men: The Mercenary Identity in the Middle Ages.* Leden: Brill, 2009, pp. 62–88.

D'Amato, Raffaele. *The Varangian Guard 988–1453.* Oxford: Osprey, 2010.

DeVries, Kelly. "Medieval Mercenaries: Methodology, Definitions, and Problems" in John France, ed., *Mercenaries and Paid Men: The Mercenary Identity in the Middle Ages.* Leiden: Brill, 2008, pp. 43–60.

Diverres, A.H., ed. *Froissart: Voyage en Béarn.* Manchester: Manchester University Press, 1953.

Douglas, David D. *William the Conqueror.* New Haven: Yale University Press, 1999.

Dymmok, John. "A Treatice [sic] of Ireland." www.aughty.org/pdf/treatise_ireland.pdf. Accessed 28 May 2012.

Early Modern England. "Sports scientists examine the medieval marchers of the Mary Rose." http://earlymodernengland.com/2012/sports-scientists-examine-the-medieval-archers-of... Accessed 29 July 2012.

Ekdahl, Sven. "The Teutonic Order's Mercenaries During the 'Great War' with Poland-Lithuania (1409–11)" in John France. *Mercenaries and Paid Men: The Mercenary Identity in the Middle Ages.* Leiden: Brill, 2008, pp. 345–361.

Favier, Jean. *La Guerre de Cent Ans.* Paris: Fayard, 1980.

Fordham University. "The Text of Magna Carta." http://www.fordham.euc/halsall/source/magnacarta.asp. Accessed 27 May 2012.

Fowler, Kenneth. *Medieval Mercenaries: Volume I, The Great Companies.* Oxford: Blackwell, 2001.

France, John. "Crusading Warfare and Its Adaptation to Eastern Conditions in the Twelfth Century" in *Mediterranean Historical Review,* 15.2, pp. 49–66. http://dx.doi.org/10.1080/09518960008569778. Accessed 24 October 2012.

_____. "Mercenaries and Capuchins in Southern France in the Late Twelfth Century." A paper given in earlier forms at Kalamazoo in May 2006 and the Crusades Seminar at the University of Historical Research, University of London, in June 2006.

_____, ed. *Mercenaries and Paid Men. The Mercenary Identity in the Middle Ages.* Leiden: Brill, 2008.

_____. "Mercenaries and Paid Men. The Mercenary Identify in the Middle Ages. Introduction." in John France ed., *Mercenaries and Paid Men. The Mercenary Identify in the Middle Ages.* Leiden: Brill, 2008, pp. 1–13.

_____. *Western Warfare in the Age of the Crusades 1000–1300.* Ithaca: Cornell University Press, 1999.

Froissart, Jean, trans. John Bourchier, also known as Lord Berners. "The Chronicles of Froissart — Chapter 2: The Battle of Poitiers." http://www.fordham.edu/halsall/basis/froissart-full.asp. Accessed 2 August 2012.

Géraud, Hercule. "Les Routiers au douzième siècle." Bibliothèque de l'école de chartres. 1842, tome 3, pp. 125–147. doi: 10.3406/bec.1842.451648. http://www.persee.fr/web/revues/home/prescript/article/bec_0373-6237_num_3_1_451648. Accessed 6 September 2012.

_____. "Mercadier: Les routiers au treizième scièrle." Bibliothèque de chartres. 1842. Tome 3, pp. 417–447. doi: 10.3406/bec.1842.451658. http://www.persee.fr/web/revues/home/prescript/article/bec_0373–6237_1842_num_3_1_451658. Accessed 8 September 2012.

Goodrich, Norma Lorre. *Medieval Myths.* New York: Mentor, 1961.

Grummitt, David, ed. *The English Experience c. 1450–1558: War, diplomacy and cultural exchange.* Aldershot: Ashgate, 2002.

Gush, George. "Renaissance Warfare. Part 9: Swiss." http://greatestbattles.iblogger.org/Renaissance/09_Swiss.htm. Accessed 13 December 2012.

Haldon, John. *The Byzantine Wars.* Stroud: History Press, 2011.

Hardy, Robert. *Longbow: A Social and Military History.* Thrupp: Sutton, 2006.

Heath, Ian. *The Vikings.* London: Osprey, 1987.

Hicks, Ashley. "The Urbino Studiolo."

http://www.ashleyhicks.com/places/the-urbino-studiolo.html. Accessed 29 November 2012.

Historical Academy for Joan of Arc Studies. "Royal Financial Records Concerning Payments for Twenty-Seven Contingents in the Portion of Joan of Arc's Army Which Arrived at Orléans on 4 May 1429." Joan of Arc: Primary Sources Series, PSS021406. Accessed 13 November 2012.

Hobbes, Thomas. Quotation from *Leviathan*. http://www.phrases.org.uk/meanings/254050. Accessed 20 December 2012.

Holmes, Richard (ed.). "Agincourt, battle of" in *The Oxford Companion to Military History*, Oxford: Oxford University Press, 2001, p. 9.

Holland, Tom. *Millennium*. London: Abacus, 2009.

Hosler, John D. "Revisiting Mercenaries under Henry Fitz Empress, 1167–1188" in John France, ed., *Mercenaries and Paid Men: The Mercenary Identity in the Middle Ages*. Leiden: Brill, 2008, pp. 33–42.

Hoyos, Xavier Bonillo. "Ramon Mutaner." http://www.visat.cat/transductions-literatura-catalana/eng/autor/30/05/medieval-classics/ram. Accessed 25 July 2012.

"Hundred Years' War: Battle of the Herrings." http://military.history.about.com/battleswar14011600/p/battle-of-the-herrings.htm. Accessed 5 November 2012.

"The Hundred Years War: Battle of Agincourt." http://www.britishbattles.com/100-years-war/agincourt.html. Accessed 5 November 2012.

Janin, Hunt. *Medieval Justice: Cases and Laws in France, England and Germany, 500–1500*. Jefferson, NC: McFarland, 2004.

Jenkins, Geraint H. *A Concise History of Wales*. Cambridge: Cambridge University Press, 2008.

Jolliffe, John, trans. and ed. *Froissart's Chronicles*. London: Penguin, 1967.

Jordan, William Chester. *Europe in the High Middle Ages*. London: Penguin, 2002.

Keen, Maurice. *English Society in the Later Middle Ages*. London: Penguin, 1990.

_____, ed. *Medieval Warfare: A History*. Oxford: Oxford University Press, 1999.

_____, ed. "The Changing Scene: Guns, Gunpowder, and Permanent Armies" in Maurice Keen, *Medieval Warfare: A History*. Oxford: Oxford University Press, 1999, pp. 273–291.

Kelly, Thomas E. "Eustache the Monk" in Thomas H. Ohlgren, *A Book of Medieval Outlaws: Ten Tales in Modern English*. Thrupp, Sutton, 2000, pp. 61–98.

"Knighthood Training." http://www.middle-ages.org.uk/knighthood-training.htm. Accessed 19 August 2012.

Knights, Alexander J. "The Battle of Agincourt." http://www.allempires.com/article/index.php?q=battle_agincourt. Accessed 16 August 2012.

Koenigsberger, H.G. *Medieval Europe 400–1500*. Harlow: Longman, 1998.

Kreis, Steven. "Jean Froissart on the *Jacquerie* (1358)." Last revised February 28, 2006. http://www.historyguide.org/ancient/jacquerie.html. Accessed 23 October 2012.

Kreutz, Barbara M. *Before the Normans: Southern Italy in the Ninth & Tenth Centuries*. Philadelphia: University of Pennsylvania Press, 1991.

Krüssman, Walter. English summary of his German book *Ernst von Mansfeld (1580–1626)*. http://www.walter-kruessmann.de/zum-buch. Accessed 12 July 2012.

Labarge, Margaret Wade. *Gascony: England's First Colony, 1204–1453*. London: Hamish Hamilton, 1980.

_____. *Medieval Travellers: The Rich and the Restless*. London: Phoenix, 1982.

Latzko, David A. "The Market for Mercenaries." http://www.personal.psu.edu/~dx131/research/presentations/mercenary.html. Accessed 24 May 2012.

Le Goff, Jacques, and Jean-Claude Schmitt. "Guerre et Croisade" *Dictionnaire Raisonné de L'Occident Médiéval*. Paris: Fayard, 1999, pp. 434–449.

Lindholm, D., and D. Nicolle. *Medieval Scandinavian Armies (1) 1100–1300*. Oxford: Osprey, 2003.

_____. *Medieval Scandinavian Armies (2) 1300–1500*. Oxford: Osprey, 2003.

Loud, G.A. *The Age of Robert Guiscard: Southern Italy and the Norman Conquest*. Harlow: Pearson, 2000.

Machiavelli, Nicolò. *The Prince*. London: Penguin, 1999.

_____. "The Prince: Chapter XII, How Many Kinds of Soldiery There Are, And Concerning Mercenaries." http://www.constitution.org/mac/prince12.htm. Accessed 25 May 2012.

_____. "The Prince: Chapter XIII, Concerning Auxiliaries, Mixed Soldiery, And One's Own." http://www.constitution.org/mac/prince13.htm. Accessed 12 April 2012.

Malory, Sir Thomas. *Le Morte d'Arthur*, Vol. II. Harmondsworth: Penguin, 1986.

Mallett, Michael. "Mercenaries" in Keen, Maurice. *Medieval Warfare: A History*. Oxford: Oxford University Press, 1999, pp. 209–229.

_____. *Mercenaries and Their Masters: Warfare in Renaissance Italy*. Barnsley: Pen & Sword Military, 2009.

_____, and Christine Shaw. *The Italian Wars 1494–1559*. Harlow: Pearson Education, 2012.

"Mamertines." www.livius.org/maa-mam/mamertines/mamertines.html. Accessed 12 April 2012.

Markham, Paul. "The Battle of Manzikert: Military Disaster or Political Failure?" http://www.deremilitari.org/resources/articles/markham.htm. Accessed 8 August 2012.

Marsden, John. *Galloglas: Hebridean and West Highland Mercenary Warrior Kindreds in Medieval Ireland*. East Linton: Tuckwell Press, 2003.

Matthews, Jeff. "Lucera, a Muslim Colony in Medieval Italy." http://ac-support.europe.umuc.edu/~jmatthew/naples/Lucera.htm. Accessed 27 August 2012.

McCullough, David Williams. *Wars of the Irish Kings*. New York: History Book Club, 2000.

McKitterick, Rosamond. *The Early Middle Ages*. Oxford: Oxford University Press, 2001.

Mediateca di Palazzo Medici Riccardi. "1478 — The Pazzi Conspiracy." http://www.palazzo-medici.it/mediateca/en/schede.php?id_scheda=160. Accessed 11 November 2012.

"Medieval Crossbow." http://www.castles.me.uk/medieval-crossbow.htm. Accessed 30 May 2012.

Medieval Sourcebook. "Roger of Hoveden: The Revolt of 1173–74," from "The Chronicle." http://www.fordham.edu/halsall/source/1173hoveden.asp. Accessed 14 March 2012.

"Medieval Warfare." http://www.medievalwarfare.info/ Accessed 17 January 2012.

"Medieval Weapons & Armour." http://www.medievalwarfare.info/weapons.htm. Accessed 1 April 2012.

"Merovingians." http://fmg.ac/Projects/MedLands/MEROVINGIANS.html. Accessed 7 May 2012.

Morillo, Stephen. "Mercenaries, Mamluks and Militia: Towards a Cross-Cultural Typology of Military Service" in John France. *Mercenaries and Paid Men: The Mercenary Identity in the Middle Ages*. Leiden: Brill, 2008, pp. 243–259.

_____. *Warfare under the Anglo-Norman Kings 1066–1135*. Woodbridge: Boydell, 1994.

Muhlberger, Steven. "Deeds of Arms: A Collection of Formal Deeds of Arms of the Fourteenth Century." http://www.nipissingu.ca/department/history/muhlberger/chroniqu/texts/thirty.htm. Accessed 29 March 2012.

Murphy, David. *Condottiere 1300–1500: Infamous Medieval Mercenaries*. Oxford: Osprey, 2007.

Nelson, Lynn Harry. "The Rise of the Franks, 330–751." Lectures in Medieval History. hhttp://www.vlib.us/medieval/lectures/franks_rise.html. Accessed 25 October 2012.

Newark, Timothy. *Medieval Warfare*. London: Bloomsbury, 1988.

Nicholson, Helen. *Medieval Warfare: Theory and Practice of War in Europe 300–1500*. Basingstoke: Palgrave Macmillan, 2004.

Nicolle, David. "The Failure of an Elite — The Genoese at Crécy." http://www.ospreypublishing.com/articles/medieval_world/failure_of_an_elite_the_genoe... Accessed 27 May 2012.

Norgate, Kate. "Dictionary of National Biography, 1885–1900, Volume 61, William of Ypres (BND00)." http://en.wikisource.org/wiki/William_of_Ypres_(DNB00). Accessed 16 March 2012.

Norman, A.V.B. *The Medieval Soldier*. New York: Barnes & Noble, 1993.

Oksansen, Elijas. "The Anglo-Flemish Treaties and Flemish Soldiers in England, 1101–1163" in John France, *Mercenaries and Paid Men: The Mercenary Identity in the Middle Ages*. Leiden: Brill, 2008, pp. 261–273.

Ohlgren, Thomas H. *A Book of Medieval Outlaws: Ten Tales in Modern English*. Thrupp: Sutton, 2000.

ORB: On-line Reference Book for Medieval Studies. "The Second Crusade." http://www.the-orb.net/textbooks/crusade/secondcru.html. Accessed 6 September 2012.

Oxford Companion to Military History. "landsknecht." http://www.answers.com/topic/landsknecht-1. Accessed 18 November 2012.

Paz, Carlos Andrés González. "The Role of Mercenary Troops in Spain in the Fourteenth Century: The Civil War" in John France, *Mercenaries and Paid Men: The Mercenary Identity in the Middle Ages*. Leiden: Brill, 2008, pp. 331–343.

Pernoud, Régine. *Lumière du Moyen Age*. Paris: Éditions Grasset et Fasquelle, 1981.

Prendergast, Muríosa. "Scots Mercenary Forces in Sixteenth-Century Ireland" in France, John. *Mercenaries and Paid Men: The Mercenary Identity in the Middle Ages*. Leiden: Brill, 2008, pp. 363–380.

Prestwich, Michael. "The Challenge to Chivalry: Longbow and Pike, 1275–1475" in Matthew Bennett, ed., *The Medieval World at War*. London: Thames & Hudson, 2009, pp. 161–181.

_____. "The Gunpowder Revolution, 1300–1500" in Bennett, Matthew (ed.), *The Medieval World at War*. London: Thames & Hudson, 2009, pp. 183–203.

_____. "Mercenaries, medieval" in *The Oxford Companion to Military History*, ed. Richard Holmes, Oxford: Oxford University Press, 2001, pp. 569, 575–576.

Pryor, John H. "Soldiers of Fortune in the Fleets of Charles I of Anjou, King of Sicily, ca. 1265–85" in John French, *Mercenaries and Paid Men: The Mercenary Identity in the Middle Ages*. Leiden: Brill, 2008, pp. 119–141.

Rabb, Kate Milner, ed. *National Epics: The Story of the Poem of the Cid*. http://www.authorama.com/national-epics-24.html. Accessed 3 September 2012.

Reiter, Timothy. "Carolingian and Ottonian Warfare" in Maurice Keen, ed., *Medieval Warfare: A History*. Oxford: Oxford University Press, 1999, pp. 13–35.

"Responses to the Threat of Invasion, 1085." *The English Historical Review*. Abstract. (2007) CXXII (498): 986–

997, doi: 10.1093/ehr/cem255. Accessed 20 May 2012.

Reynolds, Susan. *Fiefs and Vassals: The Medieval Evidence Reinterpreted*. Oxford: Clarendon, 1996.

Rice, Andrew. "Mercenaries of the Angevin Empire: Reputations and Power." http://fch.ju.edu/FCH-2009/Rice_mercenaries_of_the-angevin-empire.htm. Accessed 22 May 2012.

Richard, Jean. "An Account of the Battle of Hattin Referring to the Frankish Mercenaries in Oriental Muslim States." *Speculum* 27. 2 (Apr. 1952), pp. 168–177. http://www.jstor.org/stable/284490. Accessed 24 October 20l2.

Roberts, Michael. *The Early Vasas: A History of Sweden, 1523–1611*. Cambridge: Cambridge University Press, 1986.

Rogers, Clifford J., ed. "Black Army of Hungary" in *The Oxford Encyclopedia of Medieval Warfare and Military Technology*. Oxford: Oxford University Press, 2010. http://www.oxfordreference.com/view/l0.1093/acref/9780195334036.001/acref-97... Accessed 14 November 2012.

Soldiers of Misfortune. "The Varangian Guard: The Vikings in Byzantium." http://www.soldier-of-misfortune.com/history/varangian-guard.htm. Accessed 4 August 2012.

Stenton, Frank. *Anglo-Saxon England*. Oxford. Oxford University Press, 2001.

"Squires." http://www/middle-ages.org.uk/squires.htm. Accessed 28 August 2012.

Tsin, Matthieu E. Chan. "Jean de Breuil: Reactionary Knight." http://docs.lib.purdue.edu/dissertations/AAI3185738. Accessed 18 August 2012.

Tuchman, Barbara W. *A Distant Mirror: The Calamitous 14th Century*. New York: Ballantine, 1978.

Turnbull, Stephen. *Tannenberg 1410: Disaster for the Teutonic Knights*. Oxford: Osprey, 2003.

U.S. Naval Academy. "Fourteenth-Century Mercenaries." http://usna.edu/Users/history/abels/hh381/mercenaries.htm. Accessed 4 November 2012.

Vegetius, Flavius Renatus, trans. Lieutenant John Clarke. *On Roman Military Matters*. St. Petersburg: Red and Black, 1767.

Verbruggen, J.F. *The Art of Warfare in Western Europe During the Middle Ages*. Woodbridge: Boydell, 2002.

Wikipedia. "Albrecht von Wallenstein." http://en.wikipedia.org/w/index.php?title=Albrecht_von_Wallenstein&printable=yes. Accessed 17 December 2012.

_____. "Andrea Doria." http://en.wikipedia.org/w/index.php?title=Andrea_Doria&printable=yes. Accessed 29 November 2012.

_____. "Antrustion." http://en.wikipedia.org/w/index.php?title=Antrustion&printablle=yes. Accessed 12 November 2012.

_____. "Arnaud de Cervole." http://en.wikipedia.org/w/index.php?title=Arnaud_de_Cervole&printable=yes. Accessed 2 November 2012.

_____. "Auld Alliance." http://en.wikipedia.org/w/index.php?title=Auld_Alliance&printable=yes. Accessed 13 November 2012.

_____. "Bataile de Manzikert." http:fr.wikipedia.org/w.index.php?title=Bataille_de_Manzikert&printable=yes. Accessed 1 September 2012.

_____. "Battle of Biocca." http://en.wikipedia.org/w/inde.php?title=Battle_of_Biocca&printable=yes. Accessed 28 November 2012.

_____. "Battle of the Cephissus." http:en.wikipedia.org/w/index.php?title=Battle_of_the_Cephissus&printable=yes. Accessed 25 October 2012.

_____. "Battle of Ceresole." http://en.wikipedia.org/w/inde.php?title=Battle_of_Ceresole&printable=yes. Accessed 30 November 2012.

_____. "Battle of Grunwald." http://en.wikipedia.org/w/index.php?title=Bat

tle_of_Grunwald&printable=yes. Accessed 25 August 2012.

_____. "Battle of Manzikert." http://en.wikipedia.org/w/index.php?title=Battle_of_Manzikert&printable=yes. Accessed 20 August 2012.

_____. "Battle of Nájera." http://en.wikipedia.org/w/index.php?title=Battle_of_N%Aljera&printable=yes. Accessed 5 November 2012.

_____. "Battle of Nancy." http://en.wikipedia.org/w/omdex.php?title=Battle_of_Nancy&printable=yes. Accessed 16 November 2012.

_____. "Battle of Pavia." http://en.wikipedia.org/w/index.php?title=Battle_of_Pavia&printable=yes. Accessed 24 December 2012.

_____. "Battle of the Herrings." http://en.wikipedia.org/w/index.php?title=Battle _of_the_Herrings&printable=yes. Accessed 5 November 2012.

_____. "Black Army of Hungary." http://en.wikipedia.org/wiki/Black_Army_of_Hungary. Accessed 14 November 2012.

_____. "Black Band (landsknechts)." http://en.wikipedia.org/w/index.php?stitle=Black_Band_(landsknechts)&printable=yes. Accessed 27 November 2012.

_____. "Byzantine Army." http://en.wikipedia.org/w/index.php?title=Byzantine_army&printable=yes. Accessed 4 August 2012.

_____. "Byzantine Empire." http://en.wikipedia/org/w/index.php?title=Byzantine_Empire&printable=yes. Accessed 6 August 2012.

_____. "Catalan Company." http://en.wikipedia.org/w/index.php?title=Catalan_Company&printable=yes. Accessed 23 July 2012.

_____. "Chivalry," quoting Huizinga, *The Waning of the Middle Ages* (1919) 1924:58. http://en.wikipedia/org/index.php?title+Chivalry&printable=yes. Accessed 19 April 2012.

_____. "Combat of the Thirty." http://en.wikipedia.org/w/index.php?title=Combat_of_the_Thirty&printable=yes. Accessed 1 August 2012.

_____. "Components of Medieval Armour." http://en.wikipedia.org/w/index.php?title=Components_of_medieval_armour&printable=yes. Accessed 2 October 2012.

_____. "Crossbow." http://en.wikipedia.org/w/index.php/title=Crossbow&printable=yes. Accessed 2 December 2011.

_____. "Eustace the Monk." http://en.wikipedia.org/w/index.php?title=Eustace_the_Monk&printable=yes. Accessed 10 September 2012.

_____. "First Barons' War." http://en.wikipedia.org/w/index.php?title=First _Baron%27_War&printable=yes. Accessed 10 September 2012.

_____. "First Crusade." http://en.wikipedia.org/w/index.php?title=First_Crusade&printable=yes. Accessed 21 November 2012.

_____. "Jean Froissart." http://en.wikipedia.org/w/inde.php?title=Jean_Froissart&printable=yes. Accessed 21 December 2012.

_____. "Fulk III, Count of Anjou." http://en.wikipedia.org/w/index.php?title=Fulk_III,_Count_of_Anjou. Accessed 29 August 2012.

_____. "Garde Écossaise." http://en.wikipedia.org/w/index.php?title=Garde_%C3%89cossaise&printable=yes. Accessed 13 November 2012.

_____. "History" [of the Landsknecht]. http://www.landsknecht.com/html/body_history.html. Accessed 19 November 2012.

_____. "Italian Wars." http://en.wikipedia.org/w/inde.php?title=Italian_Wars&printable=yes. Accessed 27 November 2012.

_____. "Jean V de Bueil." http://en.wikipedia.org/w/index.php?title=Jean_V_de_Bueil&printagle=yes. Accessed 4 May 2012.

_____. "John Hawkwood." http://en.wikipedia.org/w/index.php?title=John_Hawkwood7printable=yes. Accessed 30 September 2012.

_____. "Landsknecht." http://en.wikipedia.org/w/index.php?title=Landsknecht&printable=yes. Accessed 26 August 2012.

_____. "Matter of France." http://en.wikipedia.org/wiki/Matter_of_France. Accessed 28 July 2012.

_____. "Medieval Warfare." http://en.wikipedia/org/w/index.php?title-Medieval_warfare&printable=yes. Accessed 17 April 2012.

_____. "Mercenary." http://en.wikipedia.org/wiki/Mercenaries. Accessed 24 September 2012.

_____. "Muslim Settlement of Lucera." http://en.wikipedia.org/w/index.php?title=Muslim_settlement of Lucera&printable=yes. Accessed 30 July 2012.

_____. "Battle of Novara (1513)." http://en.wikipedia.org/w/index.php?title=Battle_of_Novara_(1513)&printable=yes. Accessed 19 November 2012.

_____. "The Prince." http://en.wikipedia.org/w/inde.php?title=The_Prince&printable=yes. Accessed 24 August 2012.

_____. "Rainulf Drengot." http://en.wikipedia.org/w/index.php?title=Rainulf_Drengot&printagle=yes. Accessed 12 July 2011.

_____. "Rodrigo de Villandrando." http://en.wikipedia.org/w/index.php?title=Rodrigo_de_Villandrando&printable=yes. Accessed 3 November 2012.

_____, "Rodrigue de Villandrando." http://fr.wikipedia.org/wiki/Rodrigue_de_Villandrando. Accessed 6 November 2012.

_____. "Roussel de Bailleul." http://en.wikipedia.org/w/index.php?=title=Roussel_de_Bailleul&printable=yes. Accessed 2 September 2012.

_____. "Schwedentrunk." http://en.wikipedia..org/wiki/Schwedentrunk. Accessed 10 December 2012.

_____. "Second Crusade." http://en.wikipedia.org/w/index.php?title=Second_Crusade&printable=yes. Accessed 6 September 2012.

_____. "Siege of Constantinople (1204)." http://en.wikipedia.org/w/index.php?title=Siege_of_Constantinople_(1204)&printable=yes. Accessed 28 August 2012.

_____. "Swiss Mercenaries." http://en.wikipedia.org/w/index.php?title=Swiss_mercenaries&printable=yes. Accessed 18 December 2011.

_____. "Teutonic Knights." http://en.wikipedia.org/w/index.php?title_Teutonic_Knights&printable=yes. Accessed 30 October 2012.

_____. "White Company." http://en.wikipedia.org/w/index.php?title=White_Company&printable=yes. Accessed 30 September 2012.

Wilson, Peter H. *Europe's Tragedy: A New History of the Thirty Years War*. London: Penguin, 2010.

Wright, Nicholas. *Knights and Peasants: The Hundred Years War in the French Countryside*. Woodbridge: Boydell, 2000.

Xenophon Group. "The Battle of the Herrings (12 February 1429)." http://xenophongroup.com/montjoie/rouvrary.htm. Accessed 6 November 2012.

Index

Index

Index